BAINISTEOIR

The 10 Greatest GAA Managers

Finbarr
McCarthy

**MENTOR
BOOKS**

First published in 2009 by
Mentor Books Ltd.,
43 Furze Road
Sandyford Industrial Estate
Dublin 18
Republic of Ireland

Tel: +353 1 295 2112/2   Fax: +353 1 295 2114
e-mail: admin@mentorbooks.ie
www.mentorbooks.ie

A catalogue record for this book is available from the British Library

ISBN: 978-1-906623-41-8

Cover: Kathryn O'Sullivan
Typesetting and layout: Mary Byrne
Editor: Treasa O'Mahony

Printed in Ireland by ColourBooks Ltd

Contents

Foreword

The role of An Bainisteoir has grown enormously in recent years. Prior to the 1970s, managers did not attract much attention and many fans would have trouble recalling the former managers of their own county team. Yet in recent decades, the role of the manager, in terms of achieving results, is seen as being as important as the team itself.

This is due, in no small measure, to the identification of certain managers with consistent success – Mick O'Dwyer, Seán Boylan and Brian Cody, to mention just a few. The importance of the modern manager's role is clearly illustrated by the recent trend of GAA Boards headhunting managers from outside their own county, e.g. Mick O'Dwyer from Kerry to Kildare, Laois and Wicklow; Ger Loughnane from Clare to Galway; Joe Kernan from Armagh to Galway; Páidí Ó Sé from Kerry to Westmeath and Clare.

What makes a 'great' manager? How do GAA fans assess the effectiveness of a manager? What are the secrets of the successful managers? Are those secrets common to each? Is a successful playing career at inter-county level a prerequisite to winning All-Irelands as manager? What part does discipline and an arduous training regime play in winning titles? Or is it all down to luck?

In the final analysis, it is inevitable that the success of any manager is measured in terms of trophies – whether Championship, League, Provincial or Club titles. Using these criteria, the ten greatest GAA managers of recent decades is practically self-selecting. The ten greatest managers featured in this book have all enjoyed tremendous success, not just in winning All-Ireland Championship titles but also winning Provincial titles and in some cases enjoying great success at Club management level also.

The list of 'Ten Greatest GAA Managers' is constantly under review and changes as each season or new controversy passes. New names will force their way into the top ten. Not everyone will agree on who should be included – although few could argue that the ten managers in this book don't deserve their place in the top ten – but 'discussing with passion' the pros and cons of a particular manager is nothing new to GAA fans!

Finbarr McCarthy
November 2009

Dedication

This book is dedicated to my wife Mary, for always being there.

I would like to take this opportunity to acknowledge the commitment and hard work of all the managers throughout the country who sacrifice so much to help our young hurlers and footballers across the country week after week, in wind and rain, far from the glare of the media and big match days at Croke Park.

They are the bedrock of our organisation and stalwarts of the GAA.

Finbarr McCarthy

Acknowledgement

My involvement in the GAA is both long and varied but to be given the opportunity to meet so many of the iconic figures within the game is a pleasure I will retain for a while yet, possibly forever.

Sincere thanks to all those Bainisteoirs who freely gave of their time to assist me with this book.

Mick O'Dwyer, Brian Cody, Kevin Heffernan, Seán Boylan, Ger Loughnane, Mickey Harte, Páidí Ó Sé, Billy Morgan, Joe Kernan and Jimmy Barry Murphy, I am forever in your debt.

Many of them went out of their way to meet me and were always available if I needed further information.

Special thanks to Bob Honohan, Nicholas Murphy, Larry Tompkins, Seanie McGrath, Ted Owens, Jimmy Keaveney, Mickey Whelan, Brian Mullins, former GAA President Nickey Brennan, Owen McCrohan, Tom Keane, Tomás Mulcahy, Kieran Shannon, Peter Canavan and TV3's Kieran McSweeney.

My colleagues in the media were of great assistance, in particular Fintan O'Toole, Eamonn Murphy, Jim O'Sullivan, Michael Clifford, Gordon Manning, Peter Sweeney and of course my great friend Damian Lawlor whose advice and support steered me in the right direction when at times I might have been drifting off course. Thanks also to Tom Humphries for use of material from his interview with Kevin Heffernan.

The Sports crew of 96FM/C103 as always gave me huge encouragement, and Sportsfile's extensive photo library adds greatly to the book.

Writing this book has been a wonderful experience - what an idea by publisher Danny McCarthy, a genial Kerryman!

Thanks to Treasa O'Mahony for once again displaying marvellous editorial skills – seriously I will miss those daily emails. And to Kathryn O' Sullivan for creating a fantastic cover.

To all in Mentor, this is our third venture together. May there be many more.

Special thanks to all my clubmates in St Nick's and Glen Rovers, male and female.

It would not have been possible to complete this book without the continued support of my family, especially my wife Mary.

An oft-used phrase is that the 'GAA is a family'. As I travelled the length and breadth of Ireland to meet these icons of the GAA, I discovered that it is indeed.

Míle Buíochas do gach éinne.
Finbarr McCarthy

1

Mick O'Dwyer

The Early Years in Waterville

4 July 2009 – Wicklow v Fermanagh in Round 3 of the All-Ireland Football qualifiers. Rain cascaded down from the grey skies. It was an evening in keeping with the dreadful summer of 2009.

However, close to 8,000 spectators inside the GAA pitch in Aughrim were oblivious to the pouring rain. Wicklow had just won this match, continuing their extraordinary run in the qualifiers. But then they have an extraordinary manager – 73-year-old Mick O'Dwyer from Waterville in South Kerry.

This game also marked an important milestone for the Wicklow manager. As player and manager he had now played and defeated all competing counties in inter-county football.

Mick O'Dwyer has rendered the game of football remarkable service, first as a player with his native Kerry, then as a manager. Apart from nurturing the greatest team ever (Kerry in the 1970s), he has worked miracles wherever he went – Kildare, Laois, Kildare again and now Wicklow.

Yet he was never offered the job as International Rules team manager. Assistant manager yes, but not the manager's position.

Does that annoy him?

'Well I was too busy with Kerry for a start. But it would have been nice to be asked. I didn't give it much thought all the same.'

Probe a bit further and you quickly find that actually yes, it did hurt.

'Seán Kelly (ex-GAA president) asked me to be assistant to Pete McGrath. Now if I was good enough to be assistant I was surely good enough to be manager. Anyway I don't fancy being anyone's assistant.'

Oh yes, it hurt and annoyed him alright.

Up to the late 1950s South Kerry were one of the weakest of the Kerry Divisions, but they produced two iconic figures of the game. Mick O'Connell from Valentia Island is regarded as the best midfielder ever to wear the famed 'green and gold'. Mick O'Dwyer is without doubt the game's greatest manager.

And he could play a bit as well.

Derrynane, a club south of Waterville, is where it all began for Micko.

'My uncles, the Galvins on my mother's (Mary Galvin) side, played with the club out there. They all then went on to play for Kerry. And it is from them that I got the love of football.'

Surprisingly his father John never played football.

'No, he never played. He was a keen sportsman but not football. He was into beagle hunting which is very big down around here. Shooting and fishing were other pastimes of his.'

Like many of his age, Mick's father was caught up in the early troubles of the state.

'He was involved in the fight for Irish freedom. He ended up going to Canada and America before coming home and marrying my mother.'

The Waterville Club is still very dear to Micko's heart and one of his regrets is not winning a County Senior medal wearing their colours.

'It is really. I won three with South Kerry (divisional team), but we lost in three finals which was heartbreaking. We had a very small panel, but we managed to win the Junior and Intermediate Championship. We were reluctant to go up to senior level but we had to. We lost one final by one point and then a second final by two points. That's how close we came to winning the big prize in Kerry football. Very disappointing. We eventually had to return to the Intermediate grade because of the lack of numbers.'

In all three final appearances Micko was the player-coach – an early grounding in management. He is proud of the contribution that South Kerry has made to football in the Kingdom.

'Since 1975 it has been the top division and we very nearly won four county titles in a row recently. Look at the players who came from down here – Jack O'Shea, Maurice Fitzgerald, Ger O'Driscoll, Ger Lynch and of course not forgetting Mick O'Connell.'

Modesty prevents him from mentioning himself.

Playing for Kerry

From the early 1950s, it was clear the Waterville native would quickly graduate to the Kerry team.

'I played minor in 1953. But we lost to Dublin in the All-Ireland Final.'

It was to be one of his rare defeats to the Dubs as a player or as a manager over the next 40 years of involvement in Kerry football.

His senior career spanned 18 years. He began as a defender and ended as an attacker, with outstanding success. The medals soon stacked up – 4 All-Ireland Senior medals, 12 Munster Championships, 1 National League, 1 Railway Cup with Munster, Texaco Footballer of the year in 1969 – and for 3 years he was top scorer in the Championship.

Not bad for a defender who converted to an attacker.

'I had a great career really and I enjoyed every minute of it. I started as a half-back and won two All-Ireland medals (1959 and 1962) in that position. Then I was moved into the forward line and won two more (1969 and 1970).'

In the midst of his career he broke both his legs playing football in 1966. Tough times.

'They were but sure that's part and parcel of playing football. I recovered and that's when I made the switch to playing as a forward.'

As with most Kerry folk, Munster Final day was special for Micko.

'It was really. While we all wanted to get to Croke Park, we had to beat Cork first. That meant a Munster Final every year and they were great occasions. Killarney is a unique venue as everyone knows. But playing in the old Athletic Grounds in Cork was special. The crowd was packed into a tight venue – it made for a great day. We didn't always win but we loved playing there.'

Dublin v Kerry is another unique rivalry.

'For Kerry it is anyway. Much is made of it, but if you look at the records, Dublin haven't fared that well. I think it is only about 4 wins in 50 odd years. So we (Kerry) can't complain.'

It is fitting then that this interview took place in Waterville just three days after the Kingdom had inflicted another drubbing (1-24 to 1-7) on the Dubs in the 2009 quarter-final. A result Mick enjoyed.

'Crikey it was an outstanding display, the best from Kerry in a long time. The trick now is to see if they can repeat it.'

Mick retired as a player in 1974, bowing out after a low-key challenge game against Sligo in Killorglin.

'I played my last All-Ireland Final in 1972. We lost to Offaly after a replay. And my last Munster Final was in 1973. It was time to go. I had done my bit and I felt it was time to move on.'

But Kerry and football had not heard the last of Mick O'Dwyer. For several years he combined playing with selecting the Kerry senior team – an unusual occurrence in those times. A hint of what was to come perhaps?

'I was player-manager for one year when we beat Mayo in the National League final. And I was a selector for about seven years, on and off, while still playing.'

Was that dual role difficult?

'I found it OK and never had any real problems with it.'

Jokingly he remarked, 'It was easy to pick myself which was the most important thing.'

Becoming Kerry Manager

Micko was a reluctant manager.

'I never had any real ambition to be a manager I suppose, but when I was asked I decided to give it a go. Well I had been manager here in Waterville so that helped.'

The Kerry under-21 team was the first to come under his influence.

'That was a good grounding. We won three All-Irelands, and I was aware that there was good young talent available in the county.'

The Munster Football Final of 1974 was a factor in O'Dwyer becoming Kerry manager. Picture the scene – rain and mist enveloping Fitzgerald Stadium in Killarney. Cork were well ahead on the way to a second successive title. In a last throw of the dice the Kerry selectors introduced the now veteran Mick O'Connell in an effort to save the game. It failed. But worse, O'Connell was taunted by a Cork player. Dinny Long played 'keep ball' in front of O'Connell. It incensed the Kerry crowd.

Word has it that the watching O'Dwyer said that day, 'No one will ever do that to a Kerry player again – if I have anything to do with it.'

Fact or fiction?

'Well it happened and it should not have. It was not nice. O'Connell was a marvellous footballer. At the end of his career he did not deserve that. I suppose he broke their (Cork) hearts for years. But it (Long's actions) had no place in the game.'

Did it influence his decision to become Kerry manager?

'In a way it did I suppose. It made it easier to say "Yes".'

The man who asked Micko the big question was the then chairman of the Kerry County Board, Ger McKenna. It took more than one call before McKenna got his man.

'He called me three or four times. I had no real ambition to be manager at the time. I was in charge of the under-21 team. We had lost the Munster Final to Cork by one point, so I was disappointed with that. The other thing was of course – not many wanted the job. There was no big rush I can tell you.'

Cork had won two Munster titles in 1973 and 1974 and many feared a valley period for Kerry.

'Cork had a great team. Apart from the senior successes, they had also won a couple of under-21 titles. That would explain why so few in Kerry were interested in becoming manager at that time. But sure it was a great time to take over. Low expectations took some pressure off.'

Eventually he took the job and set about building a new team – a team that would go on to break old records and create new records.

'I stayed managing the under-21 team as well as the seniors in 1975. I knew what I wanted. I got rid of a lot of the older players and I went with a group of young players. Some of these had been with me in the under-21s and were good and keen.'

Back then training was less scientific and when the panel reported for their first session they got a rude awakening.

'I'm sure they did. I worked them hard and, boy, were they tired afterwards.'

At one stage of the season the team trained for 21 nights on the trot.

'We did. It was all designed to build stamina over the winter. Then when the evenings stretched we would concentrate on our skills. I am a firm believer in that. Put enough fuel in the tank and you can go forever.'

Cork were beaten by revamped Kerry in the Munster Final.

Did Cork underestimate O'Dwyer's new-look team?

'They probably did. We got a lucky goal but won well in the end.'

Sligo were hammered by them in the All-Ireland semi-final.

All-Ireland champions Dublin were the opposition in the final of 1975.

It was the beginning of a new era in Gaelic Football.

'I suppose it was, but all we were worried about was winning the final. None of our team had played in a final before. We had to deal with that.'

How?

'We kept our heads down, trained away and went about our job of beating the champions. You see, down in Kerry you're expected to be in All-Ireland Finals.'

And beat them they did – even coping with the loss of their captain early in the game.

'Mickey Ned (O'Sullivan) got a bit of a clatter from Seán Doherty and ended up in hospital. Pat Spillane took over as captain. Sure we won handy in the end.'

A satisfactory ending to his first year as Kerry manager?

'Of course – and we also won the under-21 All-Ireland – so a few of the team had two medals in the one year.'

The task in 1976 was to defend the title. But it nearly came unstuck in Munster – in a final that shaped the Championship for years to come. It was a Munster Final Cork should have won. Had they, would the great Kerry team ever have been heard of again?

Cork goalkeeper in that final, Billy Morgan, thinks it might have been the last anyone would have heard from Kerry for some time.

'He could be right and probably is. Cork had the talent. I kept saying that. Now Billy thought it was me playing the old soldier. But we got a few breaks in the match and it swung it for us.'

As for the match itself?

'My recollection is that the free we got the goal from turned the match. It was a big call, but over the years you get some (calls) and you don't get others, and we went on from there.'

They did. Kerry won the next seven Munster titles. Kerry and O'Dwyer were back.

The Golden Era of Kerry Football

Success in the Munster Final was sweet, but the 1976 All-Ireland Final and 1977 semi-final did not go according to plan.

'No, they did not. We lost them both to Dublin. They got their revenge for 1975 in the 1976 final and in 1977 they got the break.'

That game (1977) is remembered as one of the classics of Gaelic Football.

'Oh it was a great match. It was up and down the field and a small thing turned it. John O'Keeffe reached for a ball but only got a finger on it and it fell to Tony Hanahoe. Now Tony had a great football brain and in a flash he had set up the goal that put Dublin on their way.'

With these two defeats did he come under pressure to resign?

'There was a bit of noise alright but nothing came of it and we drove on.'

Drive on they did. Cork were kept in check in Munster while up to 2009 Dublin have yet to record another Championship victory over Kerry since 1977.

The All-Ireland Finals of 1978 and 1979 were won by Kerry with Dublin providing the opposition in both years. Roscommon fell to Kerry in the 1980 final. O'Dwyer and Kerry now had their three-in-a-row. The critics were silenced. So were Dublin, as the fresh challenge of Meath emerged from Leinster. But the Dublin rivalry was one he relished.

'Ah sure it was great. The players on both sides loved it. The crowds were huge and the GAA benefitted greatly.'

What about his rivalry with Dublin manager Kevin Heffernan?

'It was good. We wouldn't have met that often outside of matches, but what a man. He was a fabulous player with his club St Vincent's and then with Dublin. Kevin has done more for the GAA in Dublin than anyone I know, and for that they should be grateful. An outstanding man.'

Four-in-a-row, the first for Kerry since 1929 to 1932, arrived in 1981. Kerry beat Offaly that year, but Offaly were not, in those famous words, 'gone away you know'. Coincidentally it was Offaly who had denied O'Dwyer the player a fifth medal in 1972. Micko had won four All-Ireland medals up to that point and then he played in the 1972 final when Kerry lost to Offaly.

What was the secret behind the success Kerry were now enjoying?

'Well, apart from being brilliant footballers, they were a joy to deal with, not too many problems in all my years with them. Of course they were young and grew up together and understood one another. Anything they got from the game they deserved.'

Picking the team was easy?

'Easiest job in the world. Sure there was times when we would not even have a meeting. It picked itself.'

What they craved now was the five-in-a-row and with it a place in football folklore.

What they got was the biggest regret of O'Dwyer's career.

The team were on the cusp of history.

Kerry v Offaly – the All-Ireland Football Final of 1982.

The ballads were written. The t-shirts were printed. The five-in-a-row was on. Nothing it seemed could stop Kerry. But Offaly never read the script. Even now, 27 years on, it still hurts.

'Heartbreaking' is how Micko describes it.

'We certainly had the winning of the match in our grasp a few times. Mike Sheehy had a penalty saved by Martin Furlong. That would have put us six or seven points up. Offaly would not have come back from that.

It was a great game though.'

It was. In fact on that horrid afternoon – it rained for the entire match – the six half-backs all scored from play. But the small things again came into the equation.

Seamus Darby's goal. The little nudge on Tommy Doyle as the ball came in. And the chance to force a replay with the last attack.

His reaction?

'Ah sure you can imagine it was tough to take. I can tell you it was a long journey home on Monday. But as I said – that's sport. You must take the good with the bad. The Kerry support came out for the team though and that was important.'

For a long while after that defeat Micko was in a state of shock.

'I looked at the video a good few times and saw the things that went against us. Some of our more experienced players made basic errors that you would not normally expect of them. OK, maybe we should have got a couple of frees that would have made a difference. It was tough to take.'

Take it he had to. Then a tragedy altered his thinking.

Matt Connor was an outstanding footballer who played with Offaly in the All-Ireland Final of 1982. A member of the Garda Síochána, he was involved in a tragic accident and is now confined to a wheelchair.

'When I heard about Matt Connor's accident I said to myself, "I've little to be worrying about". In many ways Matt deserved his medal. The other thing of course was that the Kerry team did not need to create any new records. They had done enough.'

It is said that lightning never strikes twice. In Kerry's case it did.

The Munster Final of 1983. The game is in injury-time – Kerry two points ahead of Cork. Safe?

'Well we thought we were. Then Tadhgie Murphy from Cork got a goal and we lost by one point. I could hardly believe it. It was like Croke Park in September 1982 – all over again.'

So for the first time since 1976 Kerry's season ended in July. No football in August or September for Mick O'Dwyer.

A strange feeling?

'It was I suppose, and we were not used to that. We just had to accept it.'

With Kerry out of the way, Dublin slipped in for an All-Ireland in 1983.

Did Micko ever think of packing it in during that year of 1983?

'No, and we had a huge incentive to carry on.'

The coming year, 1984, was the Centenary Year of the GAA.

Was it hard to motivate players given what had happened in 1982 and 1983?

'Not at all, in fact the opposite. The players were dead keen to get going. I suppose the unexpected break gave them renewed enthusiasm. In fact we won the League and then won another All-Ireland.'

A nice double in 1984.

'Very nice and the fact that it was Dublin who we beat in the All-Ireland Final made it that bit sweeter.'

A year later (1985) Dublin were beaten again by Kerry in the final and in 1986 a second three-in-a-row was completed. This time Tyrone were Kerry's victims.

'That was a remarkable feat. Another three-in-a-row after all that we had already won shows how committed the players were. And that was evident in the 1986 win against Tyrone. We were behind and they had a penalty that would have put them seven points up. They only got a point from it and we kicked on from there. (Pat) Spillane was brilliant that day. A marvellous comeback. We won by 7 points which is a 14-point turnaround in football. That is some achievement.'

It was Kerry's eighth All-Ireland victory under O'Dwyer in ten final appearances.

Little did he know that when he would next manage a team in an All-Ireland Final it would not be Kerry.

Cork won in Munster in 1987 and cracks were now appearing in

O'Dwyer's team. It did not get any better in 1988 and 1989 and for the third year in a row Kerry failed to emerge from Munster.

Time To Go

O'Dwyer knew it was time to go.

'I decided after the 1989 Munster Final that I would retire. The team was struggling and the difficulty I had was my loyalty – my loyalty to the lads who had been brilliant for me. I wouldn't have had the heart to drop them, so I got out.'

Did he stay too long?

'I possibly should have left after the 1986 All-Ireland win – gone out on a high after the three-in-a-row, but I didn't. Then I should definitely have left after the 1988 Munster Final, but again I stayed on. That was a mistake. The other problem at the time was that because the team was so successful, replacements were hard to find.'

A generation lost perhaps?

'Without question. It was almost impossible to break into the team and players left the panel in frustration. It made building a new team that bit harder.'

There was one other disappointing moment in his tenure as Kerry boss. It happened in the 1984 All-Ireland Final. Even now it upsets him.

'Late in the game, about nine minutes from time I think it was, it was decided to take off John Egan. Now I was totally against the move, but I was outvoted. It took the good out of the win for me. I did not even enjoy the celebrations.'

O'Dwyer had huge respect for Egan.

'One of the best I ever had. He trained harder than anyone. And I can tell you we would not have won the All-Irelands of 1975 and 1978 without him. There was no justification for what was done to him.'

When the team and cup arrived in the dressing room after the match,

Egan had showered and was gone. He never played for Kerry again.

So after 14 years at the helm and an unprecedented run of success, it was over. One week after the Munster Final defeat in 1989 Mick O'Dwyer quit as Kerry manager.

'It was a fantastic era for Kerry football – unlikely to be seen again. I was just glad to have been a part of it.'

But his love of football would see him return to the manager's hot seat, this time with Kildare.

Down through the years O'Dwyer was never afraid to express his opinions on matters – the GPA, payments to managers, pay for play, Croke Park, the Dublin job.

A firm players' man, he supports the GPA.

'They are the best thing to happen to the players. If the GPA was around in my time, I would have been the first to join. The players are the heart and soul of the GAA. I don't think we can sustain "pay for play" especially in the current climate, but players must be looked after. I am on record as saying the players who play in an All-Ireland Final should get €10,000 a man. Look at the money it generates. Even the President of the GAA is now getting paid.'

'The GAA should also be more proactive in ensuring players get jobs and scholarships which are very important nowadays. To be fair, players are well looked after. It's a bit of a joke though giving them 50 cents a mile in expenses. The very least they should get is €1 a mile. It is they, after all, who generate the most money for the GAA nowadays.'

Do managers make a fortune out of the game from managing teams?

'I can tell you this much – if I stayed at my business here at home (a hotel in Waterville) I would have made a lot more. I got my expenses but as for making a fortune, far from it. I have retired from business now anyway.'

The opening up of Croke Park – was it long overdue?

'It should have happened long ago. Took too long. Look at the money it has generated for the association since it opened up. It's a wonderful facility and as a small country why should it be closed for most of the year?'

'Mick O'Dwyer to manage the Dublin footballers' ran the headlines. Was it true and how would it sit with die-hard Dubs?

'It was true. I had the job. John Bailey was the chairman of the Dublin County Board and I had a meeting with him. John offered me the job and said if I accepted it, he would ensure it got passed by the board. So I agreed to take the job. I was looking forward to it, a challenge yes, but one I wanted.'

But it never happened! Why?

'I'll tell you why. As I was driving home to Waterville I started thinking about the consequences. All those Dublin fellas waiting to have a go at me if it failed. Then there was the Kerry reaction.'

Which was?

'Dublin and Cork are our two biggest rivals. I was never going to be asked to manage Cork. Now I was going to train a team that could seriously trouble Kerry. So by the time I reached Waterville I had changed my mind. I rang John Bailey and told him I wouldn't be taking the job. He was fine about it really. I have no regrets. It was probably right not to go there.'

Gilding the Lilywhites (The Kildare Years)

Two years out of the game at inter-county level had whetted his appetite for more and when the call came in 1991 he said, 'Yes'.

It was from an unexpected source. A sleeping giant of Leinster football.

Kildare were next to come under the wing of the Waterville maestro.

How did that come about?

'Simple enough really. A gang of Kildare fellows came down here to me and pushed me to take the job. I was reluctant but eventually agreed to go there for six months.'

His appointment and return to football management was greeted enthusiastically in the land of horses and horsemen.

Six months turned into three years.

'The plan was to go up there and set up a system that they themselves could continue with.'

What made him stay?

'I got the bug again I suppose. The energy and enthusiasm for football in the county really struck me. The team had marvellous support. They followed them everywhere and I stayed with them.'

It also helped that they started winning.

'Ah well it did, and we got to the League final and should have won it. Dublin beat us by two points. They got a lucky goal. Our goalkeeper misjudged a high ball and it ended up in the net.'

Louth ended their Championship ambitions.

'We kicked that one away. We had a few injuries but still dominated the game and lost.'

Not one to walk away, Micko stayed on for another couple of years. Ironically, for the next three years an old adversary came back to haunt him – Dublin.

'They did – they beat us in two Leinster Finals and in a first round of the Championship – so I decided it was time to move on.'

Two players who would have been of huge benefit to O'Dwyer and Kildare were now plying their trade elsewhere – Larry Tompkins and Shay Fahy. The two talented Kildare footballers were now donning the colours of Cork.

'I have no doubt that had we Tompkins and Fahy we would have won an All-Ireland. Look what they achieved with Cork. They would have been brilliant for me and the experience they would have given Kildare. I don't know why they weren't playing with us, but it was a great pity. Sure they were Kildare's two best players – a huge loss.'

On leaving Kildare in 1994 Micko returned to coach his club Waterville. But once more the lure of inter-county football proved too strong to resist. Kildare came calling again in 1997. He answered because of his passion for football and that passion was matched by the Kildare supporters.

'Unbelievable really – they go everywhere to follow the team. Even at training sessions you get a crowd. For the two years that I was out, Kildare struggled. They had first round losses to Laois and then to Louth. So maybe they felt this O'Dwyer fellow wasn't too bad after all. So I went back up there.'

Is football in Leinster and Munster very different?

'For a start it's tougher for a Leinster football team to win the Championship. Realistically there are only two teams down here, Cork and Kerry. Every now and again one of the others will make a shape but they cannot sustain it. The bottom line is that Munster is a hurling province.'

He makes an interesting observation.

'One year with Kerry I won an All-Ireland by playing three games. We got a bye to the Munster Final, beat Sligo or someone in the semi-final and then won the final. In Leinster you might play three games just to get to the provincial final.'

Second time round with Micko, Kildare enjoyed great success.

'We had an excellent run. We won two Leinster titles and were very unlucky not to win an All-Ireland – injuries deprived us. Remember we also won a Leinster under-21 Championship which was a huge boost as well.'

It was the 1998 final – Kildare against Galway. In his second year back with the Lilywhites they reached their first All-Ireland Final since 1935. Back then Cavan beat them by 3-6 to 2-5.

En route to the 1998 final, a semi-final with his native county Kerry stood in the way.

Was it strange managing a team to try and beat Kerry?

'It was of course, especially with Páidí (Ó Sé) in charge. I would have preferred if it did not happen. But that's football. I had a job to do and that is how I went about it.'

How did he feel after the game?

'I was delighted we (Kildare) won of course. A degree of sympathy for Páidí naturally, but Kerry always recover from defeats. Kildare haven't been in a final since while Kerry have added a few more titles to their list.'

He has little doubt but that they could have won the final against Galway but for the injuries. Galway beat them 1-14 to 1-10.

'No question but it was a great campaign. We beat teams that had won All-Irelands – Dublin, Meath and Kerry. The whole county got behind the team and I really felt that we could win. Galway played well, but we had key men injured, especially Glen Ryan. He played through the pain barrier. Before the game he got a cortisone injection so he could start. Then at half-time we had to literally lift him up off the seat so he could go out for the second-half. There was no way he was coming off. He was that determined, but he could barely move. Had he been fully fit, we would have won. Ronan Quinn and Niall Buckley were also injured. The spine of our team was gone.'

One other factor did not help Kildare.

'We played seven games to get to the final. Galway had only three games and with limited resources it told in the final. Galway beat us by four points (1-14 to 1-10).'

It did have its benefits, which O'Dwyer now believes are showing.

'I left when we were knocked out of the Championship in 2002. I felt I had done my stint. But the passion for football in Kildare is huge and that helps. Also they put a lot of work into developing the game at under-age level and it is now bearing fruit. The young lads got renewed interest as a result of reaching that final. It showed what can be done with hard work and now they are coming strong again. Kildare will be a force at senior level shortly I can tell you.'

Leading Laois to Glory

One regular car journey was now over, and boy, has he done some miles in his managerial career! But another new car journey was about to begin. Before 2002 ran its course he was back in inter-county management. The year 2003 would see him once again patrolling the sideline in

Championship football – same province, different county.

Laois were next to benefit from O'Dwyer's guile, cunning and long experience.

Yet another challenge for the genial Waterville man. And it was a challenge.

'Every county is different but Laois were in the doldrums for over 60 years. It was a challenge alright. But remember they had good success at minor and under-21, so the raw material was there.'

'A good friend of mine, Declan O'Loughlin, asked me to go down there in 2002. He said, "Micko, you're doing nothing. Can't you come down and help us out?" So I said "Why not?" I love a new challenge and I was determined to try and get them to fulfil their potential.'

As it had done with Kildare, the O'Dwyer magic worked with Laois.

'We won the Leinster Championship in my first year down there – Laois's first Leinster title in over 60 years. We were very unlucky then in the All-Ireland semi-final. Armagh beat us by one point I think. Had we beaten them we could have won the All-Ireland.'

The feeling of euphoria in the county was something special?

'It was, and it was the same when Kildare won the Leinster Championship. Look, Cork and Kerry take winning the Munster Championship in their stride. It's different for these counties. They celebrate as if they had won the All-Ireland. Back in Kerry the cup is put in the boot of the car or somewhere till next year. Up there (in Laois and Kildare) they go mad.'

The homecomings were special.

'They were. I thought when Kildare won the first one (Leinster title) it could not be surpassed. But when Laois won – my God, the crowds that followed the bus home from Croke Park were unbelievable. I never saw anything like it. Then when we hit Portlaoise it was incredible. But it just shows what the GAA means to people in these counties.'

Once again in his stint with Laois he crossed swords with that other Kerry great.

Páidí Ó Sé was now managing Westmeath.

'Amazing it should happen for the second time and so soon after we clashed while I was with Kildare.'

This time though Páidí would emerge as the winner.

'We had two great games. It was a draw the first day but they got the better of us in the replay. Westmeath went on to win the Leinster Championship and I can tell you that was some achievement by Páidí. It was also his first year in charge which made it all the more remarkable.'

There was a fair bit of trouble in the build-up to that match.

'In our (Laois) camp anyway. Well a few players did not turn up for training on the week of the replay. That never happened with teams I trained before. It did not help matters I can tell you. We dealt with it at the time, but it's no way to prepare for a big match.'

Did it affect the outcome?

'Let's just say we could have done without it. It was an unwanted distraction.'

The year 2003 was a special one for the men from the O'Moore County.

'Of course it was, and we really enjoyed it. Played some terrific football and enjoyed a huge profile which was good for the game in the county.'

One other aspect of Leinster football that attracted him: the rivalry.

'Nearly every game is a local derby in a sense. That made for some fantastic battles. Playing the games in venues other than Croke Park also helped.'

It was announced that 2006 would be his last year with Laois.

'I had done three years and decided to leave. I learned my lesson in Kerry – never overstay your welcome. Players also need to hear a new voice.'

Laois were knocked out of the Championship in 2006 but regrouped for the qualifiers. All the time efforts were being made to get O'Dwyer to change his mind. But he was adamant he was leaving.

'We had a good run in the qualifiers after losing to Dublin in Leinster.'

The big scalp though was Tyrone. A week after losing to Dublin, they went in as 'no hopers'.

'It was a huge win. No one gave us a chance. We won a tight game by three points on a dreadful wet and windy night in Portlaoise. I felt if Tyrone got over us that night they could have gone on to win the All-Ireland.'

Laois went on to beat Meath, Offaly and drew with Mayo.

'Mayo beat us in the replay in the quarter-final of the All-Ireland. It was my last game and I was determined to go. We did not play well that afternoon. The team looked stale and I knew they needed someone else to take them on.'

There were some rumblings that the players were getting restless under O'Dwyer.

'Maybe there was, but I knew it was time to go and I resisted all efforts to get me to stay.'

Mick stuck to his guns and as he left Croke Park that afternoon, the GAA world was convinced it had seen the last of the man from Waterville.

Once again though, it was wrong.

Interestingly, since O'Dwyer left Laois they have lurched from one crisis to another.

'I had a few problems when I was there and I dealt with them very quickly. I have learned over the years that it is best to nip things in the bud and not allow them to fester.'

What about players being asked to sign a code of conduct agreement.

'I don't buy into that at all. If a player is giving you bother, or not putting in the effort, the remedy is simple. Take him off the panel. That also sends a clear signal as to who is in charge – the manager and not the players.'

Laois won two Minor All-Irelands and the players on those teams appear to be still celebrating.

'That may be the case. It's the wrong path to go down and very quickly your career will have passed you by. Laois have plenty of talent and unless they harness it they will slip back into the pack.'

With all his football commitments, Micko's family were left to run the business back home in Kerry.

'They did, and they made a fine job of it too while I was away.'

Micko's three sons – Robbie, John and Karl – all played for Kerry, but there's a tinge of regret that Karl did not get an extended run. Micko suspects that he (Karl) got a raw deal.

'I have no doubt he did. I don't know why, but maybe it had something to do with me. After all he proved himself to be a good footballer with Kildare. The day we beat Kerry he had a great game – helped win us the match really. He won a Leinster Championship medal with me and also picked up an All-Star award – not bad for an unwanted Kerry footballer.'

Wherever he went Mick enjoyed the full support of players and officials alike.

'It's as simple as this really. If everyone is not pulling in the same direction you are in trouble. County boards want to win as well and I always got great help, especially in Kerry. It has been the same since. I do not always agree with officials but I respect them. I would much rather be out in a muddy field training a team than stuck in a committee room. But I appreciate the time and effort they put in.'

The bond between Mick and the Kerry team he guided to eight All-Ireland titles is a strong one.

'Well you don't go through what we did and not have some sort of bond. I meet a lot of them regularly at games and we enjoy each other's company. It's great too that so many of their sons are now part of the present Kerry team. Jack O'Shea, Ogie Moran and Seanie Walsh all have lads playing and they are the future of Kerry football.'

There were, of course, times when all was not well.

'Ah, a few times. Páidí fell out with me for a bit when we didn't pick him. Then Jack (O'Shea) played with his club in Kildare a week before an All-Ireland Final and it upset us for a while. Given that we were together as a group for over 10 years a couple of little problems were bound to crop

21

up. But at the end of the day we are still very good friends.'

In all his years in the game O'Dwyer has always been accommodating to the media.

'I never stopped anyone coming to my training sessions. They were always welcome. It helps raise the profile of our games. Some players, especially younger lads, need a bit of protection. However, as a rule, I have no problem with players giving interviews before games.'

As for trial by television?

'There is nothing wrong with it at all. They show up mistakes in games – that is all. Referees also come under the microscope as well. If it improves the quality of our games then all the better.'

Mick is also strongly opposed to the ban on winter training.

'A complete joke. What will players do if they are not playing our games – they go off playing either soccer or rugby. Young fellows want to play games and it is our duty to provide them. A joke – the guys that came up with this have got it all wrong. Most inter-county players look after themselves anyway and banning collective training will not change that. It also gives you little time to prepare for the National League which starts in February. I feel myself it was done to save money which is the wrong reason. If you're not fit you'll get injured and if it's a serious injury it will cost a lot more. This is one decision that in my opinion should be revisited.'

Not surprisingly, with a lifetime involvement, he has a few moments that stand out – good and bad.

'My proudest was winning my first All-Ireland as a player in 1959 against Galway. As a manager it had to be beating Dublin in 1978, having lost in 1976 and 1977. I did regret the 1982 loss to Offaly (the five-in-a-row lost opportunity), but as I said, Matt Connor getting his medal and then his accident – that put my disappointment into perspective. Overall I have very few regrets.'

Winning with Wicklow

Then of course there's Wicklow.

'Ah yes, Wicklow! The Garden County.'

Yet another chapter in an amazing career.

Mick O'Dwyer stepped down as Laois manager on 26 September 2006. Two weeks later on 7 October 2006 he was appointed Wicklow manager and the story goes on. Again his appointment came about when Wicklow GAA people made the initial approach.

'I suppose in many ways I could not say "No" when they asked me. This was a real test though. Wicklow were (still are) in Division 4 of the League and no real Championship pedigree to go on. But I was impressed by their plans and the energy that the people in charge had. So off I went.'

Immediately on his appointment, Wicklow's profile increased. Media interest heightened, and they (Wicklow) even appeared on television.

'It was crazy really. Our first couple of games in the O'Byrne Cup were televised live. That never happened to Wicklow before.'

The O'Dwyer factor at work once again. Box-office material.

'I suppose if I wasn't in charge, they (RTÉ) wouldn't have bothered with Wicklow.'

His first task was to alter the mindset of the players. Remember they were ranked number 31 in the country.

'Yes, because the majority of them would have felt that there was little to be gained from playing with the county. Club football is strong up there and that is where their loyalties lay. Now there is nothing wrong with that. But I wanted success for the team and the players needed to be made aware of my plans. I needed to get them thinking county before club.'

Mick, with the help of local knowledge provided by Kevin O'Brien and Arthur French, began laying his plans.

'We started off with a series of trials and the response was incredible. Over 120 players turned up on the first day. Basically every player got three trials before we made up our minds. The level of interest was incredible. I knew straight away that I would enjoy myself in Wicklow. We gradually whittled it down to 40 before settling on a panel.'

Then came the hard work of getting the team ready for competitive action.

'I laid out my plans and told them exactly what was required. To be fair the response was excellent – the players really bought into it.'

They have not yet managed to escape from Division 4, but that is not a concern to Micko.

'We experimented a lot during the League in 2009. The Championship is the thing really. That was my priority along with the Tommy Murphy Cup.'

The Championship and the Tommy Murphy Cup are a bone of contention with O'Dwyer. A couple of years ago the GAA in an effort to streamline the Championship decided that counties in Division 4 of the League could not participate in the qualifiers unless they made their Provincial Final. This incensed O'Dwyer.

'Another crazy decision. How are counties going to improve if they cannot play against the top teams? They might never win the All-Ireland but they are surely entitled to play in the Championship. We should not be elitist, all counties should be equal.'

To illustrate the point he makes the following observation.

'A few years ago Fermanagh came from a very low base to reach the All-Ireland semi-final, beating Armagh in the process. Now that is how it should be. This is the beauty of Championship football. The qualifiers were brought in to improve teams – not to exclude them.'

And to strengthen the argument look at what happened to Wicklow in 2008.

'A crazy situation really. We beat Kildare in the Leinster Championship, lost the next round to Laois and then could not go into the qualifiers. Kildare then went on to reach the All-Ireland quarter-final after losing to us. Now tell me, is that right? It smacks of a decision made by people who never played the game.'

Accepting their fate, Wicklow approached the Tommy Murphy Cup with the intention of winning it.

'Well we took the attitude – if a competition is worth entering, it's worth winning. The players have the same approach. Remember Wicklow don't win much and this was an opportunity to change that.'

It was an exciting campaign, but the manager had only a peripheral role.

'I had a few health problems during 2008. A hip replacement and a few stints put in. But I got over that, thank God, and we reached the final which was great for a county like Wicklow. The GAA, to their credit, played the final in Croke Park and we beat Antrim. I felt a bit sorry for Antrim but it was a special day for the Wicklow players.'

How highly did he rate that win?

'Look, it was a marvellous achievement really, and the players deserved some reward for their hard work.'

By now the Wicklow support had grown.

'They followed the team in huge numbers and for them to win a trophy in Croke Park was also a bit special.'

Micko pays generous tribute to his backroom team. A backroom team that is much slimmer than most counties.

'Kevin O'Brien and Arthur French are marvellous men. Kevin was a great player. He was Wicklow's first All-Star, while Arthur knows every footballer in the county and those two lads were invaluable to me.'

The change in modern training methods is something that has intrigued many for years, and O'Dwyer adjusted suitably.

'I still go on the basic principle that you must be fit to play. So that meant hard work over the winter. I listen to the physios and their likes a bit more nowadays. I also accept the advice of the dieticians. But as for statistics, I don't need a stats person. I have seen enough football to know exactly what's required to win or indeed change a match. I have adopted the new methods alright I suppose, but I still trust my own judgement above anyone else.'

The year 2009 was an incredible year for Wicklow despite being one of the few counties that have yet to win a provincial title.

'The best ever I suppose. We played six Championship games. We won a Championship game for the very first time in Croke Park. And thanks to our run in the qualifiers we reached the last 12 in the All-Ireland.'

Not bad.

'Not bad? Bloody marvellous with such a small squad! We used the same 15 players in the last 4 games simply because they were all playing so well and trying so hard we felt it would have been harsh to take anyone off.'

Westmeath knocked them out of the Leinster Championship after extra-time – in another televised match. That was after Wicklow had beaten Longford – a team playing in a division above them in the League. Had they beaten Westmeath, the prize on offer was a semi-final clash with Dublin. Now there's a prospect!

'By God, I can tell you I would have enjoyed that. That is what we were aiming for – to get into the big stuff. But we missed a late '45' to win the game. A great pity – there would have been some craic if we got to play Dublin.'

Then came the qualifiers. A case of Ulster opposition in three games on the bounce. And it came as no real surprise that Wicklow won all three. Fermanagh, Cavan and Down all bit the dust in the battles at Aughrim – a tight compact ground, where according to Niall Carew of Kildare, 'even the All Blacks would find it hard to win there'.

O'Dwyer was delighted with the progress.

'Look at the three teams we beat. Fermanagh, All-Ireland semi-finalists a few years ago. Cavan and Down are two big traditional football counties. They are all teams we would not be expected to beat.'

The win over Down gave him particular pleasure.

'It did, yes. They have been doing very well at under-age level in the last few years. Of course they gave Kerry a few beatings in my playing career so that was a nice win.'

It could not last though. Successive weeks of action finally took its toll on his brave but limited squad – limited in terms of numbers of personnel.

'Kildare beat us, but despite everything we had chances to win. We should have got two goals and we missed two easy points. But look, they gave it their all and the games just caught up with us in the end.'

So Wicklow's great run was over and it left an indelible mark on their manager.

'What I achieved with Wicklow in 2009 gave me huge satisfaction. Even more than what I won with Kerry. It created a great atmosphere in the county. Young boys and girls, and not so young, mind you, are all going around wearing the Wicklow jersey which is fantastic.'

That is some statement.

'It might be, but it's true. You see, Kerry expect to win. Wicklow hope to win. We got no trophy at the end of it but for the first time in their history they won four Championship games in the one year. That was good enough for me.'

'They as a team wanted more which is a good sign. Only one team can win the All-Ireland but if you can produce a team to play football like they did, then you're on the right road.'

A Last Tango?

His philosophy throughout his career has been, 'play football the way it should be played'.

'I don't know any other way to play. I never worry about the opposition. I set out my team to play good attractive football and I am not going to change now. I have no time for the cynicism that some counties adopt. That's not the way football should be played.'

Micko is a fan of all sports, plays a bit of golf – 'golf and football, they are my pastimes now'.

He also enjoys hurling and struck up a friendship with the great Christy Ring.

'He used to holiday in Ballinskelligs and often called in to Waterville for a chat. We had many a good afternoon discussing hurling and football. He used to say to me, "They should get rid of the footballs in Cork and concentrate on hurling".'

Sir Matt Busby of Manchester United fame was the only manager who influenced Micko.

'A great friend of mine, Billy Behan from Ringsend in Dublin, was a big fan of Kerry football. Billy was United's scout in Ireland. He made arrangements for me to go over and watch United in pre-season training. He introduced me to Matt and he advised me on a few things and I took them on board for Kerry training.'

It was a beautiful sunny day in Waterville as we concluded our chat. It was bristling with visitors. We walked across to the beach. Along the way Mick had a word for most people who passed by. It was as if he knew everyone. Looking out at the sea, he pointed out the various spots.

Portmagee to the right. Waterville Golf Links a bit further on. Valentia Island straight ahead. The sheer beauty of the place was breathtaking. Miles of golden sand as the tide drifted out.

'I walk that stretch every morning. Fantastic exercise that keeps me in shape.'

Two final questions. Will you ever retire from football and how do you cope with the driving?

'I love driving, I'd want to with all the miles I've done. But I enjoy my own company in the car. My family think I am mad to be still involved but what else would I be doing? I have to retire some day, but not yet.'

In October 2009, O'Dwyer announced that he will continue as Wicklow manager, to the great delight of all GAA fans in that county.

So he will once more stride into the dressing room, deliver his pep talk, roll the match programme into his hand, don the manager's bib and take his place on the sideline.

Why?

'Football, and the love of it. That's what it's all about. Always was, always will be. I'm just glad to be a part of it.'

There are many who appreciate what Mick O'Dwyer has done for Gaelic Football.

When he does call it a day, the GAA will be poorer without him – the maestro from Waterville.

2
Brian Cody

All-Star Anger

The text message arrived to confirm the appointment. 'I will meet you at 4.15 in Hotel Kilkenny.' Less than 24 hours later, the automatic door in the hotel lobby slides open. Brian Cody enters. We greet and shake hands. It is Thursday 15 October 2009. The Vodafone All-Stars hurling team has just been announced. I ask the Kilkenny manager if he had heard who made the team.

'I'm still trying to get over the shock. Six on the team – come on, what do you think?'

'Well', I said, 'given what Kilkenny won I thought you would get maybe eight, but definitely seven. Six seems small.'

His anger subsides, slightly. 'How anyone could leave JJ Delaney off an All-Star team is beyond me!'

I press on.

'Is there anyone else who should have got on?'

'Eddie Brennan had strong claims as well. How any group of – what is it, 14 or 15 – could pick a team never ceases to amaze me. But then the All-Stars always seem to get it wrong.'

Brian acknowledges that at last a Kilkenny goalkeeper (PJ Ryan) got picked.

'Well, they got that right. Look at the way James McGarry was treated over the years. He played in all our big games – won every honour – yet never got an All-Star. This thing about good defenders in front of him doesn't stack up. Good goalkeepers are vital. James was one of the best.'

It is the only time during our chat that Cody is angry. He is relaxed and in good form. Despite his busy schedule, he answers any question put to him in a calm and assured manner. A bit like his demeanour on the sideline – relaxed and in control.

These are great times for Kilkenny hurling and their manager Brian Cody.

'Yeah, it's a bit special alright, but things can change quickly so we'll enjoy it while we can.'

Did he ever think when he took the job back in 1998 that they would be where they are today?

'Not in a million years. The ambition was to win one All-Ireland and then see where we go from there.'

That one All-Ireland has turned into an unprecedented run of victories. Seven All-Ireland titles, ten Leinster Championships and five National League titles.

The Club & College

Hurling is a way of life in Kilkenny, a bit like football in Kerry. Cody was always destined to be a hurler – for school, club and county. School was, of course, the famed St Kieran's College in the heart of the Marble City. The 'black and white' striped jerseys are as famous as the 'black and amber' ones.

Then there is his club, James Stephens – or 'The Village' as they are better known. It's a strange nickname for a club that is but a stone's throw from the main street of the city centre.

Brian Cody is immensely proud of his club. His late father, Bill, was the club's vice-chairman for 17 years. Brian himself held that position for a brief period.

'The club is very important to me. I am immensely proud that I had the privilege of playing for them. Winning County and All-Ireland Club titles with The Village are among my most treasured memories. I also had the honour of managing the senior team.'

The day we spoke he was thinking ahead to the Kilkenny County Final – James Stephens v Ballyhale-Shamrocks. A tough one to win?

'Very tough – we're really up against it. Shamrock's have a great team. Henry (Shefflin), Cha (Fitzpatrick) and Eoin (Reid) – any one of them a match winner.'

Brian's son Donnacha will play in the final despite having just recovered from a cruciate knee injury.

'He probably shouldn't be playing. It was a serious operation, but he worked hard to get himself fit. It would be great to win, but we're up against it.'

Ballyhale-Shamrocks won the final, 1-14 to 1-11, notching up an impressive four-in-a-row club titles.

As with most hurlers he graduated through the ranks on and off the field.

'I took the usual route. Start at a young age and move on through the ranks. Great men working with us helped develop our skills. Carried that on then in Kieran's and eventually got picked for the Kilkenny minors.'

Hurling is a very important part of the ethos of St Kieran's College. The college has made a huge contribution to the very healthy state of Kilkenny hurling.

'Some of the best hurlers in the county learned their trade in Kieran's. It helped me enormously and made me a better player. That and the amount of work going on in the clubs all combine to put the county on a strong footing.'

Among Brian's teammates in St Kieran's was former GAA President Nickey Brennan, who has huge regard for Cody. 'A great guy. Lovely hurler himself. I played with him on various teams, we kind of came up together.'

Brennan is in little doubt that Cody has transformed Kilkenny hurling.

'No question about that. The way he has gone about it has impressed everyone. He is hard but fair. He commands respect and in return he respects the players. Once you have that in the dressing room, you're well on the way to winning titles.'

Cody also helped fulfil an ambition for Brennan during his three years as GAA President.

'I had hoped that during my term of office that I would get the opportunity to present the Liam McCarthy Cup to a Kilkenny captain. It was a thrill to do it once, but three times – I owe Brian for that.'

In 2009 Brennan, now retired as GAA President, sat back and enjoyed All-Ireland Final day as the four-in-a-row was completed.

Following his stint in St Kieran's, Brian headed for St Patrick's College, Drumcondra, in north Dublin, to begin training as a National School teacher. It was here that Brian Cody and Ger Loughnane first crossed paths.

'We did. Ger was a year ahead of me, but we played on the one team. A great player even then.'

Years later as a TV pundit Loughnane would be critical of Kilkenny's style under Cody, while as Galway manager Loughnane would face Cody in a Championship encounter.

The Kilkenny Hurler

Brian Cody tasted success early in his playing career with Kilkenny.

'I was captain of the minor team that beat Cork in the 1972 All-Ireland Final. On the same afternoon Kilkenny won the senior title, also beating Cork, a special day for the county. I was thrilled to be part of it.'

A short few weeks later he was called into the senior team.

'A real baptism. Back then the League began in October. I was picked at centre-back against Limerick in Nowlan Park. A real honour to make the senior team. It's the ambition of every player to play for your county at senior level; I was thrilled at being selected.'

For the record Kilkenny won that league game by 1-16 to 4-2. Cody scored two points. He was just 18 years of age. It heralded the beginning of a long career in the famed Kilkenny jersey that lasted until his retirement in 1986.

As with most players, he experienced peaks and valleys along the way.

In the Championship of 1973 Cody tasted All-Ireland Final day as Kilkenny faced Limerick in the decider.

'At 19, I was the youngest hurler playing in the match. I played at left half-back, but we were badly hit with injuries. Having beaten Wexford in the Leinster Final, in between we lost key players for the All-Ireland. Limerick won. It was their first title in 33 years, so that made a lot of people happy. But as you can imagine, it was disappointing to lose in your first senior final.'

One year later, the teams met again in an All-Ireland Final. This time Cody was only a substitute as Kilkenny had an almost full-strength squad. They won comfortably enough.

The 20-year-old from 'The Village' had his All-Ireland Senior hurling medal, but ambitious as ever he wanted to win one on the field. He would not have long to wait.

Cody also picked up successive All-Ireland under-21 medals as Kilkenny defeated Waterford and Cork respectively in 1974 and 1975.

1975 was to be another special year. Kilkenny once again contested the All-Ireland Final. Galway were the surprise winners over Cork in the All-Ireland semi-final and it made for a unique final – Galway v Kilkenny.

Later in his career, Cody always wondered why Galway could play so well in semi-finals yet fail to deliver in the subsequent final. This trend was set in 1975 and Kilkenny were easy winners. It was another milestone of his playing days.

'Your first medal on the field is always special, but I also got to play with great Kilkenny hurlers – Eddie Keher among them. Eddie was pure class as a hurler. It was in fact the only time we played together on a winning team in an All-Ireland Final. Eddie missed the 1973 Final loss to Limerick while I was only a sub in the 1974 win.'

1976 and 1977, though, were disappointing years for the 'Cats' as their fierce rivals Wexford beat them in the Leinster Championship. In those years it was always Kilkenny and Wexford in the Leinster Final. Big crowds, high scoring, great battles. Exciting times in Leinster hurling. Cody has fond memories of those days – especially his tussles with the big man from Wexford, Tony Doran. Cody was full-back, while Doran was a full-forward.

'Tony was an outstanding player. Big and strong and a great man to go for goal. Over the years we had some wonderful battles. Both of us enjoyed them and of course the matches were very exciting. Tony was one of the toughest players I marked but very fair as well. That's a mark of the man.'

Comparing the Munster and Leinster Championships is a favourite topic nowadays. More so among those who feel the Southern province is far superior than its Eastern equivalent.

'Okay, the Munster Championship is fantastic. The people down there are rightly very proud of it. I go to as many Munster Championship games as my time allows and love the occasions. But don't knock the Leinster Championship. The counties here are very proud of our Championship. Kilkenny value it very highly and I am sure the other counties are the same.

Winning your Provincial Championship is a huge honour and should not be ignored.'

Wexford might be struggling right now, but Cody has huge respect for the 'yellow bellies'.

'All the time, we treat every team with respect and Wexford with more. They are, after all, our neighbours and there is no greater rivalry in the GAA than a local derby. I never underestimated a Wexford team as a player and I carry that with me as a manager.'

That said, Cody is of the opinion that for the benefit and promotion of hurling it may very well be time for change.

'The GAA have shown by the manner in which they introduced the qualifiers in hurling and football that they are not afraid to make changes. While a lot of people feel the Provincial Championships should not be touched, I think hurling would get a huge boost with a new format.'

He expands on his plan.

'What would be wrong with Kilkenny and Cork playing in the 'Park' (Cork's home ground – Páirc Uí Chaoimh) in a Championship game? Or Clare v Wexford in Ennis? Look at the interest it would generate. Sometimes the same pairings in the Provincial Championship can get a bit stale and a change might be worth considering.'

That would suggest that he thinks the Provincial Championships should be scrapped.

'If it was for the benefit of hurling, why not? A properly constructed group-set might just work. To get the best counties playing on a regular basis.'

Yes, but does he see it happening?

'Probably not, but it should not be dismissed out of hand. We need to promote the game as best we can at every available opportunity. Put aside the notion that what was successful for so long might last forever.'

It should come as no real surprise then that Brian welcomed the introduction of Galway and Antrim into the Leinster Championship.

'Of course, as I said, the GAA are not afraid to change. I am sure that in time both Galway and Antrim will see the benefits. Antrim being so far away from the hurling counties (geographically) – they deserve every bit of help they can get. There are wonderful hurling people working hard in that county and they deserve immense credit for their efforts.'

Captain Cody Collects the Cup

It was 1978 before Kilkenny emerged from Leinster again. By then Cork were on the cusp of the three-in-a-row. Cody had now been deployed in the unfamiliar position (for him) of full-forward. How did that switch come about?

'Heading into the Championship that year, the selectors just decided to play me there. No problem – you play where you're picked and if they felt that I could do a job, so be it.'

It started off well enough. Cody bagged a total of 2-3 in the Leinster Championship and then scored 1-2 in the All-Ireland semi-final win over Galway. Cork were next in the All-Ireland Final, the 'Rebels' chasing the three-in-a-row.

'For obvious reasons we really wanted to stop them doing that. But they were a powerful team with some great players. It didn't work out – we lost by four points. We only managed to score a total of 2-8 and that score would not be good enough to win a match at that level.'

Interestingly, Cork's match-winning goal that day was scored by Jimmy Barry Murphy. A bit like Loughnane and Galway, Jimmy Barry Murphy and Brian Cody would collide again.

The decision to play Cody, a recognised defender as an attacker, did not work and the match reports concentrated on that issue. Cody, though, moved on.

'The reality was that as a unit the attack failed. That and a good Cork team beat us – simple as that.'

1979 was a disappointing year for Brian, not helped by an injury.

'It probably cost me an All-Ireland medal. I broke my ankle playing with the club. It meant I missed a lot of the year. I did make it back for the Championship but I was only a sub for the Final.'

The 1979 Final saw Kilkenny beat Galway, who had shocked Cork (now seeking a four-in-a-row) in the All-Ireland semi-final. Once again Cody wondered about Galway's inability to string good back-to-back performances.

Offaly replaced Wexford as Kilkenny's main rivals for a period in Leinster and they (Offaly) won the Championship in 1980 and 1981. Kilkenny bounced back in 1982. Cody was now back in defence, with an added honour – he was now captain. James Stephens had won the County Championship in 1981 and named Brian Cody as their captain. It's a tradition that, as manager, Cody is fully behind.

'I was named captain because of my club's success and I see no reason to alter that. We (Kilkenny) have had great captains as a result and it is never an issue. It is one tradition I'd never change.'

He has good memories of 1982.

'Yeah, fantastic really. We got out of Leinster and then faced a highly-rated Cork team in the All-Ireland Final. Cork had hammered everyone out of sight and were raging favourites for the final. But Christy Heffernan got a couple of goals and we won handy in the end.'

Ten years after climbing the steps to collect the All-Ireland minor cup he was now making that very same climb. But the prize was much bigger.

'An outstanding feeling – to collect the Liam McCarthy Cup – for myself and especially for my club. Not too many 'Village' men had done it, so that made it extra special.'

Brian was to win one more All-Ireland when Cork were beaten again in 1983.

Heading into the GAA's Centenary Year (1984) Kilkenny, as in 1978, were hot favourites to complete the three-in-a-row. But once again they failed to emerge from the province. The wait for the three-in-a-row would go on.

Brian Cody's inter-county career came to an end in 1986 with no regrets.

'Not really. I would like to have won more, but sport is sport – you take what you get and look to the next challenge.'

For Brian Cody that would be giving something back to his beloved James Stephens. The Village would now command his full attention. With his inter-county playing career over, Cody immersed himself in his club.

'I had always intended giving something back to the club, so that is what I did. I got involved in coaching teams at various levels. I had been doing that with the school teams anyway so I just carried on with the club. It is very important to give something back to your club. You start and end your career there and fellas should never forget that.'

The club scene is something Cody as Kilkenny manager places great store in, and he is not one for denying clubs access to their inter-county stars.

'Absolutely not. We always allow our players play with their clubs. We're not much into challenge games with the Kilkenny county team, the odd one or two maybe. But as a rule we find good competitive club games are much more beneficial than inter-county challenge games. Players also are well aware that club form is important when the county panel is being picked, so they know what to expect. If you don't perform at club level you might not get picked for the inter-county team.'

Something rare happened in Kilkenny hurling between 1983 and 1992 – they failed to win an All-Ireland Senior Championship. A famine in Kilkenny terms. A few managers failed to deliver the goods. One of them was Nickey Brennan (the former GAA President) and he recalls that period.

'It was strange alright, not winning All-Irelands, but sure that's the nature of sport. There was a bit of pressure on but then there is always pressure on the big counties to win.'

Brennan was followed in the job by Kevin Fennelly. Fennelly stepped down after the Championship of 1998. Then the Kilkenny County Board set about getting their man – and Brian Cody was to be that man.

Brian Gets the Call

Was he surprised to get the call, considering that he had never managed an inter-county team at any level?

'In a way I was, but at the same time I was honoured. I went for the interview and then the County Board came back and offered me the job.'

Did the fact that there was an interview process influence his decision to go for the job.

'Not at all, that's the procedure here in Kilkenny, so I was happy to go along with that.'

With no All-Ireland title win in the previous eight years, was there pressure on him?

'Not really. I believe Kilkenny are good enough to win the All-Ireland every year and that is the way I approached the job.'

On his appointment he chose Ger Henderson and Johnny Walsh as his selectors – two men who he could work well with.

'I had known them both. I hurled with Ger. They were also two very independent-minded guys, exactly what you need in a selection committee. "Yes men" are no good to anyone.'

The view of most people is that Cody calls the shots and the rest of the backroom team follow his lead.

'Ah God, no! That would never work! It's a collective thing – we all work together. I trust the trainers to get the lads fit, the physio to take care of injuries, the doctor to treat them and make sure they are all well and ready for action.'

Over the years Cody has had no hesitation in changing selectors if he felt they needed changing. It's a practice that has worked to perfection.

'The one thing you must do is to maintain a freshness – on and off the field. In that regard I have changed selectors. Some left because they had other things to do – or could not give it the time required. And believe you me, it's a huge commitment. On other occasions I myself made the call to change and that was respected. This is not about me, this is about what is best for Kilkenny hurling. I like to think that those who have worked with me would be of the same opinion. There are no hard feelings with anyone in that regard.'

Players, like selectors, have come and gone. Even some members of his own club, James Stephens, have found themselves surplus to requirements.

'Again it's the same situation as with the selectors. You must at times strive to improve your team. The decision to omit players is never an easy one but then it's part and parcel of the job.'

Is it the hardest part of the job?

'To be perfectly honest, the hardest part is telling a guy he's not on the panel. I have long since stopped worrying about letting lads off the starting 15. It's off the panel that concerns me.'

Cody places great emphasis on the squad system.

'It is something I set out to do from the start. Championships, or leagues for that matter, are no longer won by 15 players. They are won by the squad of 25 or 30 or whatever it is. I tell the players that all the time. The panel, the panel – that is the key! Telling a guy who might have trained with us for a few months that he has not made the cut – that's the difficult part.'

In his time there have been many rumours that he rules with an iron fist – his way or no way – and that has caused a number of high-profile players to leave the set-up.

'Any guy that ever left – left. That's his choice. I never went after a fella to try and get him back. If you go, you go. That's it as far as I am concerned. The strength of the panel will always absorb fellas leaving.'

In the Kilkenny wins of 1982 and 1983 over Cork, Brian Cody marked Jimmy Barry Murphy. Cody's first year as manager in 1999 saw his Kilkenny side reach the All-Ireland Final. Waiting there were Cork and their manager – Jimmy Barry Murphy.

Mutual respect?

'Very much so. Jimmy is a great guy – we have always got on well together. I was looking forward to renewing the rivalry with him.'

It did not have the fairytale ending. On a dank and dull September afternoon Cork won by 1 point, 0-13 to 0-12. The memory still haunts Cody.

'What haunts me is that if I was told beforehand that we would not concede a goal and Cork would only score 13 points, I would have said we could not lose. But we did.'

Yet with about 15 minutes left Kilkenny were in a strong position – leading by 4 points.

'We just didn't close the game out. I felt we would win from that position, but we didn't and that was disappointing. I had to learn the lessons and make sure it would not happen again.'

A year later, in 2000, Cork fell to Offaly in the All-Ireland semi-final. Kilkenny beat their Leinster rivals (Offaly) in the final.

'DJ (Carey) got a great goal early on and we were always in control after that. The winning margin was 13 points which was a reflection of our dominance. It was a great feeling to win the All-Ireland.'

Did the defeat to Offaly in the 1998 Final act as an extra motivation?

'Not one bit. The motivation is the same every year – which is to win the All-Ireland. You have no control over what went on before or after any game. Matches are won by what happens in the 70-odd minutes that it takes to play a game.'

Cody regularly trots out the line, 'The best team wins the All-Ireland every year'. It is a statement he stands over.

'Of course I do. I say it and I mean it. Whatever the circumstances of any given year, the best team will always win.'

One All-Ireland in the bag – it was time to savour the moment, and then plan his campaign for the 2001 Championship. A Championship that would not end as he would have hoped.

Cody and the Media

Brian Cody is a straight-talking individual. As he said in his autobiography, *Cody*, published in 2009, he dislikes stupid questions. He laughs when I remind him that he is on record as having made that comment.

'I suppose I do, but then guys have a job to do. I don't like the set-up in Croke Park where after a game you sit at a table and answer questions. I prefer it with my back to the wall outside a dressing room. My territory!'

That leads us into the role the media play in the GAA and how they influence decisions. Trial by television. Pundits can be judge and jury. During 2009 Kilkenny were subject to criticism regarding their style of play. One player in particular, Tommy Walsh, was singled out for what some termed his over-aggressive play. This angered Cody as did comments made by former Waterford player Paul O'Flynn before a big game.

'For Paul to come out and say those things in advance of a big game was not on really. Tommy Walsh plays the game hard and fair and to suggest otherwise is poor form. What O'Flynn said put added pressure on the referee and that too is unfair. If you're a pundit on these programmes at least be balanced in your views, and don't convict a man even before a match has started.'

Paul O'Flynn made his comments on *The Sunday Game* on RTÉ a week before Kilkenny played Waterford in the 2009 All-Ireland semi-final.

Ger Loughnane is another whose comments when he was Galway manager upset Cody.

Loughnane said that, 'Kilkenny are good at flicking and belting across the hands and get away with it'. Loughnane's comments were also made on *The Sunday Game* in advance of the 2007 All-Ireland Final against Limerick. Cody though kept his counsel.

'I was very disappointed at Ger's remarks. We've known each other a long time and I felt annoyed that he should say such things. However I didn't respond as it would take our focus off the game. That's what Ger might have wished for. But I didn't buy it.'

As it was, the Kilkenny County Board issued a statement criticising Loughnane's remarks while a succession of former Kilkenny hurlers rallied in defence of Cody and his team. It mattered little – Limerick were dispatched without fuss.

Cody's most recent brush with the media came immediately after the 2009 All-Ireland Final win over Tipperary. Marty Morrissey was the man in question. The interview has had a huge number of hits on You Tube. Cody laughs at that prospect. But the Kilkenny manager has no regrets and 'yes', he has spoken to Marty since.

'Ah, Marty's a nice guy, but I just felt the question was asked at the wrong time.'

Let's recall the events. Kilkenny had just completed an historic four-in-a-row – the county's first time ever achieving such a feat. In the process not only did they beat their great rivals Tipperary, they also emulated the Cork team of the 1940s – the last side to win the four-in-a-row.

It was a cracking final. Tipperary were ahead with less than 10 minutes remaining, but then at a crucial stage, referee Diarmuid Kirwan awarded Kilkenny a penalty. It was a big call. Henry Shefflin scored a goal and it turned the game in Kilkenny's favour.

Having first congratulated Cody on the win, Marty then asked him did he think it was a penalty. Cody was livid and quickly turned it around to ask if Marty thought it was a penalty.

Six weeks later Brian offers this view.

'Here I am, high on emotion, with Kilkenny having just created history and instead of concentrating on what we had achieved, I'm asked about something I had no control over. I just felt it was an inappropriate question at that particular time. Ask me maybe 24 hours later. But not 15 or 20 minutes after a fantastic All-Ireland Final. But as far as I'm concerned it's over and done with now.'

It reminds me again not to ask any stupid questions.

The Kilkenny and Cork Decade

2001 began promisingly enough and Kilkenny duly retained their Leinster title. But not for the first time Galway had one of those 'great days' in the All-Ireland semi-final and ended Kilkenny's reign as champions. It was a blow.

Cody sensed early on in the game that Kilkenny were in trouble. He was right. Galway won and the manager accepted full responsibility for the defeat.

'I looked at the game in the overall context and felt we were not ready for the Galway challenge. In advance I probably had let standards drop and even a slight lowering of standards is fatal at this level.'

It was a mistake he would not repeat. Lessons learned.

Galway, in keeping with their inconsistency, would once again fail in the final. Such a defeat was of little consolation to Cody. But it annoyed him that himself and his team had thrown away an opportunity to win the All-Ireland.

For the next five years, the big guns were back – Cork and Kilkenny would command centre-stage on five successive All-Ireland September Sundays. It was to be the decade of the Cats and the Rebels (2000–2009). And the Rebels certainly lived up to their name by becoming involved in two protracted and bitter disputes with the Cork County Board.

Did such disputes damage hurling?

'Well it certainly wasn't a nice thing to be reading and listening to. It was sad for those involved and not good for the image of hurling. But it was of no concern of mine – what Cork got up to was their business. Nothing to do with me.'

The latest strike in the early part of 2009 looked like it would impact on both the League and Championship with Cork's participation in both competitions in doubt.

Cody had this to say.

'I actually stopped reading about it fairly early on as it had little effect on me. As for Cork not playing – if such was the case so be it. It wouldn't devalue the competitions. It's the teams that play in a competition that make it, not those who choose to stay out.'

As it happened it was resolved. Cork played in both the League and Championship but made little impact in either. In fact Kilkenny inflicted a humiliating defeat on their rivals in a League game – winning by 4-26 to 0-11 before 15,000 spectators in Nowlan Park.

Cody, though, is quick to dispel the theory that they set out to teach Cork – and in particular this group of players – a lesson.

'No, we had a match to win in an effort to make the League Final – nothing more, nothing less. We played alright, but as for teaching Cork a lesson, it was not an issue that day. We always try to beat Cork in any game and it's the same with them I'm sure.'

The first such Cork strike was back in the autumn of 2002. But by September of 2003 Cork were in the All-Ireland Final, with Cody and Kilkenny in the other corner. The Cork v Kilkenny rivalry is a healthy one and Cody was looking forward to the Final.

'Cork were highly motivated, given what had happened earlier in the year, and it would make for a fascinating Final.'

It was a great Final, but having built a good lead, Kilkenny had enough in hand to repel the late Cork challenge and retain the title. Two-in-a-row. Now for that elusive third.

That win gave Cody particular pleasure especially as DJ Carey was captain.

'DJ had been a fantastic servant for Kilkenny, and indeed hurling in general. It was only fitting that he should have the honour of being captain. If anyone deserved it, DJ did – a wonderful hurler who played the game in the right spirit and had brilliant skill levels.'

Three times in the modern era, Kilkenny had failed to land the coveted three-in-a-row – 1974-1975, 1982-1983, and again in 1992-1993.

With Cody at the helm history beckoned.

The Cork strikes, three in all, made it easy to ask the next question.

The role of the GPA in the GAA?

'I remain unconvinced as to their motives. They say they are not pursuing "pay for play", but it appears to be in the background all the time. One thing I am certain of – the GAA cannot afford it and never will be able to, especially in the current climate.'

Cody is by no means anti-GPA.

'Not at all – after all, they are all members of the GAA, just like me. They have done a lot of good work especially for players' welfare. I would hope that the GPA can get official recognition from Croke Park and move on and work together.'

As for his own relationship with the Kilkenny County Board?

'Fantastic! We never want for anything. In this regard, county secretary Ned Quinn is an outstanding individual and makes my job so easy. I have a great relationship with Ned and with the current chairman Paul Kinsella, who was the principal of the school where I am teaching up to a few months ago before his retirement.'

The support from his family is also very important – helped by the fact that Brian's wife, Elsie (Walsh), is a former camogie player with Wexford – yes Wexford!

'She shouts for Kilkenny, though, and of course the two lads, Donnacha and Diarmuid, are playing with the club (James Stephens).'

No-Three-In-A-Row (2004)

In 2004 Kilkenny were chasing the elusive three-in-a-row. They would meet Cork in the Final. Nothing unique about that you would say, well this one was. Both had lost in their respective Provincial Finals. Wexford beat Kilkenny, and Waterford put one over on Cork. Cody and Donal O'Grady (Cork manager) were both grateful for the qualifiers.

Kilkenny were three points ahead after 25 minutes, but the lead was down to just one at half-time. In the second-half Kilkenny only scored two more points. They had little in the tank when Cork raised the tempo. In the end Cork were winners by 0-17 to 0-9. Once again Kilkenny had failed to land the three-in-a-row.

Cody had no complaints.

'None, as I say, the best team always win the All-Ireland. Cork played very well and deserved their win. Our lads were committed and brave, but on the day it was not enough.'

In the aftermath of that game, sections of the media were quick to write Kilkenny and possibly Cody's epitaph. This criticism gathered momentum after Galway beat Kilkenny in the All-Ireland semi-final of 2005. This loss incensed him.

Galway once again failed to reproduce their semi-final form in the Final. Cork retained their title with a comfortable win.

He thought briefly about stepping down, but soon decided against it, helped by outside comments.

'I read where Enda McEvoy (*The Sunday Tribune* journalist) said that the Liam McCarthy Cup would be absent from Kilkenny for a long time. Donal O'Grady who by now had resigned as Cork manager (John Allen was the manager when Cork won in 2005) suggested Kilkenny might struggle for a while.'

Such statements could not be backed up with facts.

'Okay, we had lost in 2004 and 2005, but I can tell you we were not gone away and I promised myself we would return stronger than ever.'

The Path to Glory

2006 offered huge motivation. Doing to Cork what Cork had done to Kilkenny – stop them completing the three-in-a-row. Kilkenny and Cork were now the dominant teams in hurling. They had shared the last four All-Irelands between them. It came as no real surprise that they would contest the All-Ireland Final of 2006. There was a lot at stake. This time Cody had his team in peak mental and physical condition. Much has been made of the intensity of Kilkenny's training. That may very well be the case but Cody is not one for complicating matters.

'While in terms of fitness we embrace all the modern methods, hurling hasn't changed. It is still a simple game to play. Do the basics well and prepare properly and you're on the right track.'

He does agree about the intensity of their training sessions.

'We try and create a match situation, play hard and show what you are capable of and that's it – nothing too complicated really.'

As for the theory that Kilkenny play like the Tyrone footballers – with a lot of players surrounding the man in possession – he laughs at the notion.

'Two different games entirely. That is a myth created by certain sections of the media.'

Cody does attend a lot of games and is a regular at football matches in Croke Park.

'I don't have a lot of spare time, but when I do I go to games and enjoy them. I like the way Kerry go about their business. Serious operators – as they showed in the 2009 All-Ireland Final.'

That gives me an opening. Did he ever play football?

'I did with the club and a bit with county. But the pressures of a dual player in Kilkenny forced me to choose hurling.'

The answer is given with a broad smile. I would think it would be considered one of those stupid questions he professes to hate. He did though clarify that he played football for James Stephens.

Whatever about playing like Tyrone, Cody devised a plan for the 2006 All-Ireland Final with Cork. They worked hard on it in training. Cork had developed the running game into an art form. It was hard to stop, but then Cody was a driven man in 2006. He wanted to answer the critics. As for the plan to stop Cork, it was – as all good plans are – simple and effective.

'We were going to harass Cork at every chance. Be in their faces. Stop them getting the handpasses away. Stifle Donal Óg Cusack's puckouts. I wanted two men there when the ball landed. It would call for total commitment for the 70 minutes.'

He got it. Kilkenny were always in front. Cork did peg them back in the second-half, but at the end Kilkenny were three points ahead, 1-14 to 1-11.

'That win was sweet. Any All-Ireland win is sweet but this was extra sweet.'

Cody acknowledges Cork's part in a great final.

'There was an honesty about that match and Cork were excellent. On another day that display would have won them the title. But on this day it was not enough.'

As he would say himself – the best team always wins the All-Ireland every year.

An added bonus was the fact that Jackie Tyrell from Cody's own James Stephens was the captain on that day. That and denying Cork the three-in-a-row – yes, a good day all round.

Cork and Kilkenny would then go their separate ways. Kilkenny in pursuit of more glory, Cork into a third bitter dispute with the County Board.

The year 2007 brought yet another title to the Marble County. This time Limerick were the beaten finalists. But it was a year tinged with sadness. Events a few days before the quarter-final with Galway impacted greatly on the Kilkenny panel.

Vanessa McGarry, the wife of James McGarry – the team's outstanding goalkeeper – was tragically killed in a car accident. Hurling and All-Irelands were put to one side. Cody has clear recollections of the tragedy.

'It was awful. It hit us hard, of course – James and his son Darragh more than anyone. But Vanessa had been so much a part of the group that it was like a death in our family. As a group we dealt with it as best we could and when the funeral was over, we went back. It was the only way we could deal with it. But you just had to feel for James.'

To the GAA's credit, all games in the Championship that weekend were cancelled as the GAA family rallied around a family in mourning.

In the quarter-final Brian Cody came up against Ger Loughnane, now the Galway manager.

'It was a cracking match. We won by 10 points in the end, but only because we got two late goals from Eddie Brennan. Given the circumstances, a week after the tragedy, it was a pleasing victory. Our own little tribute I suppose to Vanessa.'

Early goals saw off Limerick in the Final. Kilkenny had once again won back-to-back titles. Now in 2008 could they finally nail that elusive three-in-a-row? Much as he would have liked to, Cody could not get away from the talk of three-in-a-row.

'We never mentioned it, but in reality it was in the background all the time I suppose. As I have said before – one match at a time. Records are for someone else to worry about.'

The year 2008 went like a dream, and with it the dream final – Kilkenny v Waterford. Waterford had been around for a while and produced some quality hurling. Their day had finally arrived. Or had it?

What happened on Sunday 7 September 2008 will live long in the memory of those who witnessed it, either in the ground or on TV. It was the complete performance as Kilkenny displayed their vast array of skills. Waterford were literally blown away. Even the normally reserved Cody was pleased.

'It was near enough to perfection I suppose really. I knew we were going well coming into the game. But to produce that type of display in a final was beyond our wildest dreams. The other pleasing aspect was that with the game long won, the lads kept playing every ball as if it was the last. That is a measure of their approach to the game.'

There was one other little cameo that historic afternoon and Cody was central to it. Not known for sentiment, he disproved that theory as the game entered the closing stages.

James McGarry was brought on to receive his medal on the field. He received a tumultuous reception from both sets of fans.

'It was the right thing to do. James was retiring at the end of the season so it was nice to be in a position to bring him on.'

And they say Brian Cody is a hard man.

'Stop now – you'll be ruining my reputation.'

It is also a day Nickey Brennan recalls with pride.

'I remember that day sitting in the stand, Uachtarán Na h-Éireann and An Taoiseach either side of me. It took me all of my power to stay in my seat. I was bursting with pride. You know what they say – a savage loves his native land, and that day was so special.'

In it all, Cody had a tinge of sympathy for Waterford.

'You'd have to be sorry for them. Great players like Tony Browne and Dan Shanahan playing in their first All-Ireland Final. But we had a job to do and that was it.'

For the record, the final score was Kilkenny 3-30 Waterford 1-13. Kilkenny and Cody had finally landed the three-in-a-row. That night at the Kilkenny victory banquet there was another accolade for Cody. In an unusual move and in acknowledgement of the Kilkenny display that afternoon, RTÉ's *The Sunday Game* panellists named Brian Cody as their 'Man of the Match'. It is the first time a non-player has received such an award. Cody was embarrassed. But there was general agreement that it was the right choice. This time Cody could not argue with the pundits.

Catching the Dream

Now for four?

In the early part of the 2009 season they set about their business in the usual manner. The National Hurling League title was secured. Next up was the new-look Leinster Championship. Galway and Antrim were now participants. As luck would have it, Galway and Kilkenny would meet in the Leinster semi-final. O'Connor Park, Tullamore, Offaly was the venue for an historic encounter.

'A really tough match and ideal preparation for the rest of the year. Galway played very well, but we stuck to our task and won in the end.'

The first steps on the road to four-in-a-row had been taken.

A fresh challenge awaited in the Leinster Final – Dublin under new boss, Anthony Daly, the former Clare hurler.

'We were very conscious of Dublin. They had been making great strides and unless we were tuned in we could be caught. As it was they gave us a good game that we were pleased to see the back of. Hurling needs to be strong in the capital and hopefully they can continue to show improvement.'

Waterford were next in the All-Ireland semi-final – a repeat of the 2008 Final. The margin of victory was smaller but the outcome was the same. Kilkenny were back in the Final. Now not even Cody could stop the talk. It was all about the four-in-a-row. History and immortality beckoned. Apart from Cork, their greatest rivals, Tipperary, stood in their way.

Before all that came the announcement that Brian Cody was to publish his autobiography. It took a lot of people by surprise, but there was a simple explanation.

'It had been suggested that someone, I'm not sure who, was going to write about me and Kilkenny hurling. So I decided if anyone was going to do it, I would do it myself.'

The day of reckoning finally dawned. Yet another dank Sunday in September. All-Ireland Hurling Final day 2009. Could Kilkenny do it?

'I felt confident because our preparation had gone according to plan. The players were focused and determined. But we faced a massive challenge.'

The challenge was even greater with less than 10 minutes remaining.

The scoreboard told the story, Tipperary 0-20, Kilkenny 0-17, and Tipperary with only 14 men after Benny Dunne had been sent off.

Then it happened. Sensing that history could be slipping from their grasp, the wearers of the 'black and amber' responded as only Cody knew they could.

'The penalty was a factor, but the way Henry (Shefflin) stood up and powered it to the net is testimony to his strength of character. Martin (Comerford) then got another goal and we finally got the scores. People talk about the penalty but remember we scored 2-3 in the last 8 minutes.'

Kilkenny 2-22, Tipperary 0-23. How did he feel at the final whistle?

'Naturally very proud of the players for the manner in which they stood up when it mattered. Also a huge sense of satisfaction that we had achieved the four-in-a-row. It was done without losing a Championship game in the four years (2006–2009) and facing down all the challenges that were put before us.'

Time to Relax

Cody could now relax and enjoy that special feeling that comes with winning an All-Ireland. By defeating Tipperary in the Final it also meant that all the big Munster hurling counties had succumbed to Kilkenny in All-Ireland Finals under his stewardship. A nice little record to add to the many already achieved.

It is easy to see why he is annoyed at the All-Star selectors. For the record – in 2009 Kilkenny played 12 competitive matches and won 11.

In the process they won all competitions open to them – Walsh Cup, National Hurling League, Leinster Championship and All-Ireland Championship.

Outside of hurling, Brian Cody was recently appointed principal of the school where he has been teaching for the last 23 years – St Patrick's De La Salle in Kilkenny City. It's a job he really enjoys.

'Teaching is a bit like managing a team. You strive to get the best out of pupils and staff alike. You are looking to get the best results for everyone.'

But the four-in-a-row must surely be his proudest moment in hurling? 'It's a massive achievement – no doubt about that. Also seeing players like Martin Comerford and Derek Lyng develop into top-class hurlers is another source of satisfaction. Neither played under-age hurling with Kilkenny but they both worked hard at their game to make it to the very top. But the biggest achievement for me is playing hurling. It's a great game and I feel honoured to have played it.'

The game also brings its perks.

'Thanks to our success the players and I have practically seen the world on some great trips. On 28 December 2009 we're off to Malaysia. That's something to look forward to after the hard work all year.'

Any regrets?

'No, not really. It's been an exciting few years and I'm delighted to have played my part.'

* * *

It is nearly time to call a halt. It's been a fascinating chat – not at all what I had expected. Before we finish I remarked that I had been a bit nervous in meeting him as fellas had said, 'You could be a bit cranky'.

Again he laughs, 'Who told you that? . . . Media guys I bet.'

One last thing.

I broach the subject of the five-in-a-row in 2010.

Brian Cody looks at me, laughs and heads out into the Kilkenny night air.

I know . . . it was a stupid question.

3

Kevin Heffernan

The Rise of Heffo's Army

On 26 May 1974 it was Dublin v Wexford in the Leinster Football Championship with an attendance of approximately 5,000. Dublin won narrowly.

In July 2008 it was, again, Dublin v Wexford in the Leinster Football Championship – this time with an attendance of 82,000. A full house in Croke Park. Dublin won at a canter; Dublin 3-23, Wexford 0-9.

What happened in the intervening 34 years that attracted over 77,000 extra supporters – even allowing for the newly redeveloped Croke Park?

Some people would put it down to one man.

Dublin manager Kevin Heffernan, or Heffo as he is often known as today.

Whatever term you use, there is no doubt his arrival as Dublin manager changed the face of Gaelic Football. In fact there are those who would say he saved the GAA in the 1970s.

Brian Mullins, a key player under Heffernan, thinks that 'saving the GAA might be putting it a bit strong. But there is no doubt that Dublin's revival helped the game enormously in the capital.'

In the early 1970s Dublin football was at its lowest ebb. Offaly were the dominant team in the province of Leinster. The men from the Faithful County had won four of the previous five Leinster Finals. In the same period Offaly won the All-Ireland title in both 1971 and 1972. They were, up to a point, dismissive of the 'Dubs'. Heffernan soon changed that.

Heffo is regarded by many as one of Dublin's greatest players, even though he won only one All-Ireland medal. That came in the 1958 win over Derry, when he was captain of the team. Heffernan had more success in Leinster – winning four Championship medals and three National Football League medals.

A member of the famed St Vincent's Club in the Marino area of north Dublin, he was part of a golden era for that club in both hurling and football. In all he won a total of 21 senior county medals – 15 in football including a 7-in-a-row between 1949 and 1955. An accomplished hurler, he won a Leinster Minor Championship medal in 1947 later adding six Dublin county hurling medals to an impressive tally.

For all his on-field achievements, and there are many, it is what he achieved as a manager that he is best remembered for – particularly among the modern generation of Gaelic football followers. His innovative thinking dragged Dublin football off its knees. The status they enjoy today first emerged in 1974.

Yet were it not for his appointment and a crucial point by Leslie Deegan, the Dubs might still be languishing in the lower echelons of football and we might never have heard of 'Heffo's Army'. Unthinkable, maybe, but possible. Of course what also defined Heffernan was the intense rivalry between Dublin and Kerry throughout the 1970s and 1980s.

Heffernan's appointment, as with most GAA managers, was not a simple one. Prior to his arrival the selection committee consisted of five members – three from the county board and two from the county champions of the time. Jimmy Gray was the Dublin Chairman and he felt a change was needed. Gray wanted a three-man management committee. Crucially he also wanted Heffernan as the main man.

Gray explains.

'I got permission from the Board to pick three selectors. Lorcan and Donal readily agreed. Now I had to get Kevin. He turned down my first approach because he had committed himself to managing St Vincent's. I did tell him that I would be back.'

In those days the media was not as influential as it is today. However one man with a huge interest in Dublin football was Seán Óg Ó Ceallacháin. Seán was working for *The Irish Press* at the time and was a big Dublin supporter. He was constantly in touch with Gray trying to find out who the next Dublin manager would be. In an effort to advance the process, Gray told Ó Ceallacháin he was hoping to get the three lads, Heffernan, Colfer and Redmond, to do the manager's job.

The following day *The Irish Press* ran the headline, 'Heffernan for Dublin'. Gray was waiting for the call. It duly arrived. Heffernan was furious. He gave it to the chairman with both barrels.

But when he calmed down, Heffernan said, 'I suppose I'll have to do the job now.'

Smiling to himself, Gray – a bit like what Heffernan would do in later years – 'had got his man'.

Heffernan immediately changed the routine being followed in Dublin training. A players' meeting was called. Plans were laid. Heffernan let it be known they could do better and achieve something. Some nodded. Others had heard it all before. Would this time be any different? It would. Heffernan would see to that. The training was savage.

Some stayed. Others dropped out. Heffernan was pleased. If you couldn't do the hard training, you weren't going to do it when it mattered – in a Championship game. Lap after lap after lap. Press-ups. Sit-ups. Nothing scientific, just sheer hard work. Tuesday, Thursday and Saturday – that was the schedule and you dare not miss one. So it was underway, the Heffernan regime. The GAA would never be the same again.

Recalling that pivotal 1974 Leinster Football Championship, Heffernan was nothing if not honest. When asked if he 'had time for any of them' (ie, the personalities involved in the 1974 Leinster Football Championship – and not just the players, but also his opposite numbers in the other countries), the reply is frank.

'None of them.'

Eugene Magee was the Offaly manager at the time.

'Magee and I would not have got on. Our paths first crossed with UCD and Vincent's.' Later they encountered each other with Dublin and Offaly.

'We would have disliked each other intensely.'

With time though that has changed.

'We'd be civil to one another now. We chatted and found we have a lot in common about the GAA. Back then he was the enemy.'

Kerry v Dublin could also be described as O'Dwyer v Heffernan. Heffernan evades the question but smiles at the mention of O'Dwyer's name. His nemesis. The Dublin players of that era had their own take on matters. Some felt that when Kerry lost a game to Dublin, the Kerry management, and by extension O'Dwyer, were slow to offer their congratulations to the victors. By contrast, Dublin were quick to acknowledge when Kerry won.

O'Dwyer himself is full of praise for Heffernan and his contribution to the GAA in Dublin.

'The GAA should be grateful to Kevin for the work he has done on their behalf in the city. A marvellous man.'

The only other manager Heffernan commented on was Seán Boylan.

'I would have huge time for Seán – the man and what he has done. One lovely fella.'

Heffernan is long gone from inter-county management but would relish the opportunity to test himself against the present breed of modern-day managers – Harte, Kernan, O'Mahoney, McGeeney, O'Connor.

'There is a part of me that would love to have the energy and platform to try it. If you see a team sending in six players to swamp the man in possession, as Tyrone and Armagh do, the challenge then is you must change your view on possession.'

His view on this is quite simplistic.

'If half a dozen guys arrive, they have to be leaving space behind them. So the option then is rather than taking steps and soloing with the ball, kick it into the space. Instead of trying to catch the ball, fist it away.' This would basically alter the way the game is played.

'What would happen if you made the instant transfer of possession the basis of your game instead of possession itself? Would they take the risk of sending in the posse?'

That's the thing about Heffernan. He loved a challenge and was always looking for a new angle to work on. He found one at a basketball match one evening. The lesson learned that night was put to good use. Kevin was studying at Trinity College and while there he played basketball.

'We played UCG one night. We were small handy players. These guys arrived out on the court – big fat guys with American accents. This is easy I thought, we'll run these fellas into the ground. They murdered us. Moved the ball at pace. We couldn't touch them. I could not believe what they did to us. It stayed with me.'

The lesson: Build a team on the premise that a good big guy will always beat a good small guy. After that Heffernan always went for big men on his teams. He got his chance to put his theory into practice as the season of 1973/74 got underway.

'We went after certain guys. We devised a style of play and demands on those who wanted to play it. I also looked for character in players – guys that would make the commitment. They needed to be able to stand the pressure and needed to be adaptable to our needs and demands. I like to think that we ended up with an exceptional group.'

Of course in any new regime there were casualties. Lads who had played through the bad days would now miss out. But there was to be no room for sentiment in Heffernan's and Dublin's new world.

Jimmy Keaveney Returns

The League was used as a springboard for the summer Championship campaign of 1974. Fitness was a priority. It was a good League campaign as well. Fellow selectors Lorcan Redmond and Donal Colfer were able lieutenants. There were signs that the team was moving in the right direction. Brian Mullins has words of praise for Redmond and Colfer.

'Oh, they were great with Kevin. They worked very well together – bounced ideas off each other. The chemistry was excellent. Dublin and progress was all that mattered for the three men.'

Heffernan was pleased with progress.

'We were doing well. Our fitness was a help. Even though the teams in Division 2 weren't great, winning games boosted our confidence. Then with that confidence we were in a position to think about our tactical plan.'

In football at the time, the hand-pass was an integral part of the game. The Dublin manager put it to good use.

'We used it to good effect in our game. The team was fit and we moved the ball quickly through the hands.' (Remember the basketball players from UCG?)

Wexford were Dublin's opponents in the opening game of the Leinster Championship. It was in Croke Park but acted as a curtain-raiser to a replay of the Division 1 National Football League final. Kerry were playing Roscommon. The Dubs couldn't even command centre stage in their own city. Heffernan watched the League Final and immediately noticed the difference.

'It was men and boys, we looked what we were – 2nd Division.'

Dublin did beat Wexford, but they were far from impressive.

'We won playing badly. In fact John Quigley, the hurler, played that day for Wexford. He remarked to one of our lads coming off the field that neither side would see much more of Croke Park for the rest of the year.'

Famous last words as it turned out.

Bobby Doyle scored 2-1 that day. One goal came from a penalty. Doyle had never taken a penalty before. He almost closed his eyes while taking it. Somehow it ended up in the net. As Doyle left the field, Heffernan approached him.

'You're not taking any more penalties.'

Blunt and to the point, Heffernan knew no other way.

Interestingly the match report in *The Irish Press* the following day finished with the line, 'Dublin can be written off as serious challengers for Offaly's provincial crown'.

Louth were next up for Heffernan's Dublin. By then the ingenious Heffernan had pulled a rabbit or two from the hat. Jimmy Keaveney was back. So too was David Hickey. Hickey recalls the moment the call came.

'I only played once in 1973. I was then playing rugby when Kevin came after me. To be honest he was pushing an open door. All I ever wanted to do was play football for Dublin. I sensed something was about to happen. And when the train left the station I wanted to be on it.'

How Keaveney returned is well documented but worth recalling.

Heffernan was driving home after the first round of the Championship in 1974 – still in search of a freetaker. A chance remark set him thinking. A glance at the teams which were successful showed him that they all had a reliable and accurate freetaker – McTeague with Offaly, Sheehy with Kerry and Stafford with Meath.

Dublin had none – at least not yet. But soon it was to be Keaveney with Dublin.

A passenger in the car that day was seven-year-old Terry Jennings. Heffernan mentioned if only we (Dublin) had a freetaker. Young Jennings piped up, 'I never saw Jimmy Keaveney miss one (free).'

Heffernan dismissed the idea initially. Keaveney was only 29 years old but by his own admission, unfit and enjoying life. By that he meant having a few pints.

'I used to have a few pints alright, sure why not? I was finished with Dublin and I was just playing with Vincent's.'

Heffernan eventually approached Keaveney. You do not say 'No' to Kevin.

'No, you do not. It's not a request – it's more like an order. Be in Parnell Park on Tuesday night for training. That was it. That's how Kevin operated.'

Keaveney's return was an important piece of Heffernan's jigsaw, although it came as a shock to Jimmy when Heffernan called.

'Yeah, it did. I was at the Wexford match and thought Dublin weren't great, now mind. I was playing hurling and football with Vincent's at the time, but felt my inter-county career was over.'

Was he glad he went back?

'Jaysus, not for the first few nights of training. It was brutal. I was completely out of condition. But I kept at it and Kevin gave me huge encouragement.'

As for the training, Keaveney noticed a slight change.

'There was, of course, a strong emphasis on the physical side. But Kevin was always adapting. The skills of the game were also worked on, as were team tactics. He was always working on angles to outwit his opponent.'

The stories about Heffernan following Jimmy around on nights before games are also true.

'I used to have a pint or two in Vincent's club. But Kevin would call in and I had to stop. He had guys everywhere telling him if I had been in.'

Jimmy devised another plan, but Heffernan saw through that as well.

'I decided to go into town as no one would see me there. Or so I thought. But he found out and pulled me in training one night. Eventually I gave in and stayed off it (the few pints) before matches.'

Jimmy has no regrets and enjoyed his 'second coming' as a Dublin player.

'Ah, sure it was great. My first stint was miserable. We couldn't even win a match. I won a Leinster medal and played in a League Final but nothing else. No one watched our games. We were the poor relations of football. Kevin changed all that. We went on to play in six All-Ireland Finals in a row. And we also played in six League Finals in a row. So it was a great period for Dublin. I won my All-Ireland medals, All-Stars, but it was not about medals. It was about playing football and playing for Dublin.'

How would he rate his fellow Vincent's man as a manager and his legacy to Dublin football?

'His greatest legacy in my opinion will be revitalising Dublin football. You must remember soccer was big in this town and the GAA was struggling. But just about this time the big soccer teams, Drumcondra and Shamrock Rovers, were also in danger. Drums faded and with that the Dublin footballers filled the void. It gave the people an outlet that they were glad to follow. It was a case of coming along at the right time. All of a sudden everyone wanted to beat Dublin, whereas before Kevin came along, everyone beat Dublin.'

Jimmy also makes this observation.

'I have no doubt Kevin would have been capable of managing the top teams in any sport – be it soccer or rugby. He just had that way about him. He was a brilliant man manager.'

Dublin's Road to Victory 1974

As mentioned, Dublin narrowly beat Wexford in the opening round of the 1974 Leinster Championship. Then after seeing off Louth in the second round, Dublin faced Kildare in the third round quarter-final.

Earlier in the year Kildare had beaten Dublin in a league play-off. Soon afterwards Kildare invited Dublin to Naas for a challenge game. The Dubs were seen as a soft touch. Heffernan played almost half his Championship team in that game. Dublin lost by 16 points.

When they played each other again six weeks later in the Leinster Championship quarter-final, Dublin won by six points. Leaving the field, Kildare players Pat Gogarty and Ollie Crinnigan were stunned. They started muttering about Heffernan's cunning.

'We never saw that coming, Pat. That's some shrewd bastard!'

Kildare never recovered and they would be a long time waiting to win the Leinster Championship again after that defeat.

After the victory over Kildare, Dublin faced Leinster Champions Offaly in the semi-final. Heffernan was confident and pleased.

'At the start of the year I would have been looking at one match at a time and possibly a Leinster title.'

That possibility was getting ever nearer. Dublin were now fashionable again. The crowds had returned. The train was beginning to leave the station. Heffernan could sense a growing confidence in the team. Further evidence came in the team meeting the day before the Offaly game.

'It was a good meeting. The players were now beginning to motor and had self-belief. Very important in any team.'

The meeting was almost over when there was another positive development.

'We were just about to finish when Gay O'Driscoll stood up. He gave a passionate speech about the match the next day.'

O'Driscoll was only a sub but what he said struck a chord.

'Gay made the point that if anyone felt they were not up for the job, he and others were willing and able to step in. He told them not to forget that. I felt good about the match after that. It was very passionate.'

The game with Offaly in 1974 set a new-look Dublin team on their way. As in most stories it had its unlikely hero. In this case it was Leslie Deegan, who like Gay O'Driscoll, did not start the match. He was introduced early in the first-half and scored a goal. With the match level and heading for a replay, Deegan made sure his name entered Dublin GAA folklore by kicking the winning point.

Had it gone to a replay, the result might have been different. He may have won them a place in the Leinster Final but Deegan remained on the periphery of the team for the remainder of his career. However, few, least of all Heffernan, will forget his contribution to the Leinster Championship win in 1974.

By now Dublin were above the radar. 'Heffo's Army', as the Hill 16 supporters became known, was born. They were on the march. Heffernan himself was looking ahead.

'Myself, Lorcan and Donal wouldn't have been ones to get carried away but things were moving along nicely. Certainly after beating Offaly we realised we were heading in the right direction.'

Having beaten Offaly, Dublin were now in the Leinster Final facing Meath. In that decider Dublin emerged winners over Meath by 1-14 to 1-9. Heffernan had won a Leinster title and now set his sights higher. In that line of sight were Cork – the reigning All-Ireland champions from 1973 and favourites to win back-to-back titles in 1974. Cork though held no fears for Dublin and Heffernan. It goes back to his own playing days. Dublin teams never lose to Cork.

It was a frantic match and Dublin's best display of the year according to Heffernan.

'I remember that day as perhaps the greatest performance the fellas gave. I would put it up there with the 1977 semi-final. Cork even got away with a goal when they had 16 players on the field. But it didn't matter. We went down the field straight away and got one ourselves. We really played the way we wanted that day.'

Tactically and fitness-wise, Dublin outsmarted Cork that afternoon.

Midfielder Brian Mullins agrees.

'It was a combination of things that all came together on the day. We were underdogs and Cork might have underestimated us but that suited us.'

Cork had high-fielding Declan Barron in their team. He was practically unbeatable in the air. Heffernan devised a plan. A simple one really.

'We just left him catch it. But we were waiting for him when he came down. He (Barron) found himself with nowhere to go. So we just took it off him.'

Sometimes it was the simplest of things that undid teams. There was another little incident that Heffernan seized on to boost his team – a throwaway comment by Cork goalkeeper Billy Morgan.

'Billy and Jimmy Keaveney are great friends. A few weeks before the game Jimmy was spending a few days with Billy in Cork. Just before he left for home, Jimmy was told, "take a look at this (the Sam Maguire Cup) – it'll be the nearest ye get to it". Now nothing was meant by it, but we used it as an example of Cork arrogance.'

Keaveney recalls the story.

'It was just a joke by Billy. Frank Cogan was there as well. We laugh about it now when we meet up. But I think Cork actually underestimated us that day. I remember Billy's wife Mary and Frank's wife Ann talking about Cork and the final even before we played Cork in the semi-final. That's how confident they were.'

Having beaten the champions (Cork) in the semi-final, it seemed almost inevitable that Dublin would now win the final of 1974 when they faced Galway.

They did – with Paddy Cullen saving a penalty from Liam Sammon. It was a very special day for all concerned. Croke Park went wild as the new-look Dubs came of age. At one point Heffernan was on the field appealing for calm as Dublin eased to victory.

'That day in 1974 was outstanding. What we achieved, we achieved together – the county board, the management, the players and the support we got from everyone.'

Heffernan has fond memories of the scenes after the game.

'I remember the colour, the banners. Personally I was a bit uncomfortable to be at the centre. But it was spectacular. You felt you were part of something special and unique.'

The day after the match there was an open-top bus parade to the Mansion House in Dublin. Robbie Kelleher tells a funny story about the journey.

'There we were, all on top of the bus. It was just crossing O'Connell Bridge when I looked down at the crowd. I recognised this guy with a hat on. He was waving up and smiling at us. It was Heffernan.'

Shunning the limelight as ever.

He had now experienced All-Ireland success as both a player and as a manager. Which was better?

His answer is typical Heffernan: obtuse.

'Was it better playing or managing? Really the pleasure of winning is a physical pleasure for a player. As a manager it's a more cerebral business. Can you beat him (the manager of the opposition) tactically or intellectually? It's in there you get the buzz.'

Dublin v Kerry Rivalry

That year, 1974, ushered in a new era. Dublin were All-Ireland champions for the first time since 1963. But very soon a new challenge presented itself. Kerry and Mick O'Dwyer arrived in 1975. For the next few years it was all about the big two – the Dublin v Kerry rivalry.

Keaveney claims that Heffernan revelled in the rivalry.

'Beating Kerry in the All-Ireland was always a double All-Ireland to me,' Heffernan was once quoted as saying.

'I would agree with that,' says Keaveney. 'He took great pleasure in the All-Ireland win of 1976. It was his first big win over Kerry in an All-Ireland Final as either player or manager.'

And Mick O'Dwyer?

'Well now, they were both great for the game. They got on alright, even though they wouldn't meet that often. I'm sure they'd enjoy a cup of coffee together. But I suppose they were just concentrating on their own jobs of managing their teams. There's a lot of respect between the two though, I'd say.'

Like O'Dwyer, Heffernan would also do anything to win.

'I can tell you he could be ruthless. If you could do a job for him, he'd get you. Nothing would stand in his way. If you were in jail in Mountjoy, he'd break you out if it meant winning the All-Ireland. Once you understood that, you were grand.'

Strangely, Brian Mullins has a different angle on the Kerry v Dublin rivalry.

'It didn't matter to Kevin. For that period it just happened to be Kerry. It could have been anyone, but it was Kerry. You had to play whoever you had to play. The important thing was to win.'

Yet when Dublin beat Kerry in the 1976 All-Ireland Final, it was Dublin's first win over the Kingdom since 1934 (an interval of 42 years). Heffernan said to defender Kevin Moran, 'I've waited 21 years for this.'

(Kerry had beaten Dublin in the All-Ireland Final of 1955 when Heffernan was a player.)

* * *

As All-Ireland champions Dublin were fancied by many to retain their title in 1975. But there had been a significant development down south. Kerry shocked Cork in the Munster Final. That unexpected victory was to usher in a new era in Gaelic football. Heffernan, as astute as ever, saw it coming.

'I knew they (Kerry) were coming. They were a good team. Indeed time would show they were a brilliant team. Good innate footballers who could think for themselves on the field. A vital ingredient in any team.'

Small things can change the course of events. Heffernan is of the opinion that that's what happened on a wet September Sunday in 1975.

'We were unfortunate to concede the first free. A bad free, Gay (O'Driscoll) just did not hold the ball when it came in. They got a goal from it. That gave them confidence and the impetus they needed. That's not to detract from them. They were a great team. We needed to keep them under.'

Interestingly, while a huge admirer of Heffernan, David Hickey believes the manager got this one wrong.

'I think he actually worried a bit too much about Kerry coming. The week before the game we did gruelling training – one night in pouring rain – to satisfy the media. We trained on Saturday, the day before the final. On the day of the game we did 20 minutes of yoga. We were very flat going out on the pitch.'

Kerry won, but Dublin and Heffernan would return in 1976.

For the 1976 Championship Heffernan reshaped his team. There was a new-found hunger in the team. With a completely new half-back line they gained revenge over Kerry in the final. It was a comfortable win, playing quality football and setting in motion another period of Kerry v Dublin rivalry.

'The three half-backs were brilliant – three players the likes of which just don't come along together at the same time.'

Kevin Moran was the centre-back on the team. Moran went on to play for Manchester United and the Republic of Ireland soccer team in the World Cup in Italy in 1990 and in the USA in 1994.

Brian Mullins on Heffo the Manager

Heffernan was very passionate about football, although he was remarkably calm in dressing rooms – as Brian Mullins recalls.

'He was passionate alright, but never one to be banging chairs and that. His dressing rooms were calm. He pointed out what needed doing – where a guy was going wrong and got his message across that way.'

Goalkeeper on the 1983 winning team John O'Leary concurs with Mullins.

'There was nothing complicated about his teamtalks or tactics. He believed in keeping things simple and having confidence in you to do the job. He was very straightforward and always believed that a Dublin player was better than the rest.'

The way O'Leary was told he would be starting his first Championship match was classic Heffernan.

'It was the Leinster Final of 1980 against Offaly. I was convinced I was only going to be a sub that day. He threw me a jersey and said, "You're in today, John". I suppose he left it so late to tell me to make sure I was relaxed going into the game.'

Man management was another of Heffernan's great strengths.

Mullins again.

'He would speak to players on an individual basis. Kevin knew exactly what to say. If a player needed a boost he got it. A quiet word here and whisper there – he always got it right. Players respected him for that.'

There is little doubt that Brian Mullins has immense respect for his fellow Vincent's man.

'I consider myself fortunate to have played for him. I learned an awful lot from him. What I learned stood to me as a player and afterwards when I moved into management. I was lucky I suppose that part of my career coincided with his term as Dublin manager.'

As a player Heffernan had exceptional talent, as evidenced by his selection on the GAA's team of the century. Former Dublin player and manager Mickey Whelan has little doubt about Heffernan's ability.

'As good a player as I ever played with – or saw for that matter. Kevin had tremendous determination for such a small man. He was very strong though and hard to mark.'

He had one other attribute as a player: a goal scorer.

'Kevin was a real finisher. A great eye for a goal in both hurling and football. He was a fabulous hurler as well. I played alongside Kevin for both club and county and he was the best – without a doubt.'

Mickey in particular remembers the 1955 Leinster Final, Dublin v Meath.

'Meath were the All-Ireland champions. They had a good defender in a chap by the name of Paddy "Hands" O'Brien. He was the guy who was going to tie down Kevin. In the first 25 minutes Kevin scored two goals and ran your man all over the field. If you pardon the pun, he didn't lay his "hands" on Kevin.'

Dublin won 5-12 to 0-7.

Unfortunately Kevin picked up an injury before the 1955 All-Ireland Final. He should not have played. He did, but Kerry won.

Jimmy Keaveney played with Heffernan for a couple of years at club level.

'Kevin had retired in 1964 I think, but came back to play with Vincent's. We won two county medals together in 1966 and 1967. He was a great player. Ahead of his time I would say. Very determined. Tactically brilliant. He used to play full-forward but not for him the high ball (not being tall, he preferred low balls into his full-forward position rather than trying to field high balls). Kevin would go looking for the ball. Run the full-back all over the place and then take or create scores. Very clever.'

Whelan agrees with Brian Mullins about Heffernan's man management skills.

'Incredible – he never got it wrong. He also had a tremendous influence on players outside their football careers. Lots of lads benefited from Kevin's advice and guidance over the years.'

Mickey also credits his friend with persuading him to remain on as manager of Vincent's in 2006.

'He did indeed. We had lost to UCD in the county final that year. Now we had not won the county title in 23 years – which for us is an eternity. I was on the point of giving up as I felt a new voice would help the team.

Kevin though encouraged me to stay on. He felt the big breakthrough was near.'

As ever Heffernan got it spot on.

Twelve months later in 2007, on an emotional evening in Parnell Park, St Vincent's claimed the title – their 25th in all. The abiding memory is of old friends, Whelan and Heffernan, embracing after the game.

'It was a great night for us and Kevin was proved right. He felt it would be wrong to change management when we were so close in 2006. The wise old head I suppose. In fact we went on to win the Leinster and All-Ireland titles later that year, which made it extra special.'

Heffo's Shock Resignation

In 1976 Heffo had won his second All-Ireland title in three years. But the euphoria of that achievement was quickly forgotten when Heffernan announced that he was stepping down. It came as a huge shock. David Hickey well remembers the circumstances.

'We were all called to a meeting in the Gresham Hotel and he just told us. No explanation or nothing. Just "I am going". I think his leaving was a betrayal of Donal and Lorcan and the boys. It was wrong to leave without an explanation.'

Keaveney also recalls the night they were told.

'A surprise alright, but sure Tony (Hanahoe) came in and we carried on. Kevin was never away though (in other words, he was always visible around Vincent's club and the Dublin players). He used to be down in Parnell Park watching the training all the time.

Did the Dublin players resent the way his resignation was handled?

'Not at all. There was huge respect for Kevin among all the players. It was never an issue in my opinion.'

Heffernan though had his reasons. One of them was staleness.

'I know some players were annoyed but I had my reasons. In 1976 there was a lot going on. I also felt it might be time for a fresh voice. There was also issues in my working life. (Heffernan's working life was spent mostly with the ESB where he was the Personnel Manager.) I just thought it was time to step away.'

* * *

Heffernan's surprise departure seemed to have little effect on Dublin. Tony Hanahoe, who was captain of the victorious 1976 team, was appointed player/manager and under his guidance Dublin retained the All-Ireland title in 1977. In the semi-final they defeated Kerry, in what many claim was one of the best games of football ever played. Then with Jimmy Keaveney in devastating form, Armagh were hammered in the final. Heffernan had this to say on the 1977 win.

'Well it (his resignation) seemed to make little difference. The team that played in 1977 was the exact same as that which played in 1976. I would assume they were playing the same game. There would appear to have been very little disruption.'

Kerry defeated Dublin in the 1978 Final, by which time Heffernan had returned as manager.

If his departure in 1976 was considered a shock, then his return after 1977 was equally so.

David Hickey was surprised.

'The way he walked away was bad and even worse his return in 1977. We had won a League and Championship under Hanahoe. Then as if he just hopped over the wire in Parnell Park and everyone moved over to accommodate him. I believe bringing him back undermined us a little. Some of the brittleness we showed in the 1978 Final came from that.'

While outspoken at times, Hickey acknowledges Heffernan's contribution to Dublin football.

'I give him credit for what he started. I just didn't agree with the cult.

He got us to All-Irelands, and from where we were coming from that was some achievement.'

Heffernan himself has no difficulty now with Hickey.

'We'd talk the same as ever. He has his view and I have mine. It's not something to be argued about. There's nothing can be done to change things now. I find I still have very good relationships with all the lads. I'm not at loggerheads with anybody.'

Interestingly, David Hickey, a surgeon in Beaumont Hospital, was recently appointed a Dublin senior football selector by the current manager Pat Gilroy.

And so Heffernan returned. Tony Hanahoe said simply that Kevin wanted to get involved again and that he (Tony) had no issue with it. In fact Hanahoe stayed on as a selector. The 1978 Final is remembered for among other things, Mikey Sheehy's goal for Kerry. Dublin were unhappy with referee Seamus Aldridge even before the game due to a number of decisions he made in a previous match. In the final, his decision to award a free against Paddy Cullen, which led to the famous goal by Mikey Sheehy only incensed them further.

Heffernan says, 'Even though we were ahead by 0-6 to 0-1 we were not playing well. I was never comfortable. We were only scoring from frees. What I do know – if we won that match it would have damaged Kerry.'

The goal changed the match and with it went Dublin's bid for three-in-a-row.

'Had we won, Kerry might have panicked – dropped half the team maybe, even got rid of the manager (O'Dwyer). Their confidence would have gone.'

New Dublin Team for the 1980s

A year later, 1979, Dublin were again beaten by Kerry. There was only one thing to do. Rebuild. Heffernan did. He retained Mullins, Tommy Drumm and Anton O'Toole, but a raft of new young Dubs would anchor this team.

Interestingly Anton O'Toole, a rampaging half-forward, credits Heffernan with improving one important aspect of his game.

'When I joined the panel, Kevin took me aside and corrected my kicking action. It made a huge difference to my game. Very few I reckon would have spotted the fault, but Kevin did.'

Dublin had a new team. Instead of Hanahoe, Doyle, Keaveney and Kelleher it now read Duff, Rock, Hargan and O'Leary. But the vital link was Brian Mullins.

Mullins was involved in a serious car crash in 1980. There was a fear he would not walk again. Not only did he walk again, but he went on to play in three more All-Ireland Finals. Heffernan was there to support him.

'Very supportive at all times. I wanted to play again anyway so his support helped me.'

It was a different team, but with the same principles.

'Kevin did not change much. He adapted all right, but the game was still the same. Tactically he was as astute as ever. The team was now built on younger players and we made great progress.'

Brian remembers the days before DVDs or videos. Heffernan had his own idea of taping games.

'Well he used to have an extra cameraman filming one end of the field while the play was at the other end. He wanted to see exactly what one set of players were doing. Were they concentrating? Were they marking their man? Were they moving? He would quickly point out what faults he had picked out.'

Dublin – Champions in 1983

The Championship of 1983 had many crucial moments. Cork beat Kerry with a late goal in the Munster Final. O'Dwyer and Heffernan would not collide. Cork and Dublin played a thrilling draw in the All-Ireland semi-final in Croke Park. Cork demanded the replay be played in Páirc Uí Chaoimh. Dublin had no problem with that. Brian Mullins explained.

'We were told the replay was going to be in Cork. Kevin just said "Okay". You play where you are fixed to play. The venue did not matter to us. We trained just like we did for any other match.'

Heffernan had similar thoughts.

'Going down to Cork that year was a gift. They looked for it and we said, "Fine, if you want to put yourselves under all that pressure so be it".'

In the drawn game Jimmy Kerrigan, the Cork half-back, crucified Dublin with his attacking runs. It was only a late goal by Barney Rock that earned Dublin a draw and saved the day. For the replay Heffernan devised his plan.

'Well we decided to list the team as usual. But at the throw-in we'd put Barney in corner-forward and John Caffrey on the wing. The hope was that Cork would instruct Kerrigan to follow Rock. They did, and before they altered their team the game was over. We ran them off the park.'

It was like 1974 all over again. Heffernan's teams don't lose to Cork. While agreeing with the move, Mullins felt it was just one of the many tactics that won that game.

'Oh, it was important alright. But it was just one move of many on the day that worked. That was Kevin though – thinking all the time.'

The atmosphere that day was special and new to Dublin – one they all enjoyed.

'The result was the important thing that day. But it was a great occasion. It was so unusual to play away from Croke Park but the supporters loved it. The players did too but only because we won. That was paramount.'

In the Final it would be Dublin v Galway.

When Heffernan won his first All-Ireland Final as manager, back in 1974, it was also against Galway in the Final. Now, even though no one knew it at the time, his last All-Ireland Final as manager would also be against the Connacht champions. It was a Final laced with controversy.

Dublin won a bruising encounter by 2 points but they finished with just 12 men. Galway ended up with 14 men. The media went into a frenzy. The '12 Apostles', as they became known, had delivered for Heffernan.

A smiling Brian Mullins remembers it well.

'It was controversial alright, but we dealt with it. Kevin was remarkably calm all through. But at the end of the day we were delighted to win the All-Ireland. The circumstances are for someone else to worry about.'

Mullins was one of the three Dublin players sent off.

'Just one of those things that happens in the course of a match. The fact that it was the All-Ireland Final meant it was highlighted more. I don't have any problem with that. As I said, you deal with things and move on. But I do know that Kevin was immensely proud of the character the boys showed. It was after all another title that he won.'

Heffernan was actually suspended after that game for unauthorised incursions onto the pitch. Word was he was not a bit bothered by the suspension. He had got what he wanted – another All-Ireland title.

However the following two years brought little joy for Dublin and Heffernan. Kerry were to win the All-Ireland Championship in 1984 and 1985. It brought the blinds down on Heffernan's managerial career with Dublin.

Heffo's Training Regime

Heffernan was thrust back into the managerial spotlight in 1986 when he was appointed manager of the International Rules team to play Australia. It was a challenge that would appeal to him, according to Brian Mullins.

'Without a doubt. He loved a challenge. It also gave him the rare opportunity to work with players from other counties. He'd enjoy that.'

Not surprisingly Ireland won that series which was played in Australia. There was one slight hint of controversy. Some were of the opinion that Mick O'Dwyer should have been appointed. When he was not, a number of Kerry players declined to travel – not out of disrespect for Heffernan; more in support of O'Dwyer.

One player who did travel was Jack O'Shea – despite coming under pressure to withdraw. Heffernan made O'Shea captain. It was an important moment.

O'Shea remembers it well.

'I had no problem going, even when others pressed me not to. It was a chance to play for Ireland. A chance to play under Heffernan. I found him extraordinary. When I look back on it that is one of the privileges of my career. Very few men can say they played for two of the greatest managers in our game – Heffernan and O'Dwyer. But I can.'

Except for a brief period between September 1976 and late in 1978, Heffernan had spent close on 12 years at the helm in Dublin. In that time, the face of the GAA changed and Heffernan played his part. Yet through it all, the players he dealt with have differing views of their manager. Very few got close to Heffernan. He would have wanted it that way. Keep a respectable distance between player and manager. Jimmy Keaveney knows Heffernan better than most.

'Kevin is a very private man – but very loyal. In the years with that Dublin team he did a lot for players – things you'd never hear about. But that's the way he would have wanted it.'

Over the years he did things his own way. Bobby Doyle once had a fitness test outside his own front door on the morning of an All-Ireland Final. On another occasion Heffernan got Gay O'Driscoll to play the first-half of a club game on a Sunday morning, then started him in a Leinster Championship match that afternoon. The reason? O'Driscoll had been away on a week's holiday and missed training.

Keaveney was another who did not escape the training regime.

'I was working for Nortons, the office supplies company, and we were launching a new photocopier down in Cork. I told Kevin I wouldn't be at training on Tuesday night as a result. "Okay," he said, but I knew he was not happy. He then asked me what time was the launch. I told him around 1 p.m. "That's fine so," he said, "See you in Parnell Park at 7 p.m.".'

Did he?

'He did – I was there. That was it – no half measures.'

A St Vincent's Man – Always

Nowadays Dublin are a huge attraction – all down to Heffernan, the man who has had a huge influence on Dublin football and of course on St Vincent's.

How much influence?

Brian Mullins is now the St Vincent's Chairman and regularly seeks his former manager's advice.

'Kevin has been wonderful for us at all levels. His views on most matters are sought and respected. He has been a hugely influential figure in our club – on and off the field. Such is his commitment to us that at one time, in 1976, he was managing both the Dublin and Vincent's senior teams. The fact that both Dublin and Vincent's went on to win All-Ireland titles is testament to what Kevin is capable of doing. That is an amazing feat. Unlikely to be repeated I would think.'

What about Dublin football strategy?

'I am sure he'd be consulted on most things. He has a wide knowledge of many aspects of life and how things work. His advice on policy and strategy would be sought. It would be foolish not to make use of that.'

Heffernan is so highly thought of that in 2007 he was appointed as a consultant to the Dublin minor football team. It received the unanimous support of the Dublin County Board members.

Mickey Whelan agrees.

'I am not sure he was ever chairman or anything like that, but I can tell you every big decision that was to be made would have Kevin's stamp all over it. The man has done more for St Vincent's than anyone.'

Keaveney says, 'Vincent's is a bit like the mafia. Once you're in you can't get out. All the big stars in the club put something back – Kevin more than most. His mantra is "One man, one club". Vincent's is everything to him. Always will be.

To illustrate that point, Phil Markey, who later became manager of the

Dublin team and subsequently Chairman of the Dublin County Board, passed a remark that infuriated Heffernan. The 1972 Dublin County Final between UCD and St Vincent's was a tempestuous contest. Markey left after 15 minutes, because 'he was sickened at the level of violence he witnessed'. In a further comment Markey said that, 'St Vincent's are running and ruining Dublin football'.

Later in the year, Markey took over the management of the Dublin team. The St Vincent's players withdrew from the panel in protest. A decade and a half later, when Markey was elected County Chairman, Heffernan immediately withdrew his management team.

Tony Hanahoe summed it up perfectly, 'When one came the other went, and neither missed the other'.

Many honours have come Heffernan's way. In 2005 he was made a Freeman of Dublin City, placing him alongside such luminaries as U2, Nelson Mandela and former US President Bill Clinton.

One year later in 2006, Heffernan was among 25 recipients of a GAA President's Award, presided over by then GAA President Seán Kelly. He was also awarded an Honorary Doctorate from the National University of Ireland in 2004 along with Mick O'Dwyer.

Now in his 80th year and still in marvellous health, Kevin is a regular at the grounds and clubhouse in Marino. He walks in and strolls around the ground and more importantly knows everyone and everyone knows him. He commands respect.

A few years ago he 'fell in' (he was 74 years of age at the time) with the under-15 hurling team. They were, to say the least, a moderate team. Kevin explains.

'I felt sorry for trainer Mick Slattery who was coaching them. He was on his own. I said I'd go down the odd Saturday. Now they were bad. I went down and eventually got sucked into it.'

As a team they had never won anything. With Heffernan's help they survived the summer. Then with holidays over the real season began.

'They were great to train. For four months we went at it. The fellas improved out of all recognition. Again we did the simple things over and over again, and we did them well. A smashing bunch of lads.'

It ended as it did with Dublin football in 1974 – with a Championship win. They played wonderful ground hurling and beat teams they had never beaten before. In the final Ballyboden were trimmed with a glut of goals. It will probably be his last success. He is entitled to his rest.

After a lifetime of service to the GAA, to Dublin and especially to his beloved St Vincent's, few will begrudge him that.

As for those who say it is hard to get to know Kevin Heffernan?

That may very well be true, but Jimmy Keaveney summed him up perfectly when he said, 'If you are a friend of Kevin's, you are a friend of his for life.'

That is as good a compliment as you can pay to anyone.

But then Kevin Heffernan is not anyone.

He is, in the eyes of most Dublin GAA people . . . a man apart.

(All quotes from Kevin Heffernan are taken from a 2005 interview with *Irish Times* journalist Tom Humphries.)

4

Seán Boylan

A Hurler First

On a September evening in 1982 Seán Boylan's phone rang. On the line was Meath County Secretary Liam Creavin. Pleasantries were exchanged. Then came the real reason for the call.

Liam told Seán he had been nominated for the job as Meath manager. Seán was surprised. In fact he was amazed. Especially when he realised it was the football position. Seán Boylan was better known as a hurling man, acting as the hurling team masseur for several years. He also played hurling with Meath for over 20 years. Indeed for one year as an inter-county player he also acted as player-manager – probably a first at that level in any county.

'I did, and got tremendous satisfaction out of it. Hurling was, and probably still is, my first game. I won a couple of Division 2 National League medals with Meath and I treasure those medals. I relished the opportunity to play against Kilkenny, Wexford and Dublin who were a force in hurling then. I took immense pride in wearing the jersey in the Leinster Championship.'

Seán's passion for hurling can be summed up by this simple story.

In 1968 as the reigning All-Ireland Football champions, Meath travelled to Australia. Seán was due to travel. However he declined the offer.

'I said I would not travel as my late father was 87 at the time, and I didn't want to be away from home for so long. But the real reason I decided not to travel was because I would have missed two National Hurling League games with Meath. That is how much I enjoyed playing hurling, especially for my county.'

Seán's love of hurling was fostered in his native parish of Dunboyne.

'One part of the parish is Kilbride, where Jack Quinn and his brothers came from. Jack was an icon in Meath football. But Dunboyne, the area I lived in, was the hurling side so it just took off from there.'

Meath wins in the Leinster Hurling Championship were rare.

'Rare? They were as scarce as hen's teeth. But that didn't matter. Irrespective of the result of a game, I would go to training the next night with huge enthusiasm. I really loved playing hurling.'

It was by no means glamorous to be playing hurling with Meath, with heavy defeats the order of the day.

'Oh God yes! Kilkenny beat us one day by 33 points and coming off the field one of the lads said that wasn't so bad. Another day Dublin trimmed us by 21 points. But we still turned up for training on the Tuesday night. It was just the sheer enjoyment of playing the game – despite the heavy beatings.'

It was over the attendance at training that he decided to end his career as a Meath hurler.

'I was attending a World Health Organisation meeting in Cambridge. I left early and caught a plane home to be in time for a training session to find only seven or eight players there. I was told there had been a row at the County Board meeting on the Monday night, as a result of which some clubs instructed their players not to train with the Meath hurlers. So I decided to finish out the year and then retire. No one would ever tell me not to play for Meath. If a guy could be told not to play for the county, they were not going to be much good in a tight corner. It was a point of principle for me. So I packed it in.'

That was a major disappointment for a man who loved his hurling.

'Huge disappointment and I saw that as a lack of commitment to Meath hurling. That hurt me as much as anything else.'

Seán also tells an interesting story when asked the inevitable question: did hurling get the full support of the Meath County Board?

'In 1949 we won our first All-Ireland Football title. The Captain was Brian Smith, a lovely hurler but a dual player. He actually won a Junior Hurling All-Ireland medal before his football medal – as did the famous Mick O'Brien. Real hurling men. Now on the journey home from the 1949 football final, Brian said as they got to Clonea on the Meath-Dublin border, "I probably helped kill the game I love".'

Seán continues this fascinating tale.

'Up to 1939, hurling would have been the strongest game in Meath but winning the first football title changed the dynamics in the county.'

Hurling has remained the second game in the Royal County ever since.

One good thing to come from his hurling days though is the friendships that still endure today.

'There was no bitterness on my part, disappointment sure, but the friends I made in hurling are still my friends today.'

On the dual players issue, Seán is adamant they can cope.

'It is hard, but if properly managed it can be done. Do your physical training with one team. Then prepare for the next game that is coming up – be it hurling or football. Co-operation all round can go a long way to sorting out problems.'

His *grá* for hurling is as strong today as ever and he rarely misses a big match.

'The problem I had when I was Meath manager was that the games usually clashed and I could not be there. Now though with fewer commitments I go all the time. Especially to Thurles and the Munster Finals. Of course I have huge admiration for the present Kilkenny team.'

The Royal Phone Call

Back to the telephone conversation in 1982 with Liam Creavin.

'I knew Meath were looking for a hurling manager and I would have done the job. I nearly collapsed when he told me I had been nominated for the football team. "Jaysus Liam," I said, "you're joking me."'

He was not.

Eventually when Seán realised Liam was serious, what did he do?

'Well I said my natural reaction would be to say "no". But I would have to think about it. Give me a bit of time and I'll get back to you.'

Having recovered from the shock, Seán gathered his thoughts and pondered his next move.

Which was . . . ?

'I decided to contact a few people whose opinion and advice I would value and see what they thought. I got into the car and drove over to Brian Smith. Brian, a member of my own club, was going to a meeting and said he would see me later. I then went to see a pal of mine, Eamonn O'Farrell, and we discussed it for a while. After that I headed back to Brian. Eventually I left Brian's house about 1.45 a.m. in the morning – still unsure what to do.'

Now it was his turn to make a phone call.

'I got back to Liam the following morning and said, "Look, I have given it a bit of thought, and this is what I suggest. I'll do the job for a few weeks until ye get someone else. Is that okay?"'

That few weeks turned into 23 years.

Two phone calls had suddenly changed the direction of his life.

Just 24 hours later at a meeting of the Meath County Board, his appointment was ratified.

Seán Boylan, hurler and herbalist from Dunboyne, was now Meath Senior Football manager.

It was a huge challenge as Meath football was not going well at the time in 1982. Now they were placing their faith in a man with little managerial experience. And what experience he had was not in football – but in camogie.

'Yeah, my career is arseways, a bit like the great Moss Keane going to UCC to play Gaelic Football and ending up as an Ireland Rugby International. My first venture was with the Dunboyne Camogie team. They were struggling at the time. In the late 1970s Mick Reilly came to me asking would I give the girls a hand for a few years, I suppose because of my hurling background.'

He was an instant success.

'They were getting ready for a county final against Kilmessin – one of the best teams in Meath. Now they had already lost to them by 18 points earlier in the year. I trained them and we lost that final by just one point. The girls were superb. It laid the foundations for a very successful period. In fact they went on to win nine of the next ten camogie finals.'

Seán was not involved in all the victories, but it was a hint of things to come.

There is little doubt his appointment as manager of the senior football team was greeted with scepticism in the county. The hurling masseur was at the helm of the football team.

'Maybe some people doubted my ability, but as I have always done, I would give it my best shot.'

Seán would leave his own prints on the job but he had huge admiration for several managers who left their mark on the game over the years.

'Kevin Heffernan, Mick O'Dwyer and Eugene McGee were three men who were ahead of their time in football. Of course what Brian Cody has achieved with the present Kilkenny hurling team is phenomenal.'

Meath v Dublin Rivalry

Having lost to Wexford in 1981 and Longford in 1982, Meath's fortunes were at a low ebb.

The Leinster title had not been claimed by the Royal County since 1970.

Things began to improve for Meath in 1983, as they prepared to play Dublin in the Leinster Championship. The first game ended in a draw, as did the replay which went to extra-time before Dublin won the third game.

'Those games helped and it also re-established the Dublin v Meath rivalry. We were to meet on a regular basis over the coming years.'

The games actually revitalised the Leinster Football Championship.

'Well the Dubs draw huge support anyway. But on top of that we were seen as neighbours and rivals. Boy, we had some fabulous matches with them!'

Boylan's reputation was also growing. Maybe it was not such a bad appointment after all.

The year 1984 was an important one. The GAA was celebrating its Centenary Year. They also initiated a once-off competition – the Centenary Cup. It was played on an open-draw basis and Meath emerged as winners, beating Monaghan in the final. Having won the O'Byrne Cup in 1983, Seán had now bagged his second title as Meath manager.

After the Centenary Final, Seán quipped, 'Hopefully we can make a successful defence of it in one hundred years' time.'

The Leinster Championship was the target but they would have to wait a bit longer for provincial honours.

In 1984 Mick Lyons, a rock at full-back, missed the Leinster Final defeat to Dublin while Laois ended Meath's aspirations in 1985.

Briefly in 1984 Seán contemplated stepping down.

'I felt maybe I might not be able to take the team any further. But having spoken to Brian Smith I decided to stay on. In fairness a number of the more experienced players also encouraged me to remain in charge.'

Was pressure for greater success building up in the county?

'No, as I felt we were making progress. Remember also the Meath manager's job is reviewed on an annual basis – even today. So I was unopposed in those early years.'

Change was needed though and Seán had to put his stamp on team affairs, on and off the field.

The first thing that needed altering was the composition of the management team.

'On being appointed I was joined by six other selectors. That meant seven of us on the line during a big match. I accepted this initially, even though it was awkward. Now all the lads would have had the best interests of Meath football at heart. But it had to change if we were to make progress.'

Making switches must have been difficult.

'Difficult! It was crazy. Could you imagine trying to get a consensus among seven fellas in the white heat of a Championship match? Before you knew it the bloody match could be over.'

So how did he execute the change?

'It actually came with the help of some of the senior players on the squad. A few of them approached me and said, "Listen Seán, you better stop being the nice guy here and do something about this." What they were effectively telling me was – "you are the boss, start showing it".'

Did that send out the wrong signals?

'Not at all, the opposite in my opinion. What it told me was that the players believed we were heading in the right direction and they trusted me. It also showed that the players and I had developed an extraordinary respect for one another. Going forward that would benefit the team.'

Eventually he got his way and the selection committee was reduced to three – the next step on the way to success.

The Leinster Championship was finally won in 1986 – the 16-year-wait was over. Kerry beat them in the All-Ireland semi-final. It would be another year before success in the All-Ireland arena would arrive.

'It was great to win the Leinster Championship, especially for the lads. I felt we were gelling as a team, becoming hard to beat and maybe we could win an All-Ireland.'

In 1987 Meath succeeded in putting Leinster titles back to back and made it to the All-Ireland Final.

Twenty years after the county last won the Sam Maguire Cup, Meath were on the cusp of sporting history. In 1967 Cork were the opposition. In 1987 the Rebels once again stood in their way. Where once it had been Dublin v Meath, for the next four years it would be Cork v Meath. Two teams dominated the sporting headlines in August and September.

The 1987 All-Ireland Final passed off without incident as Meath landed what was only their fourth title.

Meath v Cork Battles

Five years after his appointment, Seán had silenced the doubters. The hurling man had delivered 'Sam' to a grateful county.

'Ah sure, it was great really. Especially for the older lads on the team. O'Rourke, McEntee and few others who had given an awful lot to Meath football.'

Much was made of the Cork v Meath rivalry. They were tough uncompromising contests laced with controversy on and off the field. The media lapped it up.

Relations between the Cork and Meath players were poor. Even when they coincidentally ended up twice at the same resort in the Canary Islands on holidays, there was little if any contact.

It stemmed from the 1988 All-Ireland Final replay. Meath won despite having to play with 14 men for long periods. Gerry McEntee was sent off in the first-half following an incident with Cork's Niall Cahalane.

Seán has his own take on the rivalry at the time.

'Having lost to us in 1987, we knew Cork would be back again. Then when we met in the All-Ireland Final of 1988, they were a different team, in so far as they were much more physical. So strong they actually pushed us out of the way.'

Did that surprise Meath?

'The Meath lads could not believe it. They were shell-shocked. Cork would not have been seen as a physical team.'

The game then ended in controversy.

'We got a late free. Was it a free? I don't know! David Beggy got late-tackled. Brian Stafford equalised to force a replay. Cork felt aggrieved at that decision.'

Did that alter Meath's approach for the replay?

'In a way it did. Because we felt if we didn't match Cork's physicality we wouldn't win. So our attitude was let's play hard and see what the game throws up.'

It was a bruising encounter, but Meath won.

Boylan had once again pulled the rabbit out of the hat.
Meath had now completed the double as the League title had been won a few months earlier in May. 1988 was a good year for the Royals. The All-Ireland Final though was remembered for many things – least of all the quality of the football it produced.

'Our job was to win and we did. Football is a tough hard game and that is the way we looked at it. All we could control was our own approach. What others said and did was no concern of ours.'

In the midst of all the controversy which followed that game what is not generally known is the action Cahalane took immediately after the match.

Boylan explains.

'We were inside in the dressing room celebrating. Next, in walks Niall. He heads straight for Gerry McEntee, shakes his hand and says, "Look, I'm sorry that I made a bit of a meal out of it". They hugged and that was the end of it as far as we were concerned. What happened on the field stayed on the field.'

Boylan has huge admiration for Cahalane.

'What a man! Could you meet a more committed guy than Niall? He would play on one leg for you. In fact he often did. What he did that day typified the man. I met him in 2008 in Croke Park and we had the best 15 minutes together chatting about football that I had in a long time. Great guy.'

As for the frosty relations between the players – Seán is adamant that not every player subscribed to that view. He maintains that there were other agendas at work.

'An awful lot of it (the perceived bad blood) was kept going by people with other agendas, they kept telling stories. So many of them were ultimately proved to be untrue.'

However, Seán does accept that relations were strained.

'The first year after the 1987 Final was okay. In January 1989, there was no contact – that was after the controversial draw and replay back in September of 1988.'

Then, as so often in times like this, an interesting anecdote emerges.

Seán explains.

'I remember one night Ciaran Duff and Mick Kennedy from Dublin were on holidays by chance also in the Canaries with a few friends. Duff said to the Cork boys, "Hey lads, if I was ye guys I'd be drinking with them fellas. They're after bating ye in two All-Ireland Finals. I'd be trying to find out what makes them tick." That lightened the atmosphere a bit and we laughed at Duffer's attitude.'

After the 1988 Final Seán once again thought about resigning.

'I did because I was exhausted after the replay. I hadn't slept well for weeks and I really felt I needed a break. In fact on the homecoming on the Monday night I wanted to get off the bus in Dunboyne and go straight to bed.'

What changed his mind?

'Basically it was the players. Especially the more senior lads – they urged me to stay on. So after a brief rest I decided to carry on.'

Cork and Meath did not meet in 1989. Meath failed in their bid for a hat-trick of Leinster titles. Cork though finally made the breakthrough and defeated Mayo in the All-Ireland Final. But both Cork and Meath knew there was unfinished business between them. 1990 would see them collide again. It was the All-Ireland Final. Cork were going for an historic double, having already won the hurling final.

This time it was the Rebels who would play the best part of the game with 14 men and exact revenge for the defeats in 1987 and 1988. It was a match many felt Cork had to win. Seán agrees.

'I suppose they felt they would not be seen as a good team if they did not beat Meath in a final. We just wanted to win – we didn't care who we were playing. It just so happened it was Cork.'

It was another tough game. There was a little bit of controversy when Cork's Colm O'Neill was sent off. But as ever Meath and Boylan had no complaints.

'None at all – the best team won on the day. Cork showed immense character after Colm was sent off and deserved their win.'

Seán paid tribute to Cork when he visited them in their dressing room after the game.

'I felt they deserved the tribute. They were an astonishing team. Having lost two All-Ireland Finals and then came back to win two. That's some achievement, a hard thing to do.'

In fact it was not achieved again until Kerry managed it in 2006 and 2007.

There was one other thing that impressed Seán during those four games: the physical strength of both teams.

'They talk about the condition of teams today. But look at Cork and Meath back then. Powerful men, strong in the tackle, hard to shake off, fabulous athletes.'

Throughout these four years of rivalry between Cork and Meath, one other man was central to the action – Cork manager Billy Morgan. To this day Morgan and Boylan remain good friends.

'Billy and I always got on very well. Of course we wanted our team to win, but sure that was the job we were in.'

In fact Billy paid Seán a nice tribute in a post-match interview.

'He did, I suppose. Billy's wife, Mary, suffers with her sinuses and I gave him a herbal remedy for her. Now Billy mentioned this on TV that night and bejaysus my phone never stopped for days after with people looking for the potion.'

Indeed at the 1990 Final journalists arriving to do pre-match interviews in Croke Park witnessed an unusual sight.

"They got a bit of a shock I can tell you. They arrived in the dressing room to do interviews. There they found Billy and me sitting down calm as you like having a chat. They could not understand this. Our teams had been at it hammer and tongs for the last few years. But as I said, Billy and I are, and will always remain, friends.'

Relations between the Cork and Meath players improved after that, helped by a good sing-song at the All-Stars dinner later in 1990.

'We had great craic that night. David Beggy on the piano and the boys drinking pints. Smashing night.'

A sad event also helped thaw relations: the tragic death from cancer of Cork goalkeeper John Kerins.

'John's death was so sad and the Meath lads were shocked when we heard the news. As a group we travelled in strength to his funeral. Both sets of players met up afterwards. Had a few drinks. Recalled good times and bad – on and off the field. There and then old wounds were healed and we all moved on. But it was a very sad occasion.'

Meath and Cork were not to meet again until the 1999 All-Ireland Final. Billy Morgan had moved on. But Seán Boylan was still the Meath manager.

The Herbalist from Dunboyne

Football aside, there are many other facets to Seán's life. His early education was in the local National School in Dunboyne. After that it was Belvedere College in Dublin, and while there Seán played a bit of rugby.

'I did, briefly, ironically enough on the pitch where the new Cusack Stand in Croke Park now stands. I soon decided rugby was not for me.'

Seán has run a thriving business as a herbalist for many years now. He was also a Director of the National Lottery from 1987 to 1994.

'I'd be a fifth generation herbalist in Dunboyne. We were out in Tara before that. Actually the family moved to Dunboyne in 1798. The house where we lived in Tara was burned in 1798 while the entire village was burned to the ground around the same time. My great-great-grandparents lived there and the tradition of herbalist had gone on in Tara for generations before that as well.'

While the role of herbalist can be taught to people, it is usually passed down from generation to generation in families. Seán is world renowned for his work and from that came one of the highlights of his life.

'One of the biggest things to happen to me was in 1979. I was asked to join the World Health Organisation body. It was to do with Economic and Municipal Planning which was a huge honour for our family. It was an acknowledgement of all the work the people who had gone before me had done. That was a very proud moment.'

Seán was 17 when he first began to work in the family business.

'I was in Agriculture College at the time. I came home to give my Dad a hand. He was 80 at the time. His health was not good as you can imagine at that age. I was to stay at home for six weeks and I have been there ever since.'

His father, also called Seán, was a huge influence on his life.

'The 10 years spent with my Dad were marvellous. I learnt more in those 10 years than any college could have taught me. Before that as a child in the yard with the lads, I was picking things up without even realising it. You were washing bottles, meeting and getting to know people. The best education in life is life.'

Seán was learning all the time.

'The one thing I learned was that plants have chemistry. The other thing was that if it a potion was right it was of great benefit. If not, it could cause problems. It was more to realise what you couldn't do than what you could do.'

And as for the tradition being carried on by Seán's sons?

'All I know is it's very funny when their pals come in to where the stuff is made. They are very curious to see how this is done and how that is done. But we will see, the eldest lad is showing a bit of interest; let him make up his own mind.'

Apart from Billy Morgan's wife benefitting from Seán's potions, many more people from other sports have been known to seek his help. Among them Ireland Rugby International Moss Keane who credits Seán with 'sorting my liver out' after a Lions tour.

It is with some reluctance that Seán accepts this.

'Look it, over the years you would have been in contact with so many sports people. And as you know, any sportsperson with an injury wanted a cure yesterday. Again it is a private thing with people so we leave it at that.'

He does tell an amusing story.

'It was just before the 1987 All-Ireland Hurling Final. Liam Hayes was working for *The Irish Press.* He had interviews lined up with a Galway player and a Tipperary player. Both were in the clinic in Dunboyne at the time. It was gas really – neither player knew the other was in the building. We had a great laugh over that. They were both carrying knocks and were trying to keep it quiet.'

Nowadays teams in the GAA are big into their isotonic drinks.

For the Meath teams under Seán Boylan it was herbal potions.

'How it all happened was very strange really. Fellas would have a bit of an ailment and they would look for something. They would drink it and then say, "Jaysus that's great!" and they'd be fine.'

Were they curious as to the content of what they were drinking?

'Not really. It was there at training if you wanted it, if not, no big deal. If they asked what they were drinking they would be told. But most of them didn't ask. I suppose they were afraid of what I would tell them.'

As for the modern drinks Seán has no problem with them but he was quite happy with his own mix.

'They were keeping the blood and sugar levels up. Excellent for avoiding dehydration. Even going back as far as the Olympic Games in Moscow there were 11 competitors on herbal potions. All legal and above board – would pass any drugs test.'

Today business is good. It is still based in Dunboyne, giving good employment to the area. They grow all their plants at various locations around the country. But the bulk of the work is done as Seán says 'at home' – maintaining a long standing tradition. It is what his father would have wanted.

The Old IRA Man

When Seán speaks about his father he does so with immense pride.

His father, Seán, was an Old IRA man who fought in the War of Independence.

'My father had strong connections with Cork. He was a great friend of Michael Collins and Pádraig Pearse. Collin's secretary was a nun, Sister Eithne in Gloucester Street Convent in Dublin. We used to visit her regularly up to her death in 1981, especially at Easter and Christmas time.'

Despite his father's involvement in that difficult period in Irish history, when it was over he had no enemies.

'No, because when it was over Dad did not enter public life and went on working. He was given a year to live in 1923 following injuries he received in an explosion. He retired. This was the Old IRA before the National Army was formed. Then there was the mutiny in the Curragh and he was brought back to put that down.'

'My father never spoke about those times. There was too much hurt and pain. Remember he had friends on both sides who had been killed. People would have associated him with the Blueshirts. My father was never a Blueshirt in his life. He fought for what he believed in and when it was over that was it. As I said, he had friends on both sides and they remained his friends for life.'

Life was not easy though for his father.

'He left school at nine years of age for a very simple reason. In that time, 1888, you made your confirmation before your communion. They were introducing the pledge for your confirmation and he refused to take it. Fr Brady was the parish priest in Dunboyne. He was there for 45 years. He came out to see my mother about this. But it didn't matter; my father would not take it and he left school.'

The lack of education did not hinder him.

'No, he became a general in the Army. The way he could write and put things together was extraordinary. He was a very learned man without the education.'

Refusing to take the pledge was not the only time his father would go against authority.

'He never signed an oath. He was Commanding Officer of Eastern

Command, the biggest in the country. His command had no executions during the Civil War. In 1966 the very first Golden Jubilee medal to commemorate 1916 was presented to my father by Seán Lemass, which was a great tribute to him and indeed the family.'

Seán's father was known as the 'quiet man of modern Irish history'.

'He was in jail six weeks longer than anyone else. He spent time in Wandsworth and Woking jails and refused to sign anything. He actually became a source of embarrassment.'

He may have lived until he was 91, but while in Wandsworth Prison he came very close to death.

'He did. He was next to Eamonn Ceannt for execution. He was called out one day, and the prison captain said to him, "Boylan, you're next". Then word comes through from the House of Commons that the executions were to stop. A few minutes later and he would have been shot.'

When Seán's father died he was paid the ultimate tribute by the government of the day.

'He was accorded a state funeral which was extraordinary. He had lived a great life and we were all very proud of him. When I was a young lad I would have been of a shy disposition. But he had more faith in me than I had in myself, especially when it came to working in the clinic at home.'

It was a faith that Seán has repaid many times over.

Dublin v Meath Saga 1991

The year 1991 was an amazing year for football as Meath set out to reclaim the All-Ireland title. There was drama all the way, particularly in the Leinster Championship. Meath and Dublin would meet four times before a winner emerged.

Before that campaign began, Seán took a decision regarding his team's preparation.

'The team had been on the road a long time and I needed to try something different. So we did a lot of our training that year in water. We went swimming in the pool and in the sea. The lads had a lot done and I felt this would help. They also thought I was mad, but they did it.'

Meath footballer Gerry McEntee was doubtful.

'He said to me, "Seán, if we lose to Dublin in the first round, you won't be able to face the people of Meath if they find out we've been training in water."'

That was not the first time Seán introduced unusual methods in training. For one session in the early years, he got the use of 30 bikes. The entire team was sent on a cycle ride into the Wicklow Mountains.

Of course as you would expect, Seán embraced all new training methods.

'You had to, or else you would be left behind. The days of the hard slog are gone. It's more scientific now and that is good for the players and their long-term welfare. That in itself is very important.'

It very nearly paid off. But in the end the number of games caught up with them.

'The Dublin games were wonderful, absolutely fantastic to be involved in – drama right to the end.'

How did you keep going week in week out?

'Playing in front of a full house in Croke Park every week was the incentive. Any player or manager worth his salt would have relished those games. At different times over the four games either side could have won it. Yet in the end you could say we stole it.'

They did, as Dublin led in injury-time of the fourth game. But Meath snatched victory with an amazing goal. Kevin Foley became the hero.

'Funny enough, people say that goal was a bit lucky but actually it was a move we had practised. The previous Sunday we were in Scotland. While there we worked for 40 minutes on a move just like the one that won the game. Amazing then that what we practised helped us win the match. It needed something different to win that game. We left it very late though.

'I remember when Dublin got a penalty. I ran to Liam Hayes and said to him, "Look Liam, even if they score, start throwing the ball around like ye did in Scotland last Sunday". They did, and well we know what happened.'

There must have been a strange feeling when that game ended.

'It was a bit surreal I suppose. You kind of felt sorry for Dublin, especially the way in which we won it. They had played their part in a fantastic series of games.

'To be fair the Leinster Council acknowledged the contribution both teams made to the Championship. They gave Dublin and Meath €30,000 each for a holiday for the teams. A nice gesture. They did not have to do it but they did.'

After that the Championship returned to some degree of normality. Meath also drew with Wicklow in the next game. But they eventually reached the All-Ireland Final. Ulster champions, Down, were the opposition. Could Meath summon up the energy to win or would the number of games take its toll?

'Well a couple of things happened that had a bearing. First of all we were without long-term injury victim, Robbie O'Malley. Robbie had a broken leg and was a huge loss. The week of the final Colm O'Rourke contracted pneumonia. He lost about 15 lbs and was told not even to attempt to go to Croke Park.'

A huge disruption in the week of any normal game, let alone an All-Ireland Final.

'Of course, but you deal with it as best you can. Colm was very determined to play some part in the game. He was a vital member of our team. Then the pneumonia cleared on the Friday. On Saturday he did 20 minutes on the pitch in Navan with a few of the lads. And on Sunday morning he did another 20 minutes on the beach in Portmarnock. The doctor said we might get about 20 minutes out of him.'

In the end O'Rourke was unable to start.

Down built up a seemingly comfortable lead – 11 points ahead with 20 minutes left.

Then Boylan sprung O'Rourke. It nearly worked.

'He was anxious to get on and to be fair he was a major influence in turning the game.'

But it was not to be – Down won what was a fabulous game.

'We nearly pulled it off. But fair play to Down, they were deserving winners and that was it. Sport is like that and you accept what happens on the field.'

Meath v Mayo Brawl

It was to be another five years before Meath would land Sam, and by now Boylan had developed yet another team.

'All teams reach the end and we began to build a new team.'

Did he in that time come under any pressure to step down and make way for someone new.

'Strangely no, but a funny thing happened late in 1995. The team was not going well and Gerry McEntee approached me saying, "Look, I think you should go, because I don't want to see you being forced out. You've done too much for Meath football for that to happen".'

Seán's reaction?

'I had a different take on things. I had a nice feeling about the team as I felt we were coming good and might just win the All-Ireland in 1996. I told Gerry I don't have a problem with what you are saying, but I can't step down. Go away and talk to the players and then come back to me.'

Did he?

'He did, and said, "Seán, you were right, the young fellas want you – you can't go, so carry on".'

Boylan's instincts were right. Meath would win the 1996 All-Ireland, but at a price.

It turned out to be the most talked about All-Ireland Final in years. And not for the first time Meath were in the eye of a storm. Meath won in a replay, but the main talking point was a brawl that occurred early in the game.

The drawn game was noted for a late Meath point that broke Mayo's heart.

'We were lucky. I remember the Thursday night before in training Colm Coyle said there will only be a hop of the ball in it. Little did he realise that he would be the one to get the point that saved us.'

Two players were sent off – Coyle for Meath and Liam McHale for Mayo and a host of players received yellow cards.

Over the years Meath had been involved in some tough games. Dublin and Cork spring to mind. Through it all, Boylan kept his counsel. Was Meath's reputation a worry and did his team really get the credit for what they achieved?

'I'll tell you I was very annoyed after that final. I was very upset actually. I always remember having eight players suspended for something we did not start.'

On this occasion he spoke out.

'The very first National League game after the final was against Cork down in Cork. We had great support that day. A couple of trains were full and more travelled down by road.'

Was it a statement?

'It was – by the Meath supporters. They were fully behind the team. Anyway after the match I gave an interview to Míceál Ó Muircheartaigh. I vented my anger at what I felt was the wrong done to my players. Remember the actual row lasted for about 26 seconds and the controversy dragged on. It went on for days – on radio, television and newspapers. Marian Finucane was on about it. The Minister for Justice – she was on about violence in sport. God, it was way over the top.'

As for TV pundits, in general Seán accepts they have a job to do.

'The only thing that would concern me is when they personalise their comments. What they should remember is that they were players themselves once. And of course lads have to go to work the following morning. It is an amateur game after all.'

It did have a lighter moment in the midst of all the drama.

'I remember on the Thursday after the final going out to Howth with my wife Tina just to get away from it all. A car pulled up alongside me and who was in it but Lar Foley, God rest him. He got out of the car in great form. He gave me a bear hug, congratulated me and then said, "Seán, poor Mayo, could you imagine losing the fucking row as well".'

But when the dust settled, Meath were the All-Ireland champions again. Boylan had delivered the county its sixth title, his third.

There would be one more.

Seán is adamant though that the Meath players suffered because of their perceived reputation as tough men.

'Oh there is no doubt about that. There were several times when we were overlooked for trips abroad. Especially after we had won either the League or Championship. In 1994 we won the League – no trip. In 1996 we won the All-Ireland – no All-Star trip. Some of the lads were even passed over as All-Star replacements. The GAA has its own way of working things I can tell you.'

What was he putting that down to?

'All I know is the Meath people were incredible in supporting this team. In good years and bad years. They never wanted for a holiday. All you can say is it goes back to 1988.'

1988 was the year a number of Meath players refused to accept their All-Ireland medals from then GAA President, the late John Dowling.

In the aftermath of the 1988 Final with Cork, Dowling had been critical of some of the incidents in that match. The Meath players were annoyed at this. Seán, as he has always done, defends his players.

'First off now, let me say John was a lovely man. The lads had met for a few jars before the official function and two lads decided not to go up for their medals. Liam Harnan and Gerry McEntee were the two lads. I can tell you it was a fair price to pay for what they did. Indeed it was not until Joe McDonagh became president that Meath were given a trip abroad by the GAA.'

The Final Victory

It was another three years before Meath made it back to the All-Ireland Final – in 1999.

Once again Cork provided the opposition. Unlike their last win in 1996, this was a victory without controversy.

'No thank God, it was a good tough game and we got home by three points against what was a young Cork team.'

It was, though, a significant win.

'In many respects it was a bit of a new team. Some players had retired after 1997 and 1998. So as we had done in the past, we just moved on and started the rebuilding process.'

Seán was not to know it at the time but it was also to be his last All-Ireland win.

In 2001 another Leinster title was won and they looked like All-Ireland winners after the semi-final.

'Well we played Kerry in the All-Ireland semi-final and hammered them by about 14 or 15 points. I thought, "Great, we are looking good here." But we flopped badly in the final. Galway did to us what we did to Kerry. We were well beaten by 0-17 to 0-8. The worst result for any team I managed in a final.'

Any particular reason for that?

'No, I could not put my finger on it at the time. To be fair, Galway were a good team, but I would have expected a better performance from us.'

For the next three years Meath struggled.

Even in Leinster, Dublin, and to an extent, Laois were the teams to beat. Seán offers a possible explanation.

'There was a change in format to the club Championship in Meath. I said at the time it would hinder the county team and I was right. Meath football thrived on the cut and thrust of knockout. Now with each team having two or three chances, that cutting edge was gone from our game.'

After their defeat in the 2005 Championship, Seán sensed it might be time to finally call it a day. On just three occasions in his 23 years as manager was he challenged for the position. He always wanted to go at a time of his own choosing.

'I was coming home from Seán Purcell's funeral in Galway when I made up my mind.'

It was time for another phone call.

A Wake with a Walking-Talking 'Body'

Seán Boylan phoned the Meath County Board Secretary Barney Allen and informed him of his decision to withdraw his name. His reign as Meath football manager was over.

In his 23 years as manager Meath enjoyed unprecedented success: 4 All-Ireland titles, 3 National League wins and 8 Leinster Senior Football titles.

Not bad for the hurler and herbalist. In recognition of his contribution to football, Seán was entered into Football's Hall of Fame. This took place in Croke Park on 1 July 2006. In April of the same year, he was made a Freeman of County Meath – the first person ever to be bestowed with that title.

There was one aspect of the job he would not miss – telling players they were dropped from either the team or, worse still, the panel.

'I absolutely hated it, especially telling guys who had trained hard. Over the years there were some tough calls to make. I didn't like doing it but it was for the good of the team. And I like to think that any lad I omitted understood the situation. Thankfully we are still on speaking terms today. That would be important to me.'

How did he feel when it was all over?

'Ah sure you know now, it leaves a void. But as in life you move on. It was very funny really. The day after it was announced, the neighbours at home started calling to the house. They brought cakes, biscuits and sandwiches. It was like they were holding a wake. But the "body" was walking around talking. It was gas really, but that shows the nature of people.'

Throughout his career Seán's family was a constant support.

'Incredible really, especially Tina who looked after things while I was away. As the kids came along she kept everything going when I was with the team. I never had to worry about anything and that made it easier to be away. She did not have much of a background in football – more motorsport actually. So much so that the first All-Ireland dinner she attended was in 1991 after we lost to Down. She arrived in a red and black outfit, the Down colours. What a ribbing she got.'

There are now six young Boylans in the family – Seán, Ciaran, Daire, Doireann, Aoife and Oran. Two of his sons are on Meath under-age football development squads.

As for the so-called big money floating around, none of it came Seán's way, nor did he want it to. In fact he gets embarrassed when you mention it. A little bit of probing explains why.

'Ah look, I don't want to talk about it. But let's just say that in 23 years I never even took expenses from Meath. I felt if I was getting some sort of money I would be letting people down if we did not succeed. Anyway I had so much fun doing the job over all those years. I got great enjoyment out of it.'

Even Sir Alex Ferguson said to him at a function one night, 'I can nae believe you did that job for 23 years and never got paid.'

When Boylan's autobiography, *Will to Win,* was published a few years ago, all the proceeds went to GOAL.

Seán also pays a huge tribute to Meath's sponsors – especially the late Noel Keating of Keepak.

'What that man did for Meath football can never be repaid. He was absolutely incredible and everything was upfront from the day he came on board.'

GPA & Compromise Rules

Seán also has strong views on the GPA.

'Well the GPA for me does not represent all the players. They are selective in who they back. Until they treat every player in the country – county and club – the same, they cannot claim to represent players. After all, club and county players are equal in my opinion.'

He does agree though that the GPA should receive official backing from the GAA.

'No problem with that at all. Players need to have a voice, but that means all players. The day they back every player is the day the GPA will get my support.'

Seán also lauds the GAA for allowing soccer and rugby to be played in Croke Park. 'Fantastic decision.'

In fact during the 2009 Six Nations Rugby Championship many of Seán's potions could be found at the Irish team's HQ.

Since retiring from the Meath job, as with most ex inter-county managers, his name has been linked with every vacancy that has arisen in football.

He is unlikely to return.

'No, I don't think so. Time done and all that.'

One position though did tempt him. It was too good to turn down.

Early in 2006 he was appointed manager of the Ireland Compromise Rules team for the two-games series against Australia.

'That is the one job you just could not turn down. It's the ultimate honour to be asked to manage your country. I consider it a tremendous honour. I was excited as it was a new challenge.'

Unfortunately it was not the most enjoyable of experiences.

The first test passed off without incident in Tuam. The second test before a full house in Croke Park was a brutal affair. Australia won, but on the day the result was irrelevant.

'It was awful! I never witnessed anything like it in all my years in sport. In fact it had nothing to do with sport, what went on that afternoon. The tackling by the Australians was bordering on the reckless. I really thought someone would be seriously injured.'

So much so that at the end of the first quarter he took the team off the field and did not want to return.

'The tackle on Graham Geraghty was the worst I have ever seen. I said I did not want this to continue and had no hesitation in withdrawing from the match.'

However the players insisted on finishing the game.

'The players talked me round at that break. They were adamant they wanted to continue. I admired their resilience. I was reluctant but eventually they persuaded me and the game finished. I can tell you I was never more pleased to hear a full-time whistle.'

Seán and the GAA, along with the general public, were appalled at what they had witnessed. The fallout was inevitable.

'It led to the cancellation of the 2007 series. That was the right thing to do. It could not continue after what went on.'

The GAA and AFL thrashed out new rules and guidelines and Seán was in charge for the series in Australia in autumn 2008. To the relief of all those involved, the two games were incident free and Ireland won.

'Thank God they went well and that is how it should be. We won and it was great to bring the Cormac McAnallen Cup back home.

Despite the furore in 2006 Seán believes the game has something to offer Gaelic Football.

'First of all it is fantastic that GAA players get the opportunity to represent their country, as with other sports people in Ireland. Now as for the game: the 'mark' is rewarded in their game – maybe we could reward the high fielding in our game. Also they have a definitive tackle that is something we might look at as well.'

For a man who brought so much success to Meath, he does have one regret.

'It's the fact that I never actually played Championship football for Meath. I was told at one stage that I was on the team. However the card notifying me never arrived. I found out later that it was because of my hurling that they didn't pick me. Yeah, that would be a huge regret.'

And despite all the glory days, the winning moments are not necessarily among his proudest.

'Of course I was proud and delighted to win titles. But I got more satisfaction out of seeing players fulfil their potential than anything else. That for me made it all worthwhile. Today the level of respect I have for the players, and hopefully they for me, is the most important thing.'

Interestingly, since Seán Boylan vacated the Meath job in 2005, success has eluded the Royal County. Up to 2009 they have had three managers – after having one manager for the previous 23 years.

Meath have seven All-Ireland Senior football titles and Seán as manager delivered four of them.

Seán Boylan has a warm engaging personality. He is full of life and enthusiasm and has time and a word for everyone.

The day we met in Dublin as I approached him in Heuston Station he was deep in conversation with a elderly gentleman. I assumed they knew one another. They didn't. He knew who Seán was. They were chatting about the Dublin Football team who on the previous Sunday had knocked Meath out of the Leinster Championship. That's Boylan.

The few hours I spent in his company, were as pleasurable a discussion I have had about the GAA in a long time.

We finished off with a cup of tea.

Herbal of course.

5

Ger Loughnane

The Clare Hurler

Half-time in the 1995 All-Ireland Hurling Final with the score at Offaly 1-6, Clare 0-7. In the bowels of the old stadium it's manic in the cramped dressing rooms. Then the two teams re-emerge for the second-half to a crescendo of noise from the capacity crowd. Offaly and Clare burst onto the field. Clare manager Ger Loughnane follows.

RTÉ reporter Marty Morrissey, himself a Clare native, approaches Loughnane.

'Any changes, Ger?' asks Marty.

'No Marty, still the same,' replies Ger.

'Can ye win?' is Morrissey's next question.

Loughnane looks surprised at the question. His reply is emphatic.

'We're going to win Marty, we're going to win!'. With that he is gone.

Forty minutes later Clare do win – and 81 years of frustration and heartbreak is at an end. The so-called curse of Biddy Early is finally laid to rest. It is Ger Loughnane's finest hour and there was more to come.

Yet if some GAA people in the Banner County had their way, Loughnane would never have been appointed Clare hurling manager. He may have guided the county to two All-Ireland wins in three years but he has another 'double' of sorts.

At a County Board meeting in 1992 he was sacked as senior hurling selector and Under-21 manager on the same night.

'It was crazy really. I was a senior selector with then manager Len Gaynor and under-21 manager at the same time. Now the under-21s were beaten by Waterford and I got shafted. Simply because some guys felt we should never lose to Waterford. They wanted their own man in the job. Waterford actually went on to win the under-21 Championship that year. Many of the players who backboned their senior team for the last few years were on that team.'

This decision angered him and he vented his anger at those responsible.

'I went to the next County Board meeting and let rip. Especially at the core group who led the call for my "head". I asked them to say to my face what they had said in my absence. I can tell you there was a deafening silence in the room.'

It would not be the first time Loughnane and County Board delegates would cross swords.

A few years later, after leaving the Clare job, he likened County Board delegates to 'village idiots'.

Ger Loughnane was an outstanding hurler. He was one-third of a half-back line that was rated as one of the best of its generation. But it came in an era when Cork in particular were dominant in Munster. In all his years as an inter-county hurler, Loughnane never won a Munster Championship medal. To this day it upsets him.

'I would love to have won just one Munster Championship medal. I really had a great career, but to win a Munster medal would have capped it off.'

This also meant he never got to play in Croke Park on All-Ireland final day. It was such disappointment that drove him on as Clare manager. It is also without question his biggest regret.

'Massive. Hurling was my passion and not having played on its greatest stage rankled me. I remember being at a concert there (Croke Park) with my wife Mary a few years ago. It was Neil Diamond. But all I could think of was what it would have been like to play there. The concert kind of passed me by. I barely heard the music. I was looking across at the pitch and thinking "if only". A huge regret.'

At least though the Feakle-born native had the not insignificant consolation of playing in two Munster Finals – 1977 and 1978.

'Ah yes, but we had no luck there either. But the Munster Final, particularly as it's held in the birthplace of the GAA – Thurles – is special. A huge occasion and great to be a part of it, even in defeat.'

Two Munster finals stand out for him – 1995 in Thurles, 1996 in Limerick. One win, one loss. He was manager on both occasions.

'For obvious reasons 1995 is special. That is the day all Clare folk recall with immense pride. I know we went on to win the All-Ireland that year, but in a funny way winning the Munster Championship was more important. A year later we lost to Limerick, but that was also some day I can tell you.'

It ended with a spectacular Ciaran Carey point.

'I remember the morning well. I drove into the Gaelic Grounds to have a look at the pitch. It was early and the sun was shining. I sensed it was going to be a special day. I arrived at the ground and even with only about 100 people around, I could feel the atmosphere.'

Three hours later when he returned on the Clare bus, it was different.

'It was warmer. There was a shimmering mist around the place. Thousands of people in shirt sleeves. It sent a shiver through my body.'

The match itself was a thriller. Clare lost – their near neighbours ended their reign as Munster and All-Ireland champions.

'We were two points up nearing the end even though we had not played well. I remember commenting to Liam Linehan (Limerick selector) that if we win, it will be robbery.'

Then came the point that has now gone into Munster hurling final folklore.

'Limerick had drawn level when Ciaran Carey got the ball. He took off and with the sliothar glued to the hurl, there was no stopping him. Now he was under savage pressure but he still composed himself and hit over a fabulous point. It was worthy of winning any match.'

Naturally Ger was disappointed.

'Of course I was, but the way Ciaran scored the winner tempered the pain. It was hard to get going after winning the All-Ireland the year before (1995), but in many ways it made us stronger for 1997.'

Clare would return better and more focused than ever.

Loughnane was an outstanding hurler and with Seán Stack and Seán Hehir alongside him, the three were a formidable half-back line. Yet for all their undoubted ability Clare inevitably fell short, especially in the Championship.

'We had a great team in the mid 1970s. But Cork blocked our path in Munster. We actually beat Kilkenny in two League Finals (1977 and 1978). But then we failed to build on that in the Championship. In fact we were in three League Finals in a row. Kilkenny beat us in 1976.'

Justin McCarthy was the Clare coach back then. Loughnane was immediately impressed.

'The first thing I picked up from Justin was his attention to detail. Even his very appearance was immaculate. Then his hurleys, he took particular care over his hurleys. Justin maintained it was the most important part of a hurler. I suppose in many ways he was right.'

Tactically though he felt Justin was a bit behind.

'His drills were top class and he was very good at training. Now in a match situation it was a bit different, but he was very impressive.'

Fr Harry Bohan was another big influence on that team. Like Loughnane, Bohan is from Feakle. Back then they were great friends. Not so now.

'Harry was brilliant, he really helped build that team with Justin. One fault of his though – he didn't believe we would make the breakthrough. Now if your manager doesn't believe in you, how are you going to win?'

As for his present relationship with his fellow parishioner?

'In every county there are rivalries and jealousies and Fr Harry fits into the second category.'

Communication between both now? Well there is none.

Loughnane is reluctant to expand further or even offer an opinion as to why that is the case. But the rumours persist.

Despite his contribution to Clare as player and manager, Loughnane was not selected on the best Clare hurling team of the last 25 years. He was also passed over for an award for special services to Clare hurling. Yet Fr Harry did receive one. In fact Loughnane was not even invited to the function at which these awards were presented.

The decline of the great Clare team which he was part of is something he remembers clearly.

The 1978 Munster Final is one that really got away from Clare.

'We went in at half-time two points down. It was 0-5 to 0-3 and we'd played against a strong wind. The Clare crowd cheered us into the dressing room. We thought, right, this is our time.'

They were wrong.

'By God we were! Cork, remember, were going for three-in-a-row and they just hurled us away in the second-half. It was a poor match but Cork won 0-13 to 0-11. We were okay in the backs, but we just could not score. It was the nearest we got to winning a Munster Final. League wins meant nothing that day. Cork showed what you need to do to win a Munster Championship.'

It led to the break-up of a great Clare team.

'In a few years most of the team were gone and the wait for the Munster title would go on. It was a great pity as we had fabulous players – Seamus Durack, Stack, Hehir, Noel Casey, Johnny Callanan, Colm Honan. Another generation of Clare hurlers would retire without the ultimate honour.'

Loughnane himself was included in that bracket.

'I knew after that game (Munster Final 1978) that it was over. You could feel it in the dressing room. No one said a word, but we all knew. I was only 25 at the time, but I never played as well after.'

The reason?

'Belief. Or lack of belief. We could beat Cork and Kilkenny on wet days in the League. But in the summer both these counties always knew they could beat the likes of Clare. That was the difference between the top teams and the rest.'

Even in his college days at St Flannan's, major honours eluded him – his team lost in both the prestigious Dean Ryan and Dr Harty Cup finals.

Ger Loughnane called time on his inter-county playing career in 1987. He finished with two National Hurling League medals and three Railway Cup medals with Munster. Ger also won two All-Stars – in fact he was the first Clare hurler to be honoured by the All-Star selectors.

However a medal he cherishes came in the twilight of his career with his beloved club. Feakle were not forgotten in their hour of need.

The Deal with Gaynor

As one of the leaders on the field of the Clare team of the 1970s, it was inevitable that Ger's name would be linked to the manager's position. It was a rocky road but he was eventually given the job.

Ger's first taste of management came from his profession as a National

School teacher.

'I was teaching in Shannon and started training the school team. I even got into bother then. I gave out to a referee one day and he walked off the field. Then I started coaching under-age teams in the Wolfe Tone Club. I set out to win the Féile Na Gael, a great competition for under-14s. We trained very hard for it.'

Wolfe Tones' under-14s were the template for the Clare team of the 1990s.

'One thing I noticed about Clare teams was the speed of their hurling. It was nowhere near as fast as the Corks of this world. So I set about changing that. I tried to get the young lads to hurl at pace. Also to work hard at closing down the space and putting your opponent under pressure.'

A bit heavy for under-14s?

'Maybe it was, but valuable all the same. Look, if you get good habits early on, you'll keep them forever. Simple as that.'

In 1993 Clare were hammered in the Munster Final by Tipperary. The final scoreline read 3-27 to 2-12. Loughnane, who wasn't involved with the team at the time, watched on in horror.

'It was humiliating. Nickey English and Pat Fox were literally laughing that day as they racked up the scores. The worse day ever for Clare hurling.'

Ironically the Clare manager that day was Len Gaynor – a Tipperary man and a proud hurling man as well.

'Len is a great hurling man and worked hard for Clare hurling. I felt for him that day.'

A surprise call from Gaynor to Loughnane changed the face of Clare hurling and by extension hurling itself.

'In 1994 Len asked me to be a selector. I said, "No way". I had been burned once. It was not going to happen again. However morale in the county was so low after the hammering by Tipp, Len could not get selectors.'

Gaynor returned to Loughnane. This time Ger had a proposition for Gaynor.

'I'll come on board as a selector on one condition.'

Which was?

'When you step down I want to become the manager.'

Gaynor had no problem with that, but he could not guarantee it. Enter Brendan Vaughan (RIP), then Chairman of the Clare County Board. Between them, Vaughan, Gaynor and Loughnane hatched a plan. Loughnane had harangued the County Board delegates just two years earlier. The very same delegates now held his managerial ambitions in their hands. So in 1994, Vaughan, an experienced and astute official, sprung the 'Loughnane as selector' proposal on the delegates at a meeting of the Board. There were a few dissensions, but the proposal was passed. It was met with a lukewarm response – no round of applause greeted his appointment. Loughnane smiled in satisfaction as he sat at the back of the room that night.

Another Loughnane double of sorts. This was just two years after being sacked as senior selector and under-21 manager on the same night. He had now, along with Vaughan, engineered his return not only as a senior selector, but as the next senior manager as well.

A massive coup. Hurling was about to undergo a massive change and for the better.

'Of all my difficulties as Clare manager, the biggest one I had was getting appointed.'

The 1994 Championship saw the beginning of the Clare renaissance. One year after a humiliating defeat by Tipperary, Clare avenged that result in the semi-final. Limerick, though, beat them well in the Munster Final.

Loughnane saw it coming.

'A couple of weeks before the final I knew we were beaten. The training was flat and too slow. The result was no surprise to me.'

Clare – Champions After 81 Years

Gaynor departed. Loughnane now had the job he craved. He also knew he had inherited something else.

'A desire among the players to succeed. I saw it first-hand before the 1994 semi-final win over Tipperary. Seanie McMahon, only 20 at the time, gave a speech that day. Boy, it made the hair stand on my head.'

It was no surprise that McMahon would emerge as one of the leaders as the new Clare were about to launch themselves on an unsuspecting hurling world.

From 1995 until he stepped down as manager in 2000, Loughnane and Clare would experience every gambit of emotion – from joy to heartbreak. And no shortage of controversy. It was in his own words, 'A rollercoaster of a ride that we all enjoyed.'

Controversy followed Clare and Loughnane. There was a massive row with the Munster Council over the 1998 Munster Hurling Final with Waterford. Loughnane had a lash at Eamonn Cregan live on *The Sunday Game.* He was banned from the sideline for one major game in Croke Park. Then there was the famous match with Offaly – prematurely brought to a halt by referee Jimmy Cooney (of which more later).

In the midst of all these events Loughnane produced a fabulous hurling team that in the beginning won the hearts of the nation. It turned several of their players into household names. Initially Clare enjoyed massive neutral support. But as quickly as it arrived the support dissipated.

'No question about that – people thought we were too big for our boots.'

Clare's arrival as a hurling force was welcome and breathed new life into the Championship.

'It made for a fantastic few years. The established counties had dominated for long enough. But now they were taking a back seat. Don't get me wrong – what Kilkenny, Cork and Tipperary have achieved is to their credit. Then in a short few years, Clare, Offaly and Wexford won the All-Ireland, and Limerick should have won one. Hurling needed a lift and it got it.'

Ger has only one other regret about hurling in recent years.

'It's a real pity that Waterford have not won an All-Ireland. They are a great team. Look at their style of hurling, brilliant. The excitement they have generated. The likes of Ken McGrath, Tony Browne and Dan Shanahan – they really deserved to win an All-Ireland medal. It's possible their time has now passed.'

Ger's first task was to put a backroom team in place and he picked Tony Considine and Mike McNamara. Then the preparations began. Training was tough. McNamara was in charge of fitness.

'Mike was brilliant and really got the lads fit. Then when it was time to hurl, they were fit enough to hurl the way I wanted them to. Pace and speed were the things I worked on. I knew it was coming along nicely. Tony also played a huge part, a very good hurling judge.'

How intense were the hurling training sessions?

'Savage was the best way to describe them. They were held behind closed doors in Cusack Park. Only those associated with the team witnessed them.'

However there was a setback in the 1995 League Final.

'A huge one really. Kilkenny beat us well. But something happened after the match that convinced me we were going in the right direction. For some reason, I don't know why, the Kilkenny manager, Ollie Walsh (RIP) ended up in our hotel. We got talking and I told him what we were doing (in training) and he said, "Keep at it and take no notice of today". Those few words helped because I was down after losing.'

As the Championship approached it seemed as if nothing had changed in Clare.

'It was as if people expected us to lose. Especially as it was Cork we were playing in the semi-final.'

This was reflected in the attendance on a damp June afternoon in the Gaelic Grounds in Limerick.

'There were only about 15,000 at the match and most of them were from Cork. The Clare supporters had no faith in the team.'

Clare played well. But with time running out it was a familiar story. Cork were ahead by two points and looked like winning. Worse, Clare had lost their talisman.

'Seanie McMahon had done his shoulder. He was knackered, but we had used all our subs and we had no replacement. I was taking him off and prepared to finish the match with 14 players.'

But McMahon was having none of it.

'He just refused to come off. That was typical Mac. I told him to go up to the forwards. Try and make a nuisance of yourself. You might distract one of the backs.'

'Seanie, now remember, had only one good hand. Somehow he forced a Cork defender to concede a line ball. Then when the sideline came across the goal, Baker (Ollie) knocked it into the net. We were a point up.'

Back came Cork.

'They did. Well we never did things easy, did we? Kevin Murray got the ball in front of the goal. Jaysus, he couldn't miss. But from nowhere Lohan flicked it away and we won. We were back in the Munster Final.'

After the game more encouraging words from another great hurling man.

'Johnny Clifford, sadly no longer with us, came into our dressing room and spoke. Now Johnny was a genuine hurling man and he addressed our lads from the heart. I knew he was sincere and he told us to go and win the Munster Championship. Hurling needs Clare he said, and what he saw today convinced him we had a chance.'

It was then on to Thurles and a Munster Final clash with Limerick.

'Even then we were outnumbered in support. It was as if we could not put two big games back to back. But what a day! I will never forget it.'

Clare were brilliant on the day as Loughnane's dream finally became a reality.

'We led at half-time and were hurling well. But still there was a nagging doubt that something would happen to spoil our day. We had waited so long for this day. Thankfully in the last five minutes we tacked on a few points and won handy in the end.'

Your emotions when it was over?

'Relief was the main one. Sheer relief. Then the pitch was engulfed in a wave of Clare supporters. Young and old were in tears. You just had to be there to witness it. Now winning Munster might not be a big deal to Cork or Tipperary. But this was 81 years of pent-up emotions being let loose. It was magic.'

Then another special moment. Anthony Daly lifts the cup. His speech struck a chord.

'Daly said, "We will go to Croke Park now in our thousands". Christ, I thought, we're heading for Croker. Fantasy stuff.'

What he had never achieved himself his team were now going to do for him. Play a Championship match in Croke Park. But first they had to go home. It was some homecoming.

'The County Secretary Pat Fitzgerald said every club in the county wanted to see the cup. I had a call to make. We still had an All-Ireland semi-final to play and I did not want to lose focus. I decided to allow a tour with the cup for three days. They could drink away and then we'd run the shit out of them on Friday night.'

The turnout amazed Loughnane and the players. He went everywhere but one visit was special.

'They were all great but my own place stood out. Feakle had always supplied players to Clare teams. In 1954 it was Dermot Sheehy. Then there was Seamus Durack, Val Donnellan and myself who had all played on losing teams. Now we were coming home as Munster Champions.'

The jury was still out on Loughnane's Clare, but they were gathering momentum. That momentum was maintained as Galway were beaten in the All-Ireland semi-final. One hurdle left to climb. The All-Ireland Final. Clare, against all the odds, had arrived on the biggest hurling stage of them all. The county had gone mad. Hurling fever gripped the entire population of Clare. The task was to keep the euphoria from distracting the players from the task in hand: To bring the Liam McCarthy Cup home to Clare.

'It was manic in the county, but we coped. We trained hard and tried to shield the players from the media hype. But to be fair it was a time to be enjoyed as well and thankfully we got the mix right. Remember now, this was all new to us, myself included. Clare in an All-Ireland Final was huge for the county. We love our music, but this time the music was all hurling.'

Offaly were their opponents. An unusual pairing, notable for the absence of the so-called big guns of hurling. The entire country, well almost, were rooting for Clare.

'There was huge goodwill towards us. I remember Jimmy Barry Murphy and Dr Con Murphy, they were there with the Cork minors that day, coming in to wish us well. A very sporting gesture. I had hoped we had got the preparation right. We took a flight up from Shannon that morning and we were very relaxed. Breakfast at 10 o'clock. Then a couple of hours' sleep for the players.'

As for the match itself, Clare were in front approaching half-time. Then a test of character.

'Michael Duignan got a goal for Offaly. It was a rare error by Davy Fitzgerald, but immediately, the 'Sparrow' got a point. So while behind at the break, we had got the last score of the half. That was important.'

What did he say to the players at the break?

'It was calm enough really. The lads reassured Fitzy not to worry – we would still win. Then we held up the Clare jersey and told them, 'this is what it's all about'. Opened the door and let them out. I was confident we would win.'

Does he remember what he said to Marty Morrissey?

'I do well. It was not cockiness or anything, but as I often said, you must have belief. We had it that day.'

Offaly got a second goal. The game was level. Doubts set in. Would Clare falter at the last hurdle? Enter team captain, Anthony Daly.

'We got a '65' – now McMahon normally takes these. But up stepped

'Dalo', a real leader. Straight as a dye over the bar. Point ahead. Offaly came down the field. Lohan cleared it and we won a free at the other end. Jamesie (O'Connor) pointed it. Game over.'

It had finally happened. Clare were the 1995 All-Ireland Senior Hurling champions. And in Loughnane's first year in charge as well. Where were those delegates now, those who did not want him to get the job? Probably in the masses of people that were celebrating a unique feat. And celebrate they did.

'I stood there taking it all in. Dalo made another great speech. The crowd went wild. But it was remarkably calm in the dressing room afterwards when we all got in. It took some time for it all to sink in.'

It was a short winter in Clare. The usual round of functions and presentations took place. But very soon the thought of defending their title came into focus.

Winning the Second Time

1996 was a strange year.

'We trained as much as we did in previous years. But the spark was missing. We never really got off the ground. We did make the Munster Final. But I felt for a few weeks beforehand that we wouldn't win.'

He was right. Carey's late wonder point gave Limerick victory. What happened next was a test of Loughnane's managerial skills.

'I called the players together the Wednesday after the Munster Final. I told them good teams win one All-Ireland, but great teams win more. We had to win another to be considered a great team rather than "one-hit wonders". I also said they should enjoy the summer off, because next year would be a long one.'

1997 was a dramatic season. Clare and Tipperary collided like speeding trains. Not once, but twice. Tipperary were the one county that had really damaged Clare down through the years. For that reason Ger Loughnane wanted to meet them and beat them in a major game. Tipperary and Clare negotiated a path to the Munster Final. En route, Clare once again beat Cork.

The Munster Final was played in Páirc Uí Chaoimh. As they assembled that morning Ger noticed the tension among his players.

'This was unusual. Normally they were very relaxed and calm. But I suppose playing Tipp in a Munster Final was different. The lads were conscious of what they did to us in 1993.'

Word was coming through of the enormity of the Clare support that was travelling to Cork for the match. It gave Loughnane the ideal opportunity to ease the tension.

'We went for a puck-around in the Mardyke when we landed in Cork. I spoke to the lads and told them what I had heard about the support. I also told them our reputation as a team was at stake this afternoon.'

'The match itself was played at a frenetic pace. That suited us. At the break we were ahead 0-13 to 0-8. Then early in the second-half Tipp drew level. And next their supporters started singing "Slievenamon". I can tell you that drove me mad. I jumped out of the dugout and roared at the lads. "Is that what ye want to hear – is it?" To be fair they responded. As I knew they would. We got a goal. In the end we won by a goal. That win swept away a lot of the heartbreak we had suffered at Tipp's hands over the years.'

Ger describes the win.

'The treasure of all treasures. To beat Tipp in a Munster Final was special, and that is a compliment to them as well.'

A few months later they would meet again. This time in the All-Ireland Final, when there was a lot more at stake. It was a game Clare could not afford to lose.

'Absolutely. If we lost that game everything we had achieved would have meant nothing. It was a huge match for Clare hurling. The build-up was very intense. The rivalry had turned a bit nasty, it must be said. Clare were winning championships that Tipp felt they should be winning.'

This time Tipperary made the better start. They hurled Clare off the field in the opening half. Yet Tipp only led by four points at half-time. It was a deficit Clare could cope with.

'Now I could have had a lash at them at the break, but I didn't. I was calm and assured. So were the players. I always believe if you whip guys into a frenzy, they lose their focus. We made a few points. A couple of slight adjustments and out they went for the second-half. I was happy enough we could still win.'

Then as the teams re-emerged for the second-half, he noticed something that convinced him Clare would win.

'I was last to leave the dressing room. As I was walking out to the pitch, the Tipp players ran past me. As they did, they almost to a man abused me. I was stunned at this. But in a funny way I was also delighted. Their focus was gone. I was sure we would win after that.'

They did, but it was close, and they very nearly lost it.

'It was a cracking second-half. We were fantastic – now to be fair, Tipp played their part as well.'

Two images stand out from that game – Loughnane and John Leahy were the characters involved. Picture the scene. Teams are level. Time is almost up, a replay looks certain. By now Loughnane had made his way around the pitch. As Jamesie O'Connor won possession, he (Loughnane) was just by the goalpost at the Hill 16 end of the ground.

'I knew straight away he would go for a point. He was right on the halfway line by the Hogan Stand – on the sideline as well. He struck it beautifully. I watched the flight of the ball. It was bang on target and dropped over the bar. I raised my fist to the crowd behind the goal. I very nearly waved the white flag myself but the umpire got there before me. It was the winning point.'

It was, but they nearly gave it away one minute later.

'I was almost back in the dugout, when Leahy got the ball. I thought he must equalise. But no, he went for the goal. Davy (Fitzgerald) saved it.

There was no way back after that.'

Clare were champions again. But should Leahy have taken the point, which would have forced a replay?

'I was sure he would take the point. But then again he had the chance to win the match and took a gamble. He would have been a hero had it gone in, but that's the way games go.'

It was another great day for Clare, tempered somewhat by Loughnane's feelings for Tipperary manager, Len Gaynor. It was Gaynor who effectively ensured that Ger would become Clare manager back in 1994.

'Len would have really felt that defeat. He put a lot of work into Clare when he was manager. It's a pity he was in the opposite corner that day. But that aside it was a magic feeling to beat Tipperary. Now we had proved ourselves to be a really great team. Tipp had humiliated us often enough; this was the ultimate payback.'

They certainly were a great team, and in the Championship of 1997 they had beaten the big guns – Cork and Kilkenny in the semi-final – and Tipperary twice.

'That made it extra special. The three big counties beaten in the one year. Magic.'

That night controversy erupted on *The Sunday Game.*

Eamonn Cregan, a panellist on the show and a former Clare manager, was critical of the standard of hurling in the final. Loughnane was fuming as he listened to Cregan.

'I was standing beside Ger Canning at the Clare victory banquet, listening to this drivel by Cregan. Canning sensed straight away that Cregan was out of order and said, "That's terrible isn't it?" "Don't worry about him," I replied. Then when it was my turn to go live I tore into him with both barrels. I didn't spare him I can tell you.'

Does he regret having a go live on TV?

'I regret the fact that I did not say more. Okay it was no classic, but it was after all an All-Ireland Final, it was tense. It's a pity he (Cregan) could not find anything good to say about the game.'

It was a disappointing end to a glorious day.

And the second bit of controversy that Ger was involved in as a result of the final?

'Because I went on to the pitch a few times in the semi-final, I was supposed to be confined to the bench for the final. They gave me a green bench to sit on. There was also an official observing how many times I moved. He was a busy man that day. I tried to take the bench home for the front garden but they would not give it to me.'

Ger on GAA Issues

1997 may have had its share of controversy, but it paled in comparison to events that dominated 1998 – on and off the field. And as ever, Loughnane was in the thick of it.

Hurling aside, Ger Loughnane is never slow to voice his opinion on matters relating to the GAA. His role on *The Sunday Game* is one he enjoys immensely.

'I really look forward to the Sundays when we are on. It's great craic with Tomás Mulcahy and Cyril Farrell. We get on well and bounce off each other. Michael Lyster is a great anchorman. He just lets us get on with it, up to a point anyway. The important thing though is the game itself. It's not about the guys in the studio, it's all about the lads who play the game. The programme portrays the game in a fabulous light and that can only be good for hurling.'

As for the perceived trial-by-television that players and officials are subject to?

'You have to be aware of what you are going to say and how it might have an impact on players. But at the same time you cannot shy away from controversial incidents. That is not fair either. I realise players are only amateurs, but they know the cameras are present. So if they step out of line they will be caught.'

His new media role often led him into confrontation with some of his former players and officials.

'Well you can't be selective – if they deserve criticism they get it. They might not like it but if I treat them differently to others, I would not be fair to myself. I hope they would take it in the spirit in which it is meant.'

As for his criticism of Clare officials.

'I was critical of the direction Clare hurling was going. It needed saying, maybe someone else should have said it. But I felt it was right to say it.'

Ger has huge admiration for Brian Cody, the present Kilkenny manager. Cody and Loughnane were in Teacher Training College at the same time. When Cody was appointed Kilkenny manager, Ger was quoted as saying, 'We're all in trouble now'.

'I did. And I've been proved right, haven't I?'

What did he see all those years ago in St Pat's Drumcondra?

'I saw a determination and a self-belief in a guy that I had not seen in anyone so young. I admire him as a man and a manager. Brian believes Kilkenny are better than any team. Okay he goes on about tough matches and hard games to win. But don't for one minute be fooled. Every time a Kilkenny team goes out he expects them to win.'

As we spoke, the All-Ireland Final and Kilkenny's bid for a four-in-a-row (against Tipperary in 2009) was not yet complete.

Does Cody want it?

'Does he what! He craves it. He might be playing it down in the media. But believe you me, Brian wants this more than anything else. Go back to when Wexford beat them with a late goal in the Leinster Final a few years ago. He slumped to the ground in despair. Cody hates losing no matter what game they play in. Look at the way they approach the Walsh Cup in January. They go out to win everything. So you can imagine how much the four-in-a-row means to him. I feel that if they win it he might even call it a day. It means that much to him.' (Kilkenny won four-in-a-row in 2009, beating Tipperary.)

The GPA is an area of concern to Ger.

'Well first of all what do they stand for? We all know what the GAA is about. It has its rules and regulations. Where are the GPA rules? Have they any? If they publish them and their charter, then we'll all know where we stand. Also I'm not sure they represent every player in the association. I think they focus on the inter-county guys and forget about the rest. That doesn't sit well with me. Let there be transparency. But get the GAA and the GPA to sit down and sort it out, once and for all.'

He does agree that players must be looked after. But 'pay for play' is a non-runner.

'By all means look after the players. They are our best asset. Now in this regard things have improved and that's only right. But there is no way the GAA can go down the road of paying players. It's unsustainable and would kill clubs and counties for that matter. We could not afford it. Simple as that.'

How did he cope with the media when he was manager?

'I had my moments I suppose. Generally it was okay but I took exception to some of the things that were written about us. I like the guy who writes the facts and not some concoction of his own.'

In the early days of his management, Clare were the darlings of the press. When did he feel that changed?

'I think it began when we started issuing dummy teams. That annoyed fellows but we didn't care.'

Ah yes, the dummy teams. A deliberate ploy on his part?

'Initially it was. Anything to give you an edge in an important game. I remember in the 1998 game against Cork, the team bore no resemblance to the one published. Jimmy Barry Murphy and Tom Cashman were scratching their heads – they were completely confused.'

What about the player or players who were named but not played?

'This was not about any individual. This was about Clare hurling. If anyone did not buy into it, they were no good to us. We told them early on to take no notice of the team that was published. You'll be given the real team when we're ready. They accepted that readily.'

Clare hurling has been struggling of late, but Ger has high hopes for the future.

'It's been a tough few years. But there is a lot of hard and good work going on in the county. The under-21 team is very good and I have no doubt Clare will be competitive in the years ahead.' (Clare won the under-21 All-Ireland hurling title in 2009 beating Kilkenny)

Ger agrees that the Championship in 2009 was poor but is hopeful that hurling in general is progressing.

'Well it's been a tame enough Championship really. We could do with a good All-Ireland Final. The last couple have not done much for the game. Hopefully 2010 will be better. To be fair, though, a lot of counties are working hard at all levels and that will surface in the coming years.'

He is also fully supportive of the tiered structure in the Championship.

'The best thing the GAA did was to introduce the Ring and Rackard Cups. It means teams are now competing at their own level. It's no good having them in against the Kilkennys and Corks of this world, getting hammered. A level playing field is what is needed and the so-called weaker counties have it.'

One regret though is events in Cork in the last few years.

'What happened, and I don't know the full story, damaged hurling. It has also broken their (Cork) spirit. Look, this decade should have been about Cork and Kilkenny. In past decades you had great rivalry. It was Cork and Wexford in the 1950s. You had Tipp and Kilkenny in another era. But this decade has been all about Kilkenny and that's not good. It was the collateral damage that was done to hurling that would be my worry. Cork had won two All-Irelands, then Kilkenny won two. We were set for a great finish to the decade. Instead we ended up with one team dominating. Kilkenny's biggest rivals were gone. All because Cork got involved in internal wrangling.'

Another interesting aspect of Ger's reign in Clare was that they never won the National Hurling League. Did they take the GAA's second competition seriously?

'I would say we took it seriously – up to a point. But the Championship is the ultimate goal of any team – be it club or county. I was no different. Look, can you tell me who won the League, let's say in 1990? You probably cannot. But I bet you could tell me who won the All-Ireland.'

It was said that Clare often trained for two or even three hours before league games.

'Rubbish! You couldn't do that to players. We warmed up as normal but we didn't train as hard as that. But I can tell you we learned a lot in the League. Especially about teams we were due to play in the Championship. In 1998 Cork were beating us well in the semi-final. Mike Mac came up to me and said, "Look, we better do something here or we'll get hammered". "Leave it," I said. The more they win by, the better. When it matters we will beat them, don't panic".'

His instincts were right. A few weeks later Clare ended Cork's Championship campaign in emphatic style.

1998 – A Year of Controversies

There's a great line in Christy Moore's song about 'Joxer'. It goes, 'It was in the year of '88 in the lovely month of June'. Now change that to 'It was in the year of '98 in the lovely month of June', and you could apply it to Ger Loughnane and the Clare hurlers. Even now 11 years later sitting in the Old Ground Hotel in Ennis, Ger laughs at the sequence of events that captivated the nation.

'It was crazy, absolutely crazy – what went on.'

Where do you start to document in detail what happened?

It was a long drawn-out process that left him and his colleagues drained – emotionally and physically.

'I remember before we played the third Offaly match, Tony (Considine) said to me, "Ger, I'm exhausted". Tony is never tired. I was too, but I didn't let on. But I knew then we were in trouble.'

It began with a tempestuous Munster Final with Waterford and finally ended with a defeat to Offaly. However, in between it had more twists and turns than an old country road. There was a host of characters involved, or implicated, depending on your viewpoint – Colin Lynch, Ger Loughnane, referee Willie Barrett, the Munster Council officers, Gerald McCarthy, an unnamed (initially) steward in Thurles, Joe McDonagh and, crucially, Galway referee Jimmy Cooney. It was Cooney who in the end unwittingly brought Clare's season to an end. If we were to delve into the events in minute detail, it would probably take another book.

Ger's recall of the events is impressive. So let's try and unravel the mysterious happenings that made the headlines in the summer of 1998.

'We made a big effort to beat Cork in the Munster semi-final. As a result we were flat in the Munster Final against Waterford. We led for most of the game. But Paul Flynn got a goal to earn them a draw. That meant a replay. We did not need an extra game, but we now had it.'

It was in the dressing room afterwards that he noticed something.

'The lads were furious. I asked, "What's up?" Then they told me. The verbal abuse, some of it on a personal level, that they were subjected to from the Waterford players during the game shocked me. One of our players was accused of beating his wife.'

Training for the replay was different.

'The first night I read the riot act for allowing it (the verbal abuse) to happen. Then for the next few nights it was all about getting their heads right. There was very little hurling done that week.'

Were they ready for the replay?

'Were they ready? They were jumping out of their skins.'

The atmosphere in Thurles for the replay was . . . well, we'll let Ger explain.

'Oh boy, was there an atmosphere? It was warlike! Then when the match started it exploded. In the opening minutes Brian Lohan and Stephen White were sent off. While off the ball Colin Lynch and Tony Browne flaked one another. They were both booked. Gerald McCarthy (Waterford manager) went ballistic when Browne was booked, implying Lynch started the flaking.'

The game eventually settled down. When it did, Clare won comfortably.

'In the end we hurled them off the field. With five minutes to go Gerald came up and congratulated me. Dalo got the cup. Waterford Chairman Pad Joe Ryan came into the dressing room and wished us well. That, I thought, was the end of it – let's move on.'

But it was far from over. It was only starting. In the days after the game the newspapers and radio were highly critical of what went on in Thurles. Loughnane was seething.

'It was disgraceful, it was anti-Clare, particularly *Sportscall* on RTÉ Radio.'

Clare resumed training with an eye on the All-Ireland semi-final.

'My gut feeling though was that something more would happen.'

Then the envelope arrived.

'We got a letter that Lynch was to appear before the Munster Council. I was right, we were in trouble. Yet Tony Browne got off scot free.'

Another twist in the ongoing saga.

'Robert Frost, Clare Chairman, was in the VIP section of Croke Park for the Galway v Waterford quarter-final on 26 July. He overheard three priests discussing Clare and the match the previous Sunday. They actually said that Lynch would get three months suspension. Now Colin's hearing was not until 7 August, two days before the All-Ireland semi-final with Offaly. Then, amazingly, at the hearing Lynch was suspended for three months. Effectively it ended his season.'

Clare sought an injunction against the Munster Council. It was thrown out. Sadly, Lynch's grandmother became seriously ill and he was unable to attend the Council hearing.

'Myself and a couple of Clare officials attended the meeting hoping to speak on Colin's behalf. When I arrived at the Limerick Inn over 120 Clare supporters were present. It was scary. They (supporters) were in an angry mood. I gave Marty Morrissey a quick interview and he misinterpreted what I said about Colin's grandmother. RTÉ then reported that she had died. I was livid when I was told – a good job Marty had left. To be fair when he realised he got it wrong, he went straight to the hospital to the family. It was a long night. The Clare officials never got into the meeting. They left around midnight. On the way home, we heard the verdict. The three priests were right – Colin got his three months.'

Lynch, it emerged, was suspended on the word of a local primary school teacher who was acting as a steward that day in Thurles.

'That really angered me as under the rules of the GAA, Colin should not have been suspended. But he was and that was contrary to the rules. Is it any wonder we were annoyed? I would go to any lengths to defend my players. More so when they are wronged. In this case Colin was the victim. I make no apologies to anyone for my actions.'

The Three Missing Minutes

It meant facing a semi-final against Offaly without a key player.

'Colin was a huge player for us. Any time he missed a big game we played poorly.'

The semi-final was a strange game. Clare were in front with 10 minutes to go. Offaly then scored 1-2 without reply. A late free from Jamesie O'Connor earned Clare a replay. Given what had gone on in advance of the game, it was an exceptional display.

'You're right, it was. But I knew we would be better in the replay. There would be no distractions this time.'

Loughnane was right. Clare were well in control. Even though they only led by three points with time almost up.

'Barry Murphy was going through, when all of a sudden he stopped. I was wondering what was up. Colm Flynn, our physio, said the game must be over. But I said, "There's at least three minutes left".'

What happened next astounded everyone. Referee Jimmy Cooney was about to become the centre of unwanted attention.

'I shook hands with Michael Bond, the Offaly manager. But there was a funny feeling around the place. Most people were aware that the game should not have ended when it did.'

Cooney was ushered off the pitch by security men in suits. The teams for the next match came out onto the field. They were quickly joined by hundreds of Offaly supporters who were protesting at the premature ending of the game.

Loughnane is sure of one thing.

'If the guys in the suits did not come onto the pitch, the match would have restarted. Jimmy would have realised his mistake and we would have finished the match. But these were not normal GAA stewards, these were security men with earpieces. They were more like FBI men than GAA men. That was crucial. GAA stewards would never act in such a high-handed manner.'

It was not to be. Yet another GAA soap opera was about to unfold. Once again Clare would command top billing. That night in their hotel, Clare were relaxing and looking forward to another All-Ireland Final. They were in fact having a few pints and joking with the Offaly players about giving them a replay.

'I was in the hotel when I got a call. It was from Marty Morrissey who told me RTÉ had been put on standby for the replay the following Saturday in Thurles. I then met Phelim Murphy who was a member of the GAC (Games Administration Committee) in Croke Park. Phelim said there could not be a replay as the referee's word was law. Yeah I thought, but this is Clare.'

Confusion reigned that night. But Loughnane saw an opening and he put the word out that if there was to be a replay, they wanted Colin Lynch cleared to play.

'I tried to meet GAA President Joe McDonagh but failed. I called a meeting for eight on Sunday morning. I also asked Pat Fitzgerald, the Clare Secretary, to arrange a meeting with Liam Mulvihill. The purpose of this meeting was to get Lynch cleared.'

Another operation swung into action. A meeting was called in Croke Park.

'I drove Pat Fitzgerald into Croke Park. I left him as he went off to meet GAA officials. After what seemed an age he arrived back. Pat had what I thought was good news. The GAA's Management Committee are meeting on Wednesday night and there is a chance Colin will be cleared to play.'

In the corridors the Clare and Offaly delegations met. The atmosphere was a bit tense. By now referee Jimmy Cooney admitted he had made an error. The clamour for a replay had grown stronger in the hours after the game.

'I told the Offaly lads there was going to be a replay. They seemed confused. But don't worry I said, this is a done deal. We'll see ye on Saturday in Thurles.'

Clare and Offaly met with the GAC, separately. After a while they were both called in and given the verdict. No real surprise – a replay was ordered. Marty was right, Saturday in Thurles. The gate receipts would go to the Omagh Fund (families of bomb victims) and each team would get a substantial donation to their holiday fund. There was one other significant change – Dickie Murphy would be the referee. GAA policy at the time was for the original referee to officiate at any replay. It's a policy that has since been changed.

'I jumped up and said we had no objection to Jimmy Cooney doing the replay. But I was told he had asked not to be reappointed.'

How did Ger feel about all of this?

'Well I felt if you were to win, you must win on the field. There must be no doubt. The All-Ireland after all is sacrosanct. Its status must not be jeopardised. Now mind you, there were those in Clare who did not agree with me. But that would not be unusual.'

How did the Clare players react to a replay?

'Very positive. I remember Daly saying, "Let's go and win it on the field, we do not want a hollow victory".'

It was back to Croke Park on the Wednesday for the Lynch appeal.

'Colin travelled up with Pat Fitzgerald. It was a funny meeting. Pat was not asked one question. The Munster Council then produced the mysterious witness. A Mr McDonnell, the primary schoolteacher who claimed he saw Colin hit Browne.'

There was another bombshell at the outset of the appeal.

Seán Kelly, Chairman of the Munster Council, presented their case. He had been contacted by GAA President Joe McDonagh and told to take some form of action in light of the incidents that occurred in the Munster Final between Offaly and Clare. Once Lynch heard about this direction from the top, he lost all hope; he knew he would remain suspended. Because he knew not one member of the Committee would go against McDonagh. At that point Lynch turned to Fitzgerald and said, "I'm fucked now".'

The end result was a fudge. The GAC could not grant Lynch clemency. Only the Munster Council could do that. There was little chance of the Council denying the wishes of the GAA President.

'To rub salt in the wounds Colin personally delivered his second appeal to Munster Council Secretary Doney Nealon. You know what – Doney did not even recognise him. He actually asked him who he was.'

The Council would have to convene an officers' meeting to clear Lynch.

'Seán Kelly was on holidays. The Offaly match was on Saturday, this was Thursday. It never happened. Lynch had no chance.'

In the end Lynch did not take part in the replay against Offaly. The GAA rulebook won again. As expected, relations between Clare and the Munster Council, particularly with the Secretary Doney Nealon, were fraught.

Efforts were made to restore harmony.

'Seán Kelly met me and asked me to manage the Munster hurling team. I knew Doney would be a selector. I thought my appointment as manager of Munster might help to improve relations between Clare and the Munster Council. But on hearing I was the manager, Doney resigned. So I stepped down also. That year not one Clare player lined out with Munster. I had no input into that – it was their own decision.'

What are his feelings now towards all those involved?

'I don't know. It's a long time ago. I am still angered at Colin's suspension. But you know who came out of this worse than anyone? Joe McDonagh is the person held in most disdain with Clare people over the whole episode.'

When all avenues of appeal for Colin Lynch were exhausted, Clare still had an All-Ireland semi-final to play.

'We tried our best in the game. But we were dead on our feet. All that went on beforehand took its toll and Offaly won. There was no bitterness towards them. I went in and congratulated them and to be fair they were very gracious. Joe Dooley, the manager, said it had been a funny week. A week? It was a funny few months.'

As they left Thurles they got a rousing reception.

'The fans were brilliant. They waited for us after the match and cheered us onto the bus. Some of the lads were in tears. In the hotel I met Dick O'Neill, a selector for Kilkenny, who were in the final. I said to him, "Ye guys are in trouble now".'

What did Ger mean?

'I couldn't see Offaly losing the final. They had momentum after the games with us. They'd be unstoppable.'

Loughnane was right. A few weeks later, after all the trauma, Offaly were crowned All-Ireland champions for 1998. One of the most controversial Championships in the GAA's history was finally over. But Ger is adamant about one thing.

'We got a raw deal and I have no doubt it was a "get Clare" thing.'

Who was out to get Clare?

'Ah come on! It had to be from the top. Who else would want us out? Why were we forced to replay a match that ended prematurely. Why did Colin Lynch get three months, without anyone seeing what happened? Why did an Offaly player get off scot free after hitting one of our players?

'You might not believe me when I tell you this. 1998 was a great year. We won the Munster Championship, played six matches and played well in most of them. It was only fatigue that beat us against Offaly in the last game. From a hurling point of view it was great. The rest, well it's consigned to history now.'

Ger might not have known it then but Clare's great run was over. A final thought on Jimmy Cooney.

'I'll put it like this. Jimmy did not deprive us of the All-Ireland that year but he did deprive us of getting there.'

A Team in Decline

The years of hard work were now telling on the Clare team. In 1999 an emerging Cork team beat them in the Munster Final. But Clare did produce one outstanding display.

'We scrambled a draw with Tipp on the first round. However a week later in the replay we literally blew them away. It was one of the best performances Clare gave in my time as manager. The complete display is the best way to describe it.'

When they lost the Munster Final to Cork Ger knew it would be difficult to win the All-Ireland that year. For one thing, it meant having to play an extra game instead of proceeding directly to the semi-finals.

'We did not need the extra game. A draw with Galway in the quarter-final only compounded matters. The direct route would have suited us. Now, had we got to the final we might have taken Cork. Because the one thing these guys (Clare players) loved was getting revenge. But Kilkenny beat us in the semi-final.'

A year later it was all over.

When Tipperary, ironically enough, ended their Championship ambitions in 2000 he called time on his role as Clare manager.

'I spoke to Tony Considine about giving up after 1998. But we stuck at it. Now this time I knew it was game over. The team needed a new voice – a new direction. It was just the right time to go. So I went.'

It was an amazing tenure in charge. Clare had revitalised hurling. Loughnane added a new dimension to the game. Love him or loathe him – and there were many of those in both camps at times – you had to admire him. This is best summed up by the remark attributed to a well-known journalist during the Championship of 2001 – the first without Loughnane since 1995. 'Christ, I'm missing him already!'

But he would return.

And as you would expect, it was a return not without its share of controversy. Throughout his entire career Ger has received wonderful support from his family, especially his wife Mary.

'Mary has been outstanding. I couldn't have done it without her.'

As for the lads Barry and Conor?

'It was great for them as well. If you look at it, they grew up in a fantastic era for Clare hurling – the best ever. They were involved with the team as waterboys. Conor was booked in Croke Park for going onto the pitch. Like father like son, I suppose.'

While he had his run-ins with officials down through the years, Ger has nothing but praise for the Clare officers.

'Outstanding is the only way I could describe them, particularly Pat Fitzgerald the Secretary. Anything I asked for, I got.'

Which brings up another issue.

Having left the Clare position, a few short years later he had a major run-in with the chairman Michael McDonagh. This also created a bit of tension with former captain Anthony Daly. Daly, the Clare manager at the time, even said, 'It's time for Ger to realise he is no longer the Clare manager.'

'I was annoyed at a few things. The best Clare hurling team was picked and then there was an award for services to Clare hurling. I did not agree with either of them and spoke my mind as I always have done. Maybe I should have just kept quiet and said nothing. But then that's me.'

One thing that has not altered is his admiration for many of the players who he worked with in Clare. The word used to describe them is 'respect'.

'They were exceptional. I would have the utmost respect for them. Especially Dalo. What a leader! Then you look at the Lohans, Brian and Frank, Jamesie and Seanie McMahon – fabulous individuals. A pleasure to have worked with them. We didn't always agree, but we agreed on one thing – Clare hurling.'

Daly was his captain from day one and now he is the Dublin hurling manager.

'He will be brilliant for them – a great guy. I can actually see him back again as Clare manager. I know he had it already, might not have been the right time to take it. But if it comes his way again, Clare will prosper.'

As with most GAA folk Ger's interest began in his local club Feakle. It is only fitting that his playing career should end there. His final act on the playing field was to help them in their attempt to win a coveted county title. Ger's late father, John James, was a well-known cross country runner and won four national titles. Coming from Clare, where they love their traditional music, he was also a renowned fiddle player. His mother Veronica, who gave him huge encouragement throughout his career, is still hale and hearty today.

At 20 years of age Ger won an intermediate title, but like everyone in the club, it was the senior medal he craved. That opportunity arrived in 1988. Before that he had been playing with Wolfe Tones of Shannon.

'I was working there so it was convenient for me to play with them. But Feakle had won 4 under-21 titles in a row and had good players coming through.'

Ironically enough it was Fr Harry Bohan who approached Ger about returning.

'It was. He felt the team had huge potential but lacked experience. I was on the verge of retiring anyway, so I decided to give it one more year.'

Unfortunately they lost to Clarecastle in the final.

'The final had everything, including a massive row. That suited Clarecastle and they won in the end. But we vowed that night to give it one more year.'

It was a wise decision.

'The following year was brilliant, We eventually got our hands on the county title. It was a bit like the Clare breakthrough though; we did not believe it until we actually got the cup.'

What made it special was that it was won with his lifelong friends.

'It is without doubt one of my proudest moments in hurling. Had we not won, it would have left a massive gap in my career. Bringing the cup home and seeing the joy on people's faces made it all worthwhile. We had not won it since the 1930s and that is a long wait for a proud club. I had worked with and gone to school with some of these people and they are a very special group. Winning with your club was more personal.'

Outside of hurling, Ger is principal of St Aidan's Primary School in Shannon. In fact he was one of the youngest principals ever appointed.

'I kind of drifted into it. A couple of years in St Flannan's as a boarder was like being in prison. Training in St Pat's, Drumcondra, was a holiday camp after that. I love teaching. Had a few offers to go into private work but no chance – wouldn't swap it for the world.'

The Galway Rambler

In his official biography *Raising The Banner* published in 2001, Ger said he had no intention of ever returning to inter-county management. But whoever penned the maxim 'never say never' got it right in this instance. In October 2006 Loughnane made a sensational return to hurling. He was appointed Galway Senior Hurling manager. His return was watched and awaited with interest. How he ended up there came about as he says himself 'as a bit of a fluke'.

'I was playing golf with Brendan Lynskey, a former Galway hurler, who I rarely play with, mind, and he asked if I'd be interested in managing Galway.'

The offer was a total surprise, but it intrigued him.

'I said the only way I would go anywhere else would be if there was nobody else. I had no intention of getting involved in an election or a canvass for the job. I dismissed it completely because Galway has so many factions I didn't think it would happen.'

However Galway persisted and a high-powered delegation soon arrived in Clare.

'John Fahy, the County Secretary, Michael Murray, a Galwegian GAA official, and Lynskey came down. We had a discussion. I gave it a bit of thought and then said, "Why not? I'll give it two years and try and win an All-Ireland".'

However, before he eventually got the job, the politics of Galway hurling kicked in. Initially there were five other nominees for the job. On hearing this, Loughnane withdrew his name. The Galway hurling panel issued a statement in support of Loughnane. Gradually all five nominees removed themselves from the race for the job. In an ironic twist, Loughnane got support from Jimmy Cooney, the referee in the middle of the Offaly v Clare controversy in 1998. Eventually with the free run he wanted, Ger was given the job. On accepting the position, he stated, "If I don't win the All-Ireland in two years I'll have failed".'

Did that put added pressure on him to deliver?

'Not really, I felt it was attainable. Given the success Galway had had at under-age level, it seemed a realistic goal. But that was before I started the job.'

While he has no regrets about taking the job, he quickly realised during his very first night in Galway as manager that it was not going to work.

'No regrets about going there. But I felt I was walking into a quagmire. There are too many factions in Galway. There's the progressive faction, led by John Fahy and Joe Connolly. These lads are anxious to move things forward. Then there is the old guard who are against everything. Fellows who were officers before and did not want to let go of the reins of power.'

There were even doubts that he would see out the two years.

'On the way back from training, we used to laugh about it. The open rivalry that we witnessed between club players stunned us. There are rivalries everywhere, but usually at least they are concealed. Not up there. I said to the lads on my backroom team, "This won't last till Christmas".'

One other factor was the Portumna incident.

A controversial county final (Portumna v Loughrea) resulted in a number of suspensions and tension in the county. As a result one of Galway's better players, Ollie Canning, refused to commit himself to playing for the county.

Ger also discovered aspects of Galway's hurling that surprised him.

'First of all, Galway are not as good as they think they are. I had to tell them that. A number of the skills you take for granted in other counties, they just do not have. The ability to win the ball in the air is not there. Getting to the pace and speed of the modern game is another while an ability to compete in highly intensive games is also just not there. And in vital games these simple things cost you.'

Ger had no difficulty in pointing these out, but the response surprised him.

'I told the County Board these things, but they felt I was insulting them. But their record over the years will bear this out. They invariably fade in the closing stages of big games.'

The obvious answer to that problem would have been an earlier move into the Leinster Championship, which would provide Galway with some opposition before meeting the big names who won their provincial title and notched up some essential experience at the same time.

'They should have done something years ago. Waiting around until August for an All-Ireland semi-final is no good. You need competitive matches to sharpen your skill. Again certain factions in the county opposed that move, and if they hadn't, they would be stronger today as a result.'

Ironically, in 2001, the year after Loughnane left, Galway entered the Leinster Championship for a three-year trial period. Despite the problems, they (Galway) produced a number of excellent displays.

'In the first year we were very close to Kilkenny in the quarter-final. It was level, I think, with about ten minutes to go. Noel Hickey just got a touch to stop Damien Hayes getting a goal that might have won us the match.'

One match he has particularly fond memories of is the 2008 Championship game Galway played against Cork, even if it was in defeat.

'Cork were brilliant that night, and to be there was a pleasure. Down to 14 men and to win like that, they did fantastic. If Cork could have played like that all the time, they would be very close to Kilkenny. But it goes back to what I said earlier – when the game goes to a certain level they (Galway) won't get there. Until such time as they rectify that problem, they will struggle to win All-Irelands at senior level.'

In his two years with Galway there was one match he did not want – but as sure as night follows day it happened – Galway v Clare. His good friend and former selector, Tony Considine, was the Clare manager.

'I suppose it was inevitable.'

Yet he found the atmosphere that evening in Ennis very strange.

'Artificial is the best way to describe it. It was a round robin game. We were both qualified and there was nothing at stake. It was a false match really.'

The issuing of 'dummy teams' may have been accepted when he was in charge in Clare, but it wasn't so welcome in Galway and it brought criticism.

'Maybe it did, but people who did not want me in Galway were only looking for excuses.'

His tenure in Galway came to an end after the loss to Cork in 2008, even though he was prepared to give it another year.

'I would have stayed on, as I still believed that for all the problems there is huge potential in the county. I would also have enjoyed a crack at the Leinster Championship. But the delegates thought otherwise and they voted not to give me another year.'

Was he disappointed?

'I suppose I would have been, but look that's life and sport. I quickly put it behind me and moved on.'

The Hunter from Feakle

This time he is adamant that he will not be back. Now he has found a new passion. Or you could say he has returned to a passion that got lost in his hurling years.

'Beagle hunting – yes, it's something I used to do before the hurling and now I am back at it. I just love it. No matter what type of weather, you just forget about everything. We always had beagles at home in Feakle. We used to go off every Sunday with my father. Walk for miles, you'd be knackered after it, but it was something I looked forward to. Then when I started hurling I just hadn't got the time for it.'

It was a relative of his who enticed him back, and for that he is grateful.

'My cousin Pat asked me to come out with him one day and that was it, the hunting bug was back. It's a bit like an alcoholic – you're off the drink for so long and then you take one and that's it. Once I heard the cry of the hounds, that was it. Now there's a group of us – we have a pack of about 30 hounds. I have six myself, and we go out every Sunday. It is just brilliant. Hunting rather than hurling for me now.'

His interest in hurling though remains.

'Oh God, yes! I regularly go to games. The League wouldn't appeal to me now, mind you. But the Championship is a different thing.'

As for other sports?

'I enjoy all sports. Munster in rugby now are great. I used to be a big athletics fan. Especially the brilliant Finnish runner, Lasse Virén. But with all the cheating and drugs in the Olympics, I lost interest.'

Ger Loughnane has been good for hurling. No doubt there are those who will say hurling has been good to him. I am sure he would agree. He has been colourful and controversial, all at the same time. A great hurler and a brilliant manager. As a player he may not have won a coveted Munster or All-Ireland medal, but he brought honour and glory to his beloved Clare. And that is something they will not forget, regardless of their views or opinions of the Feakle native. Would they have won the two All-Irelands without him? It is doubtful. Should they have won more? Probably. But when you are 81 years without a title, then two in three years is a real bonus.

So Ger Loughnane, family man, hurler, manager, teacher and TV pundit has now returned to his favourite pastime – beagle hunting.

One thing is certain.

If the birds, rabbits and hares around the hills of Clare are pursued in the same relentless fashion that he pursued the Munster and All-Ireland Championships, they are – a bit like what he said about Brian Cody – 'all in trouble'.

6

Mickey Harte

The Birth of Errigal Ciaran

The story of Mickey Harte is not just about managing Tyrone teams. Through dramatic and sometimes tragic circumstances, Harte has weathered many storms outside of football during his tenure as manager of club and county, at minor and senior levels.

Mickey Harte was born in Ballygawley in 1952, one of a family of nine. From a young age Gaelic football dominated his life. His early education was at that famed football academy Omagh CBS. Harte trained to be a teacher in St Joseph's Training College in Belfast, where he also played university football.

In his own words he was 'a modest but honest footballer'. He played senior for Tyrone from 1975 to 1982. It was a period when Ulster titles did not visit the county. The closest they came was in the Final of 1980, but in a cracking contest, Armagh emerged winners by 4-10 to 4-7.

He called time on his playing career in 1985. But football, and particularly Tyrone football, was to benefit from Harte's expertise almost immediately. He played his football with St Ciaran's, Ballygawley. Due to a dispute between Harte, Glencull (a football club in his local area) and the Ulster club committee, a new club was born in 1990 called Errigal Ciaran. Despite being a relatively new club, Errigal Ciaran made an instant impact on Tyrone and Ulster Club football.

'Errigal was born out of a split within the GAA. Or maybe it was born out of me. Back in the winter of 1982, we decided to keep lads active and started a league. The club in the parish was St Ciaran's, Ballygawley. There were four church areas in our parish. Garvaghey, Ballygawley, Dunmoyle and Glencull. Ideal, four teams all playing against one another. I was the manager of Glencull. During a game against Dunmoyle I was sent off. I was then suspended by the committee. Not only from playing but from managing. I did not agree with that and as a result several members left the club.'

It led to a prolonged and nasty dispute. It divided the parish. All avenues were explored in an attempt to break the impasse. Conventions were picketed. GAA Presidents were approached. It looked as if Harte and others would be lost to the GAA. Seven years without competitive football had taken its toll. They were getting tired. Were it not for the intervention of two men they might have been lost to the game.

'St Ciaran's lost a Tyrone county final in 1989. Had Peter Canavan been playing they would have won. Then Fr Sean Hegarty the local curate with a bit of cunning brought the two sides together. Basically he told lies. Even he would admit that now. Brendan Harkin was now County Chairman and he saw the need to resolve the issue. As a result in 1990 we all came back together. Errigal Ciaran was born.'

In 2003 having defeated Crossmaglen Rangers in the first round and then Ballinderry in the Ulster club semi-final, Errigal Ciaran now faced Enniskillen in the final on 1 December. It was to be an historic afternoon for the fledgling club from Tyrone.

'Pretty it was not, but as a statement it was massive. Steel and heart won it for us. Nine years after our formation we were now Ulster champions.'

They were crowned county champions in 1993, 1994 and 1997.

Mickey and the Minors

Harte was appointed manager of the Tyrone minors in 1991. In his first year in charge Donegal beat them in the Ulster Final. It was a narrow loss, 1-10 to 1-9, but the Tyrone County Board had no hesitation in re-appointing Harte. This proved to be a wise move.

In 1993, Tyrone captured their first Ulster minor title since 1988 by beating Derry 1-9 to 1-5 in the final. However, Mayo ended their All-Ireland ambitions in the semi-final. By now Mickey Harte was beginning to see the bigger picture. Ulster titles no longer satisfied him. He craved an All-Ireland Minor Championship and given the talent within the county he felt it was attainable.

But Harte had to wait until 1997 for his second crack at the All-Ireland minor title. 1997 was also the year in which the St Ciaran's Ballygawley schoolteacher would encounter his first sporting tragedy. Ten minutes into the first round of the Ulster Minor Football Championship in Omagh between Tyrone and Armagh, Paul McGirr dived at a ball and fisted it into the Armagh net. He had already scored a point, now he had 1-1 to his name. In scoring the goal he collided with the Armagh goalkeeper. He did not get up. Initially it was thought he had broken ribs. Team doctor Seamus Cassidy took Paul to the hospital in Omagh. The game continued and Tyrone won 1-10 to 0-9.

The seniors were playing afterwards and the minors stayed on to watch the match. They also won – a Tyrone double. A short few hours later, it would mean little.

After the team meal, Mickey Harte drove to the hospital to check on Paul's well-being. As he walked towards the hospital he was met by Stephen O'Neill, a member of the team.

'Upon seeing O'Neill's face, I immediately asked, "What's wrong?" He said, "Paul's dead". I could feel the blood draining from my face.'

He describes how he composed himself and continues, 'I went upstairs and there he was, lying in his Tyrone gear. His mother Rita, his father Francis and his sisters were all by the bed. They were beside themselves with grief.'

Three hours earlier he had gone out to play a match with Tyrone. Now he was dead.

'It shook me to the core, and you know we won the match by 1-1, the exact amount Paul scored.'

What happened to young Paul McGirr was a freak accident. In the collision with the goalkeeper's knee, Paul suffered a rupture under his ribcage and his liver was punctured. His death sent shockwaves through the GAA fraternity in Tyrone and beyond.

Harte recalls watching *The Sunday Game* 24 hours later.

'Paul Bealin missed a last-minute penalty and Dublin lost to Meath. Dublin were out of the Championship. One of the pundits, I can't remember which one, commented, "Dublin may be out, but what happened in Tyrone – that's a real tragedy". Too right!'

Harte and the Tyrone County Board brought in specialist help for the young players.

'No group of 17-or 18-year-olds should have to deal with something like that. To their credit they were brave and resilient. They were involved in everything – wake, removal and burial. It bonded them together.'

When they did get back to playing football, they once again displayed tremendous resolve. They wanted to win the All-Ireland for Paul McGirr. They very nearly did. The first match after Paul's death was hugely emotional.

'Paul's parents wrote to the team and thanked them for all they had done. We beat Monaghan by 10 points to qualify for the Ulster Final.'

It was in the next two games that the bonding of the previous few weeks surfaced.

'In the Ulster Final, we were eight points down at half-time to Antrim. We ended up winning by seven. Then in the All-Ireland Minor semi-final with Kerry we were three points behind with five minutes to go. We managed to get a draw. Two weeks later we won a fabulous match by 0-23 to 0-21 after extra-time. It has been described as one of the best minor matches ever.'

However they eventually lost to Laois in the All-Ireland Minor Final. In a wonderful sporting gesture, the Laois team formed a guard of honour for the Tyrone team, who were distraught at having lost, as they left the field.

That night Mickey Harte decided he would step down as minor manager. However the players had other ideas – one in particular, Stephen O'Neill. It was O'Neill who persuaded Harte to remain on. Unfinished business. Twelve months later in 1998 they closed the deal. Tyrone were crowned All-Ireland Minor Football Champions.

'For that Championship our polo shirts had a special crest. We had the numbers '97 printed into the crest along with '98. It was a tribute to those involved the year before, including Paul McGirr. They were all there.'

When they brought the cup home on the Monday night, they had a pleasant but welcome surprise.

'In Aughnacloy, Francis McGirr (Paul's father) came on stage and shook hands with every player.'

Another incident in 1998 impacted on the minor team – the Omagh Bombing.

'That day we were in Benburb with the minor team getting ready for the All-Ireland semi-final. Word came through about the bomb. I was worried because my wife Marian used to go shopping there every Saturday. It was an anxious time as I could not make contact with anyone. Eventually I drove home and could only relax when I saw Mattie playing football on the road.'

Friends were lost that horrible afternoon, and Tyrone in the shape of their footballers would try and bring joy to the town in the years ahead. Mickey Harte moved on to manage the Tyrone under-21 team.

'In 2000 we won the Ulster and All-Ireland titles. The day they won the All-Ireland in Mullingar, Francis McGirr was there again. The spirit of Paul lived on in the team.'

One year later in 2001, the under-21 All-Ireland title was retained. Harte was leaving an imprint on Tyrone minor football. The senior job would surely come his way. But as ever in the GAA, things are not that simple. In September 2002 Art McRory and Eugene McKenna were re-appointed joint managers of the Tyrone senior team. Within a week McRory resigned for health reasons. The County Board re-advertised the position and stated that McKenna would have to re-apply. This did not sit well with some GAA people in the county. The Tyrone County Board issued an apology to Eugene McKenna for the hurt and anxiety the process caused him.

Eventually the Tyrone County Board made their choice. It was one they would not regret.

The Top Job

Thursday 14 November 2002 – a date to remember. Harte was at home preparing for a training session with Errigal Ciaran, who were in the Ulster Club semi-final in 10 days' time. The phone rang. It was County Secretary Dominic McCaughey. McCaughey confirmed that Mickey Harte was to be the new manager of the Tyrone Senior Football team.

In his book *Kicking Down Heaven's Door,* Harte revealed a nice little story. In September 1997 his daughter Michaela made a poster. It read,

1 . . . We (Tyrone) will win the All-Ireland Minor Final in 1998.

2 . . . We will win the All-Ireland Final in 2000 with the Under-21s.

3 . . . We will win the Senior All-Ireland Final in 2003.

By the night of Harte's appointment as senior manager, two of the three predictions had come true. Now the Harte family were about to see if they could complete the set.

Not long after being informed of his appointment Harte took an Errigal Ciaran session and did not tell the players his news. One task at a time. The club was still his priority. However, his appointment did not meet with universal approval in the county. Some felt McKenna was shafted. Others questioned not only Harte's ability, but his motives for taking the job.

In time Harte would prove them all wrong. With his backroom team of Fr Gerard McAleer and team trainer Paddy Tally, Harte immediately set about altering the mindset of the Tyrone players.

Five nights after his appointment, he was introduced to the media and he fielded all sorts of questions. It left no one in any doubt that the Mickey Harte era was underway. The next step was to pick the panel. When that was done there was another initiative. Modern technology was introduced and purchased with the full support of the Tyrone County Board. Every Tyrone game and training session would be recorded. Harte's attention to detail is legendary.

Harte explains, 'Some county boards, will ask you "What do you want?" Others will say, "What do you need that for?" In Tyrone's case it was the former. That showed me they wanted success as much as I did.'

Whatever else would happen the Tyrone team under Harte would want for nothing.

On Monday 6 January 2003 in Quinn's Corner, Tyrone, Mickey Harte and his panel of 30 met for the first time as a group. The odyssey was about to begin. Destination Croke Park, Dublin in September.

Harte describes it as an historic night for Tyrone football.

'Basically all in the room that night set their sights on getting to and winning the All-Ireland title. We were all in it together – players, officials, backroom team and sponsor. There was to be no more "them and us" – it was all one.'

He also outlined his plans. Training one night a week collectively until the end of March. But each player would be expected to work on strength and conditioning. It was also the first time the players met trainer Paddy Tally. Harte could see they were impressed.

'He spoke in simple terms. Explained what he wanted. Diet and hydration were important. The days of steak and chips were over. It was now white meat, fish and pasta.'

Captain Canavan

Another important decision. The appointment of the captain.

'I informed them that Peter Canavan was my choice. I knew he was the right man and he re-affirmed that when he spoke. He concluded by saying, "I don't want to be a great captain, I want to captain a great team".'

Tyrone set out to win every competition they entered that year – the Dr McKenna Cup, National Football League, Ulster Championship and the All-Ireland title.

For Canavan the captaincy was a huge honour, as he explains.

'Well it's always an honour to be asked to captain your county. But for it to come from Mickey was huge. I had known him for years as a neighbour. Then as my teacher in St Ciaran's. I knew what he expected of me. He was a very single-minded and driven man.

'Tyrone had made progress the year before under Art (McRory) and Eugene (McKenna) – winning the League for the first time. But now there was renewed optimism around. Mickey had won minor and under-21 All-Irelands with some of these lads and it was the natural follow-on to win the senior title.'

Tyrone and Mickey Harte's first competitive game in 2003 was a winning one, beating Fermanagh in the Dr McKenna Cup. A week later another victory – this time over Antrim in the same competition. Then Cavan were beaten. Three wins on the bounce. A great start. However they did lose the final to Monaghan when it was played in March.

The opening League game to Roscommon ended in defeat. But in general the League campaign went well. Only once did he let loose on the players.

'It was against Donegal in Coalisland. We were behind at half-time. I tore into the players in the dressing room. I demanded they put more pride in the Tyrone jersey. To be fair they responded and the win got our League ambitions back on track. The win over Armagh was also important.'

Armagh were the reigning All-Ireland champions. They would meet again before the year was over. Fermanagh were their semi-final opponents. Tyrone won comfortably.

On 4 May, Harte delivered his first trophy when Laois were well beaten in the League Final. Peter Canavan was delighted with the League win.

'It was good because we won the semi-final and final playing very attractive football. Now the Championship would be different but we were going into it as winners. That, from our point of view, was important.'

The Ulster Championship has long been a minefield. Mickey Harte was about to find out how hard it is to win it. Tyrone v Derry is always an intense rivalry. In 2003 it ended in a draw. But in the replay there was no contest, Tyrone won at a canter. Antrim were well beaten in the next round and it set up a meeting with Down in the Final. Another test for Mickey Harte's Tyrone.

In the match Down were reduced to 14 men when Gregory McCartan was sent off. But it made little difference because at one stage Down had opened up a nine-point lead. Tyrone were struggling. Harte could see the headlines.

'"Tyrone destroyed by 14-man Down." "Old Tyrone failings come back to haunt them." I was disappointed at the attitude. But to the lads' credit they fought back. With five minutes to go we had drawn level. Then Down got another goal. This is it, I thought – all over.'

Amazingly Tyrone once again drew level. In those added minutes they kicked three points to force a replay. Tyrone 1-17, Down 4-8.

'We even had a chance to win it, but we settled for a draw. We could still win the Ulster Championship.'

For the replay Harte switched Cormac McAnallen to full-back. It was a masterstroke. The 19-year-old never put a foot wrong. It was hard to believe the first game ended level. Tyrone 0-23 Down 1-5. The Anglo-Celt Cup was heading to Tyrone.

Since his appointment Mickey had been receiving calls from two supporters. They were to become known as the 'midnight callers'. On cue, on the night of the Ulster Final they called.

'They complimented me on my choice of full-back. I then asked them to give me their names.'

Their reply was optimistic.

'No! After you win the All-Ireland!' Only a couple of months to wait then.

The one blot on the year came in February 2003 when Harte's club, Errigal Ciaran, lost in the All-Ireland club semi-final.

'I felt good going down to Portlaoise that day to play Nemo Rangers. Now we did not play well. Nemo though were good. They got ahead of us and we could not pull it back. We did get it back to one point, but Nemo had another gear. They tacked on a couple of points to win by four. We were devastated. The dressing room was like a morgue. So was the journey home. Even when we got to Kelly's there was only a small crowd to greet us. The difference between winning and losing is huge.'

It was also his last match as manager of the club. It was not meant to end this way. The feeling of defeat was one he did not want to endure again during the year. When asked recently what sporting ambition remained, he replied, 'Errigal Ciaran to win the All-Ireland club title. We haven't won it yet, but we now have a good manager in Peter (Canavan) – it might happen yet.'

Tyrone now had his undivided attention.

Before the draw for the quarter-final the Tyrone players decided to renew their commitments to each other. This was important, because the county was gripped in excitement as the season evolved.

'The players spoke of going to another level. After a discussion they also agreed on a total ban on drink until it – the Championship – was all over.'

As a non-drinker or non-smoker for that matter, it made no difference to Harte. But he was impressed by their attitude. He then made a sacrifice of his own.

'I decided to abstain from the sweet things – chocolate, desserts and biscuits – they would now go on hold.'

Fermanagh were their opponents in the quarter-final. Tyrone brushed them aside with ruthless efficiency, winning by 1-21 to 0-5. Next up was the big one – the ultimate test – Kerry in the All-Ireland semi-final.

Conquering the Kingdom

Planning for the semi-final began immediately. Harte left nothing to chance. It even included a dry run to the City West Hotel the week before the game.

'We went through in minute detail the gameplan we felt would beat Kerry. It was to put pressure on every Kerry player when they had possession. But they had a few key men. How we handled them would shape the outcome. Work rate was also important.'

Then out of a team meeting came another idea. 'Amhrán Na bhFiann' – the national anthem.

'It was mentioned how people loved to hear it sung by the crowd on big match days. It's a pity that more players don't do the same. So it got me thinking, why can't we do it, sing the national anthem? In full blast in Irish – that would really help. Michaela printed it off for the boys. Some of them had fluent Irish, but we worked on it and that was it. We gave a great rendition of it before we left the hotel. We would do the same on Tuesday and Thursday after training. We were now ready for Kerry.'

The semi-final was a defining one. By half-time Tyrone were leading by 0-9 to 0-2. Kerry were on the ropes.

For the second-half Tyrone were out on the field first. Kerry kept them waiting. An old ploy. Tyrone countered by gathering in a circle and once more singing 'Amhrán Na bhFiann'. If Kerry kept them waiting, Tyrone were in no hurry to restart.

In the second-half, without pulling away, Tyrone remained in control. They finished winners by 0-13 to 0-6. Mickey Harte had guided his team to the All-Ireland Final in his first season. He was pleased – especially with the first-half, not so the second period.

'There was aspects of our play that disappointed me. Darragh Ó Sé won too many of our kick-outs. We gave away too many frees while our tackling at times was poor.'

The image that many took away from that game though came after about 15 minutes. Harte explains.

'It came at a crucial time. Peter (Canavan) had just gone off injured. Then for about 40 seconds we swarmed all round several Kerry players who had possession. Brian Dooher ended up with the ball. It set the trend for the rest of the half.' Kerry had never encountered this swarming form of tackle before and couldn't deal with it.

The one downside to the match was the ankle injury to Peter Canavan. He was extremely doubtful for the Final which would be against their great rivals from Ulster, Armagh.

It was to be an historic final. And Tyrone's best player was in danger of missing it. The build-up was dominated by Canavan's injury. Harte had a big call to make and at the same time prepare his team for the biggest day of their sporting lives. Tyrone got another boost as the under-21s beat Sligo to reach the All-Ireland Final.

Apart from Canavan's injury, there was one other piece of disturbing news. Harte's uncle of the same name was ill – very ill. He might not live to see the final but he was a huge Tyrone supporter. After each win the cup was brought to his house. Only one cup left to bring.

Sadly on 13 September Mickey Harte's uncle was buried in Pomeroy.

The county by now had gone wild with excitement and Harte took steps to protect the players.

'At training one night I saw 42 items to be signed. I called a halt. This was too much of a distraction. From now on anything that needed to be signed had to be approved by me. We have only one job to do and that was to win.'

Then on Sunday 14 September, Harte took the team to Donegal for a training session. It also got them out of the county for the day. A week before the final, they travelled to Dublin – another dry run for the big day. By now it was time to deal with the Peter Canavan injury situation. Peter himself explains how it was dealt with.

'First of all I was not fit to play. I had not trained since the semi-final. What little I had done, I broke down. But I was desperate to play. I played in 1995 when we lost to Dublin, so I really wanted this one. Mickey called down to the house a few days before the game. We talked for a good bit, then he produced a piece of paper. On one side were the positives of me playing. On the other side the negatives.'

They both agreed that the positives outweighed the negatives.

'It was then Mickey outlined his plan to me. He said that if it was announced before the game that I wasn't playing, it would sap the morale of the supporters. That would then get to the players. We must be positive at all times. He then said I would start the match. After about 20 minutes I'd be replaced. Get a bit of work done on the ankle. Then I'd come back on for the last 20 minutes.'

Peter readily bought into this.

'No problem at all with it. The team was more important than any one player.'

In this case though some would say Canavan was more important than the team. If he's on, he could pinch a few scores. Tap over an early free. But more than anything else he would keep the Armagh backs busy.

All was now set, Peter would start. Harte and Canavan agree on most things about Tyrone football. This one was no different.

The 2003 Final: Tyrone v Armagh

The day of the 2003 All-Ireland Football Final dawned. A day of destiny for Tyrone and Mickey Harte. The team arrived onto the field to a crescendo of noise. The warm-up began at the Hill 16 end of the ground. Peter Canavan knelt to fix his boot. Harte strolled over to him. The manager sensed straight away that all was not well.

He told Harte, 'The ankle is not good'. Harte was worried, but as ever didn't panic. They continued with the plan. Canavan started. Interestingly in the warm-up Canavan didn't kick the ball once. Take no chances – kick it when you need to, when the game is on.

First kick of the ball, a point. Tyrone ahead. The pre-match plan was working. So were the player match-ups. Harte had his tactics spot on.

Canavan kicked a few frees. The ankle held out. They reached half-time. Tyrone were ahead 0-8 to 0-4. In the dressing room they worked on Canavan's ankle but decided to rest him for the opening quarter of the second-half. So far so good.

Harte was strong in the dressing room.

'35 minutes boys. We're plus four. Now let's finish the job.'

Peter Canavan also spoke.

'We've been knocking on heaven's door boys and she's opening. Keep knocking and soon we will be in heaven.'

On the resumption Tyrone missed a goal chance. On the line Harte wondered was it a bad sign. Would the doubts set in? He need not have worried. With 15 minutes to go Tyrone were ahead by three and Armagh were down to 14 men.

Peter Canavan re-entered the game. Armagh pressed forward. Conor Gormley made a brilliant block to deny Armagh a goal. But they did get a point. Just two points between the sides now.

In injury-time Tyrone mounted an attack. Stephen O'Neill got possession, took aim and fired over the insurance point. Tyrone were champions.

Six years after he persuaded Mickey Harte to stay involved, Stephen O'Neill helped deliver the Sam Maguire Cup to a grateful county. Tyrone 2003 All-Ireland Champions – they defeated Armagh by 0-12 to 0-9. Peter Canavan accepted the Sam Maguire Cup. He was now not only a great captain but the captain of a great team. Michaela Harte's poster was also complete. In victory they also remembered the late Paul McGirr.

Harte was absolutely thrilled.

'The thrill was the journey. The fun was in the preparation and the challenge it presented. I cannot wait for next year.'

Twenty-four hours later they returned home with Sam. They finally put a smile on the faces of the people of Omagh.

One last thing from 2003. Mickey Harte met the 'Midnight Callers' – two lads from Derrylaughan – Brendan Quinn and Seán McGrath.

Harte said to them, 'Give me a call during the week and we'll have a chat.'

Cormac McAnallen Tragedy

If 2003 was all about winning Sam Maguire, 2004 would be entirely different. Harte appointed Cormac McAnallen captain as they set out to retain Sam. In January Cormac collected the Dr McKenna Cup. It was one of his last acts as Tyrone football captain.

On 2 March Cormac died suddenly at home. His death sent shockwaves through the country. Tributes poured in from all walks of life. Mickey Harte was devastated. Again, for the second time as a Tyrone manager, he had to deal with tragedy.

'He was such a good guy. A brilliant athlete. Dedicated and his maturity belied his years. He had everything you would want in a young man. He was just a gem and a pleasure to deal with.'

Peter Canavan remembers that sad time as if it was yesterday and how Harte helped them get through it.

'It was an awful time. Cormac was so young. But Mickey was fantastic. I suppose he was able to call on the experience when young Paul McGirr died. He told us to focus on the positives. It is what Cormac would have wanted he said. We tried but it was hard, very hard I can tell you. We got through it, but without Mickey we might not have. And you can be sure it was awful hard on Mickey as well. He really admired Cormac. I mean he made him captain at 23, that shows how much he respected him.'

When the funeral and mourning were over, Tyrone had to go back playing football. It was not easy. Canavan explains.

'It was what we do – play football. We just had to carry on. But it was a very difficult year.'

Tyrone also retired the Number 3 jersey for the year. It was Cormac McAnallen's jersey. It was a year in which they surrendered the Ulster and All-Ireland titles. In Ulster, Donegal defeated Tyrone by 1-11 to 0-9. Tyrone did reach the last eight of the All-Ireland Championship after beating Down, but Mayo ended their year. The year of 2004 is not one they care to remember.

2005 was very different. They put the troubles of 2004 behind them and in the process played fabulous football. Brian Dooher was appointed captain. They were on a mission. Canavan, in his last year as an inter-county player, knew it would be an emotional season. The name of one man dominated their thoughts. Cormac McAnallen.

'It was never mentioned but we all knew what we had to do. Mickey played it down as well. But it was there in the background all the time.'

Beating Kerry in the Final

History was made as Tyrone and Armagh would meet in the 2005 Ulster Final before a packed Croke Park. Armagh won. But they would meet again before the summer's end.

Tyrone got back on track with wins over Monaghan and Dublin. Next up it was their old friends in the All-Ireland semi-final – Armagh. This time Tyrone emerged winners.

Peter Canavan recalls a fantastic match, in which he proved the hero.

'That was some game and Mickey was brilliant in the build-up. He used all his experience to get us right. It was also a hugely significant game in our bid for another title.'

In a cracker of a match it was level as the game entered injury-time. A replay loomed. Canavan stood over a free. Peter 'the Great' nailed it. Tyrone won by 1 point, 1-13 to 1-12. They were back in the Final. One more game to bring an end to yet another emotional journey.

That journey was completed on a September Sunday. Tyrone 1-16, Kerry 2-10. A memorable final. Canavan scored a great goal and retired after the match. Brian Dooher climbed the steps to accept the cup. However everyone in the ground was thinking of one man – Cormac McAnallen.

In a moving speech Dooher remembered their friend. Pitch-side, Mickey Harte broke down in the middle of a television interview. On the journey home the following day, they visited McAnallen's grave.

Now they could carry on. They had honoured his memory by winning the one thing he cherished – the All-Ireland Championship.

Harte did have one regret about the year. It was Canavan's retirement.

'If I could have got to Peter before he announced it to the nation, I would have got him to hold on and think about it. He would have been invaluable to us in 2006.'

The task now was to retain the title. But injuries and fatigue were factors in 2006. Derry beat them in the quarter-final of the Ulster Championship in a poor game by 1-8 to 0-5. It hurt even more that it was on their own patch in Omagh.

There was little joy in the qualifiers as Laois ended their season on a miserable night in Portlaoise by 0-9 to 0-6.

Failure to defend the title annoyed Harte. A point made by Peter Canavan.

'He makes a big thing of that. Mickey would love to put titles back-to-back. One thing about him though, he learns a lot in defeat.'

More to Mickey than Football

There is more to Mickey Harte than football. He is a man of principle who can ignore Croke Park dictates when they're at variance with those principles. He is steadfast in his opposition to the International Rules Series, despite the fact that the trophy for the winners is called after one of his favourites players, the late Cormac McAnallen. His opinion didn't even change when his current star player, Seán Cavanagh, was named as the Irish captain. He firmly believes GAA resources could be employed to greater benefit elsewhere.

'There is nothing in the series for our game. The money could be put to better use to promote Gaelic football. I see no benefit in it.'

Harte is also extremely loyal. He refuses to speak to one particular Irish tabloid newspaper because of two articles it printed. One of those articles related to the McAnallen family – a family he still visits every month.

As for the media's influence on the game?

'Well once it's fair and balanced I have no problem. After all they are like everyone else - they're entitled to their opinion.'

For over 25 years now, Harte has been involved with Action MS. This is a Northern charity for those who suffer from Multiple Sclerosis.

Harte opposed the opening of Croke Park to soccer and rugby. However he set aside his opposition to campaign for an Ireland v Brazil soccer game to raise funds for the Suicide charity, Decide. The game never happened as the GAA ban on foreign games had not yet been lifted.

Small things make a difference and he introduced a few in his time. The practice of calling players up in the dressing room to receive their jerseys. It began with the minors, it continues with the seniors. He also gets each player to nominate their favourite song. These are then made into a compilation and played on the team coach.

The 'nice guy' image can also be abandoned. In 2005 he jettisoned team trainer Paddy Tally and replaced him with current man Fergal McCann.

Another major change came when he gave up teaching. Now he works as a property consultant. He also does motivational talks. Harte has spoken at all sorts of events – business meetings, functions, novenas and retreats. As regards leaving teaching, he says himself, 'It is probably the first time since I was four that I am away from a bell and a timetable'.

In 2007 Tyrone once again won the Ulster Championship defeating Monaghan in the Final. It was a close match with Tyrone the narrow winners by 1-15 to 1-13. However they were well below par in the All-Ireland quarter-final when losing to Meath by 1-13 to 2-8.

Was the bubble about to burst? Was Harte losing his touch? Was he under pressure? Not really is the answer to all three questions. 2007 was seen as a transitional year. The recovery from injuries was underway; they would get better. Harte was annoyed though. He felt they did not get enough credit for what they had achieved. They did after all win the Ulster Championship. This was not reflected in the Irish media and the selection of players in the Vodafone All-Stars. Harte wondered did Monaghan, who won nothing, actually win the Ulster Championship. However he did agree that they (Tyrone) were lacking something.

'You think you're doing things well, but in reality we weren't. It was routine. Maybe we (management) sat back and weren't creative or innovative enough.'

They would rectify that in 2008.

In the Ulster Championship they lost to Down after a replay. But it turned out to be a blessing in disguise. Mickey Harte was quite pleased leaving Newry after that game even though he hates losing. He's a bit like Brian Cody in this regard. The reason for his optimism was simple – Armagh were next up and with injuries Tyrone were not ready for that challenge. By losing to Down, they now had time to regroup and improve.

In the aftermath of that game against Down, there was criticism of Harte. Sections of the media and supporters were of the opinion that his time had come and he should step down. The manager was unfazed.

'I knew exactly where we were in terms of the season. People are entitled to express their views. I respect that. But for those of us in the group, we had confidence in the players and more importantly in the direction we were travelling.'

For a man who hates to lose, this is what he said leaving Newry after the loss to Down.

'It is our sweetest defeat, if you can have such a thing.'

The qualifiers ironed out a lot of their problems. Louth, Westmeath and Mayo were dispatched. Dublin lay in wait in the quarter-final. It was to be a defining game. Before a sold-out Croke Park the Dubs were ripped apart. It was almost the complete performance. Backs and forwards combined brilliantly to demolish Dublin and end Paul Caffrey's reign as manager. As the stadium emptied, Tyrone were winners, 3-14 to 1-8.

All this achieved without Stephen O'Neill who had quit the panel in January. The team's star forward had had enough. Rumours were rife that O'Neill and Harte had a falling-out – reportedly over a property deal. They both worked for the same company, Martin Short Auctioneers. Mickey Harte quickly put the rumours to bed.

'There was never an issue between us. We worked for the one company. I actually was the contact that got him to work in the mortgage section of the company. Stephen left to go back to teaching. We've never had anything but total respect for one another.'

Tyrone met the surprise packet, Wexford, in the semi-final and won comfortably by 0-23 to 1-14. A third final appearance beckoned. Kerry would once again provide the opposition.

Beards, Mindgames and Kerry

Two days after the win over Wexford there was another boost. Harte got word that Stephen O'Neill was interested in returning. Once it was confirmed by Harte's source, he phoned O'Neill to express his delight. O'Neill and Harte arranged to meet that night in Harte's house.

This posed a potential problem a few short weeks before the final. But in his own way, Harte would deal with it. The panel would also welcome O'Neill back.

'Stephen was aware of the timing and its implications. He was even prepared to wait until January. He didn't want to disrupt the team. I told him if he wanted to be a Tyrone player again, the time was now.'

Could he do a job against Kerry?

'Definitely. He oozes class. I felt he could contribute in the final. His fitness was good although he wouldn't start the match. But this was a long-term job, not just for the 2008 decider, this was 2009 and beyond.'

So 11 years after O'Neill had persuaded Harte to stay on as minor coach, he was in a way repaying the favour by returning to try and help Harte deliver a third Sam Maguire Cup.

This Final though was going to be different. It would require all of Harte's tactical know-how to overcome the Kingdom's so called 'twin towers'. Kerry's Tommy Walsh and Kieran Donaghy had blitzed all before them in the Championship. Could they now conquer the newly-bearded Tyrone defenders?

A few players decided not to shave until the Championship was over. It led to a spate of text messages doing the rounds about 'bearded men and twin towers'.

Harte hatched his plans. Discretion and secrecy were key components in the plan. It would also mean hard calls in the team selection. Some players would lose out.

'We had to be discreet. It was important to keep everyone positive. That's why we left it until the Thursday before the game to tell the players. Ciaran Gourley and Brian McGuigan would lose out. But we wanted the sessions to retain their energy, that's why we kept it quiet.'

How the players were informed was classic Harte.

On Thursday Gourley and McGuigan were getting rubs in the dressing room. Harte and captain Brian Dooher went to them and explained the plan. Both readily bought into it. Their reactions did not surprise the manager.

'That was the theme all year – team first.'

A few examples.

'Brian Dooher got married in crutches because he did not want to lose two weeks recovery from injury. Early in the year every player met with Caroline Currid, a member of the backroom team who acts as a facilitator or motivator, for an hour and set targets. The team also had a Celtic emblem on their shirt, TINE (Two Is Not Enough). We wanted a third.'

In the team reshuffle Joe McMahon was deployed to mark Tommy Walsh. Martin Penrose's pace would trouble Aidan O'Mahony and McGuigan along with the returning O'Neill would also play their parts – but from the bench. Pascal McConnell would play in goal. John Devine had gone to bury his father.

Before the game Harte made an impassioned speech. The team also wore black armbands as a mark of respect to John Devine.

Harte asked of his players, 'Do you want to be remembered as the boys that let Kerry win three-in-a-row? Or the boys that denied them three-in-a-row. I think I know what I would want.'

It was an absorbing match. Fantastic football by both sides. Quality scores, including one from Brian Dooher – the captain leading by example. Tactically once again, Harte was bang on. His defensive strategy was working to perfection. The 'twin towers' were nullified. But for all that Kerry led by 1 point, 0-8 to 0-7, at half-time. By now though Stephen O'Neill was on the field and making an impact.

Within 20 seconds of the resumption Tyrone struck. O'Neill created a goal for Tommy McGuigan. A crucial score. Harte's faith in O'Neill was repaid.

Kerry were not finished and by the 55th minute it was all square. Outstanding midfielder Seán Cavanagh kicked two splendid points as Tyrone moved ahead again. Then came the game's defining moment – from a player who in normal circumstances would not have played. But as it is with Tyrone, nothing is normal.

The game was nearing its conclusion. Kerry were on the attack. Declan O'Sullivan broke through and had a shot for a goal. For all the world it looked a winner. However replacement goalkeeper Pascal McConnell saved the shot. As McConnell said after the match, 'With a little help from the Devines'.

It drained the life out of the Kerry challenge and Tyrone finished in style.

They rattled over three points in quick succession. Game over. Tyrone were champions for the third time. Tyrone 1-15, Kerry 0-14. The presentation of the cup is yet another emotional one. Just like three years earlier. This time Brian Dooher holds the Number 1 jersey aloft. It was the jersey that John Devine would have worn. Instead he was back in Ballygawley at his father's wake.

After the game Harte paid tribute to his team.

'I cannot speak highly enough of the players that lost out in the team selection. They were immense. The key to getting a result was sheer hard work.'

As for the circumstances that saw Devine drop out and McConnell play, Harte had this to say.

'Unfortunately, we've become used to playing in difficult circumstances. The way our players performed today was all that John (Devine) and his late father would have wanted.'

He (Harte) also revealed that the defeat in the 1986 final to Kerry was a factor.

'That day Tyrone were 8 up at one stage and lost, and 22 years on the Tyrone people still regret that. Kerry stopped us winning our first All-Ireland back then. We just had to stop them winning a three-in-a-row.'

Midfielder Seán Cavanagh paid tribute to Harte.

'People doubted Mickey after we lost to Down. They said we were finished. Mickey was finished. We owed him this one. We proved the doubters wrong.'

Twenty-four hours later they went home with another sad stopover. Three years earlier it was in a quiet field in Eglish at Cormac's grave. This time it was John Devine's house in Ballygawley.

When they arrived John Devine embraced Harte and took 'Sam' inside where his father rested. He raised the cup high, evoking a cheer from those present.

Mickey Harte approved.

'I thought that was nice. It wasn't the usual place to bring the cup, but it was nice amidst all the sadness. It also allowed John's family to express some happiness too.'

Once again Mickey Harte's handling of a very sad occasion showed his compassionate side. As Peter Canavan recalled, 'He is such an amiable and honest man that he is the ideal individual to have in such tragic situations.' One other interesting cameo followed that 2008 Final win over Kerry. Stephen O'Neill refused to accept his medal because he felt he did not do enough to earn it. Harte had other ideas.

'He more than earned it. In time he will take it. He deserves it.'

The Elusive Back-to-Back Titles

Now that he has moved into management himself, Canavan has no hesitation in saying he will avail of Harte's expertise.

'Well I would be silly not to. After all, I learned so much from him. He is a clubmate of mine here (at Errigal Ciaran), so I speak to him and seek his advice when needed.'

Harte saw the year 2009 as another challenge. There is always one. This time it was to finally win back-to-back titles. They had failed to achieve that on the previous two occasions they were champions. It was all going to plan, that is until Sunday 23 August 2009. The Ulster title had been won with victories over Armagh, Derry and Antrim. Kildare were seen off in the All-Ireland quarter-final – but Cork were too good in the semi-final. As ever Mickey Harte had no complaints.

'None really. One or two funny calls by the referee, but other than that the better team won the game.'

Will Tyrone and Mickey Harte be back?

Peter Canavan has no doubts.

'Mickey's going nowhere. In fact he will come back stronger than ever. He will learn from the loss to Cork and rectify it for next year. In fact I'd say he cannot wait for next year. He'll be refreshed and ready.'

Canavan is also adamant that his contribution to Tyrone football will never be matched.

'What he has done for the game in the county is immense. Be it with club, school or county team, Mickey has nurtured a generation of Tyrone footballers to great success. Success that was not there before he got involved. It's a debt we cannot repay. But then he just loves football. Especially Tyrone football.'

Peter is also impressed by his cool demeanour on the sideline.

'He is very passionate, but never loses his cool. Mickey always says if you get excited you might miss a vital moment in a match. That calmness gets to the players and it has worked most of the time.'

Harte himself confirms as much. Speaking in Dublin at the Sudden Adult Death Syndrome (SADS) launch, just days after the Cork game, Harte says, 'I am under no pressure whatsoever. Maybe that's part of the process of living and learning what life has to offer.'

As for working with the present group of players, he says, 'It's a privilege to be with the best footballers in Tyrone. At this time in our history they are amongst the best in the country. There is more to do with this team, and if I didn't enjoy working with them I should not be here. As long as I believe in that I am going to stick around for a wee while yet.'

He also pays the players this compliment.

'They won't really know how great they are until they retire. It is only then people will really appreciate what a great team they are.'

Tyrone have enjoyed good and bad days under Harte. On and off the field they have shared many a moment. And will do so again in the future.

As part of the team's song compilation, midfielder Seán Cavanagh chose as his song Van Morrison's, 'Days Like This'.

One verse reads:
> *'When there's no one complaining, there'll be days like this*
> *When everything falls into place, like the flick of a switch*
> *Well my mama told me there will be days like this.'*

It is doubtful if the past, present and future Tyrone players would have enjoyed 'Days Like This' were it not for the guiding influence of one Mickey Harte.

7

Páidí Ó Sé

The Early Years

Ceann Trá or Ventry lies in the heart of An Gaeltacht in West Kerry and it is famous for many things. Its rugged beauty and wonderful sandy beaches are just two. Also of course there's the football. It's sometimes said there are two religions in Kerry – football and football.

Listed among the greats of the game in the Kingdom is Ventry native, Páidí Ó Sé. As a player he was a fearless and outstanding defender. As a manager he enjoyed a successful, if at times controversial, innings at the helm in Kerry.

Páidí Ó Sé was born on 16 May 1955 and from a very early age, it was obvious he would wear the famous green and gold jersey. And he would do so with distinction.

By coincidence it was the day before his birthday when we met in his thriving bar and restaurant in Ventry. The sun was shining as Páidí was busy preparing for the day ahead – washing and cleaning the floors while advising me to enjoy the beautiful scenery of Slea Head and Cuan Harbour before we commenced our chat.

During the course of our discussion and over lunch afterwards, Páidí, as the good host, spoke freely with the visitors that came and went and happily posed for photographs with tourists.

He had particularly welcoming words for those from America who marvelled at the vast collection of photographs that adorned the walls of his pub. The teak tough defender of his playing days gives way to a man who appreciates what is required in the present economic climate to keep the 'punters' happy, and hope they return.

A native Irish speaker, his early education was in the local national school, Cill Mhic a' Domhnaigh. He attended Dingle CBS for a brief period before the big decision had to be made.

Páidí explains, 'If you were interested in football there was only one place to go. For me it was easy – I went to St Brendan's College in Killarney or the 'Sem' as it is better known. I openly admit football drew me there, not the scholastic side of the school. Subsequent events would prove I was better with a football than books.'

For him it was the beginning of a great period with the school that lasted until 'they threw me out in the early part of 1974,' for in his own words, 'being a *buachaill dána* (bold boy)'.

But he has wonderful memories of the college, and as with most things in life, it had a twist in the end. There were some great men running the football teams in those days. 'Magnificent trainers in Fr James Linnane and

Jimmy Hegarty. I achieved my objective, but I did feel aggrieved at being kicked out, but sure that's the way it was.'

With St Brendan's, Páidí won four Kerry Senior Colleges titles and back-to-back Corn Uí Mhuirí (Munster Colleges) wins in 1972 and 1973. He completed his education at St Michael's, Listowel. However while at the Listowel school he was presented with an unforeseen opportunity to exact revenge on the 'Sem' for showing him the 'red card'. It came in 1974 in the Kerry Colleges' Senior Final when St Michael's faced St Brendan's.

Páidí has a clear recollection of the final. 'Well it involved three games, two that went to extra-time. In the third game at the end of normal time we were a point down. Seanie Burrows from Tralee was the referee and I said to him "you'll surely give us one more chance". Well we got a '50' and I lined up to take it. "Now," says Seanie, "here's your chance". Luckily enough it went over the bar for a point and we won handy enough in extra-time. To win that was a huge achievement for a small school against the aristocrats of colleges' football at the time.'

Three days after that game, Páidí, at just 18 years of age, was to play with Kerry in a National League Final. It made little difference to him. 'Believe it or not I was so caught up in that game with St Michael's that the League Final was the furthest thing from my mind.' The St Michael's Colleges' medal is one he really treasures. 'Without doubt a great win and one that I took a lot of pleasure from – and I have many friends today from that team – Billy Keane, Robert Bunyan and Johnny Mulvihill, and a fabulous manager in Johnny Flaherty, to mention just a few.'

Mulvihill remains close to his old school pal from Ventry. 'Throughout my career Johnny would always write to me before games with Kerry. I remember well in 1975 before the All-Ireland Final against Dublin, the letter duly arrived. As usual he wished me well, but he also gave me a great bit of advice. In that game I was to mark David Hickey, a very fast and lively player. In the letter Johnny said to watch the eye contact between Hickey and Dublin goalkeeper Paddy Cullen. Just before Cullen takes his kick-out, he'll tug the right-hand side of his shorts. That's the signal that the ball is going to Hickey. He was spot on and every time it happened I was out of the traps like a greyhound and beat Hickey to the ball. It meant I was fine and relaxed in my first All-Ireland Final – all thanks to Johnny Mulvihill.'

Páidí's career could not have got off to a better start. It was a trend that would continue throughout his playing days – a fact he readily acknowledges.

'I had a great career really. I played with very good teams and players. *Bhí an tádh agam* also (I was lucky as well).'

Strangely the only time in his career that honours eluded him was at minor level with Kerry. 'I was not picked for a few years as they felt I was too young. Then when they did pick me, we lost to Cork in 1971, 1972 and again in 1973. Ironically enough in those finals I played in three different positions.'

Unusually at that time, he went straight onto the senior team from the minors, playing in his first Munster Senior Final against Cork in Killarney in 1974.

He won the first of his All-Ireland medals in the Kerry jersey at under-21 level. Three on the bounce in fact, and they were significant wins. 'They were significant in so far as winning under-21 in 1974, 1975 and 1976 laid the platform for the senior team's dominance in later years.'

Joining the Gardaí

Football was by now beginning to shape his life, but there was another chapter evolving in the story of the defender from Ceann Trá. Ó Sé became a defender in a different uniform. He was now Garda Páidí Ó Sé stationed in Limerick City. It was a period, brief though it may have been, from which he derived tremendous satisfaction.

'At the time it was something I wanted to do. I did the usual stuff in

180

Templemore and all that. I graduated and was sent to Limerick. I enjoyed my spell in the Gardaí – a good grounding in life and of course the discipline is important.'

In terms of his playing career he got tremendous support from his Garda colleagues and indeed his superiors. 'Superb' is the word he uses to describe the help he got. 'Never was there a problem with training or work, and for that I was very grateful.'

Páidí's stint in the Garda Síochána generated a few famous, and some infamous, stories. One such story goes as follows:

'It was 1979, the year the Pope came to Ireland, and we had just played Cork in the League and won. That night I went for a few pints with the lads. Needless to say one drink led to another and another. I can tell you it was a long, a very long, night.'

The only problem was Páidí had to be on duty early the following morning.

'I arrived in the station and when the boss saw the sight of me, he was not impressed.' To limit the damage he advised Páidí to lie low for a while.

'Jaysus, I was in no mood to argue. I grabbed the patrol car and went on "patrol". As I was fairly tired I decided to have forty winks. A few miles out the road I pulled into a field. I had no sooner dozed off when there was a tap on the window.'

'Staring me in the face was a Superintendent and an Inspector. The one field I picked in which to have a snooze was being used for the Pope's visit. All the brass were in town that day and trust me to pick the field they were checking out. I think there and then my promotion prospects took a dive. Looking back at it now it's pretty funny, but then it was serious, but sure we moved on from it.'

Micko Takes Over

And move on he did. Within a short few years Páidí's career in uniform was over.

'I decided to take time out and took the option of leasing Kruger Kavanagh's Pub in Dunquin. But whatever they say I had a good and fruitful time in the Garda Síochána and consider it a happy period in my life.'

By now his other career, that with the Kerry seniors, was about to take off in a big way. Having lost the 1974 Munster Final to Cork there was a new manager in Kerry. Mick O'Dwyer was appointed. It was to change the face of football in Kerry and beyond.

Páidí had played in that final (1974) as a substitute, but he was not to taste defeat against the 'old enemy' for the next eight years. It was the beginning of the team dubbed the 'best ever' produced by Kerry. Páidí is in no doubt it was down to O'Dwyer.

Unlike nowadays the appointment of O'Dwyer as manager was a low-key affair. 'Very little fanfare really, he just arrived and started training in January.' Training under Micko was 'savage, nothing scientific, just lap after lap of the field'.

'The first thing he did was to assemble the bulk of the under-21 winning teams. He really did train us hard. I think he felt we were all very young and could take it. I never felt fitter, especially as the season moved on and it was the same with the other lads. We were running up big scores and early on I sensed we were onto something with this fella.'

They were.

Cork were well beaten in the 1975 Munster Final and the same fate befell Sligo in the All-Ireland semi-final. It set up the dream final – Kerry v Dublin. It ushered in a new era in Gaelic football and one that captured the public's imagination. The Munster Final apart, Páidí revelled in this rivalry.

'Cork v Kerry is special but this was different. It was the first time that colour appeared on the Hill. Dublin fans brought a new dimension to supporting their team and subsequently other counties followed. It was also the "culchies" against the "jackeens" and the media lapped it up.'

With it being his first final, was he nervous?

'A bit, but here in Kerry you strive to play in Croke Park and that is where we wanted to be.'

Kerry's young team surprised the then champions, Dublin, and won by 2-12 to 0-11.

'We won it with our sheer fitness and passion. We played without fear and really they had no answer to us.'

It was a wonderful achievement by O'Dwyer's men and Páidí was thrilled at winning his first senior medal. 'Well the first one is always special and while I was to win seven more, that 1975 medal, along with the 1985 medal, stand out.'

The Kerry v Dublin Era

The GAA were the big winners though – Dublin and Kerry locked horns on a regular basis for the next few years. Every encounter was played to a full house in Croke Park and the players were thrust into the limelight. They were exciting and fabulous times for Páidí and his colleagues. 'Great matches to play in, the glamour games really – and once the Munster Final was over, all thoughts turned to Dublin.'

Kerry were beaten by Dublin in 1976 and 1977, but one other game shaped the team and it was one they were lucky to survive. It was the Munster Final of 1976, the year Páirc Uí Chaoimh was officially opened.

Páidí concurs. 'Haunted is the best way to describe that win. It was a draw the first day against Cork and we were very lucky in the replay. Cork were very good and two big calls went against them. One goal given to us and another disallowed on Declan Barron – lucky, really lucky.'

Had Cork won, would it have altered the football landscape back then? 'No question, that was a good Cork team and they had the players capable of winning an All-Ireland. It might also have forced a rethink in Kerry. But on small things are matches decided.'

One other factor in 1976 was over-confidence.

'I would question our approach that year. We got a warning against Cork, but probably didn't heed it. Dublin did not let us off the hook and were deserving winners.'

The 1977 Dublin and Kerry semi-final clash has often been referred to as the greatest game ever. 'Maybe, but the one thing I remember about it – it was played at a ferocious pace. Both sides looked likely winners at various stages. Yet in the end a little touch here and there swung the game in Dublin's favour.'

Kerry bounced back in 1978 and for the next few years held the upper hand in their games with the Dubs and went on to win the four-in-a-row.

Then the first real setback on the field arrived. It came in the 1982 All-Ireland Final when Kerry were on the cusp of history. The five-in-a-row beckoned. Immortality for O'Dwyer and his players. Enter Seamus Darby – and that late goal for Offaly in the final. It still hurts even now, almost 30 years on.

'That was a real sickener. We had it in our hands and in one fell swoop Darby took it from us. It would have been O'Dwyer's, and indeed our, crowning achievement but that's sport. It was a great match – all six half-backs scored from play that day. There was a hint of a shove on Tommy Doyle for the goal, but sure them calls went our way often enough.'

Nine months later and déjà vu. This time it was the Munster Final of 1983 against Cork in Páirc Uí Chaoimh played in dreadful weather with only a small crowd in attendance. Kerry were hot favourites and were ahead with time almost up. Páidí has vivid memories of what happened next.

'We were two points in front, the worst possible lead of course. Cork got

22 September 1985: Kerry captain Páidí Ó Sé is congratulated by Kerry manager Mick O'Dwyer after victory over Dublin in the All-Ireland Senior Football Final. Kerry v Dublin in Croke Park.

11 August 1985: Kerry manager Mick O'Dwyer shouts encouragement to his Kerry players in the All-Ireland Senior Football Semi-Final, Kerry v Monaghan, in Croke Park, Dublin.

18 July 2009: Wicklow manager Mick O'Dwyer smiles in the dressing room after Wicklow's victory over Down in Round 3 of the Football Championship qualifier – the County Grounds, Aughrim, Co Wicklow.

15 September 2009: Veterans of many great Cork v Kerry battles, both as players and managers, Billy Morgan (left) and Mick O'Dwyer analyse the statistics of the paths of both counties to the 2009 All-Ireland Senior Football Final, Kerry v Cork.

25 July 1982: Brian Cody of Kilkenny in action against Mark Corrigan of Offaly, Leinster Senior Hurling Final.

8 September 2002: Brian Cody, Kilkenny manager, celebrates with the Liam McCarthy cup. Clare v Kilkenny, All Ireland Senior Hurling Final, Croke Park, Dublin.

14 September 2003: Kilkenny manager Brian Cody celebrates with Martin Comeford after victory over Cork. All-Ireland Senior Hurling Final, Kilkenny v Cork, Croke Park, Dublin.

9 August 2009: Brian Cody, Kilkenny manager, at the end of the game. All-Ireland Senior Hurling Semi-Final, Kilkenny v Waterford, Croke Park, Dublin.

18 September 1983: Dublin manager Kevin Heffernan watches the final moments of the game. All-Ireland Senior Football Final, Dublin v Galway, Croke Park.

August 1983: Kevin Heffernan, Dublin manager (right) pictured with renowned GAA broadcaster, Mícheál O'Hehir.

10 August 1999: The launch of the An Post-GAA official Gaelic Football Team of the Millennium. From left; Seán Murphy, Kerry, Seán O'Neill, Down, Seán Purcell, Galway, Pat Spillane, Kerry, Kevin Heffernan, Dublin, Mick O'Connell, Kerry, Enda Colleran, Galway and Martin O'Connell, Meath.

17 November 2002: Former Dublin manager Kevin Heffernan pictured with his grandson, Kevin, during the UCD v St Vincent's, Dublin County Football Final, Parnell Park, Dublin.

8 January 2004: L to R: former Dublin footballer Jimmy Keaveney, former Taoiseach Bertie Ahern TD, former Dublin manager Kevin Heffernan and former Dublin player Gay O'Driscoll, at the launch of TG4's Laochga Gael series in St Vincent's GAA Club, Dublin.

Spring 2004: Kevin Heffernan, left (former Dublin football manager) and Mick O'Dwyer (former football manager of Kerry, Kildare, Laois and current Wicklow manager) were conferred with Honorary Doctorate degrees by the National University of Ireland in recognition of their enormous contribution to Gaelic Football.

March 2004: Kevin Heffernan at the funeral of Tyrone footballer, Cormac McAnallen, Eglish, Co Tyrone.

27 July 1986: Meath manager Seán Boylan (left) celebrates Meath's victory over Dublin in the Leinster Football Final at Croke Park.

6 September 1988: Seán Boylan, the Meath football manager.

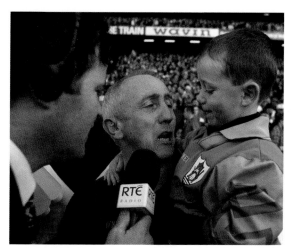

1 August 1999: Seán Boylan, Meath manager (left) celebrates victory over Dublin with Meath player Tommy Dowd (centre). Meath v Dublin in the Leinster Final at Croke Park.

29 September 1996: Victorious Meath manager Seán Boylan, with his son, being interviewed by Brian Carthy after the final whistle. Meath v Mayo All-Ireland Senior Football Final Replay, Croke Park.

15 July 2001: Meath manager Seán Boylan (right) congratulates Meath player Paul Sharkey after Meath's victory over Dublin in the Leinster Final at Croke Park.

7 October 2008: Irish team manager Seán Boylan at the announcement of the Ireland squad to take on Australia in the Coca Cola sponsored International Rules Series. Croke Park.

3 September 1995: Clare manager Ger Loughnane with the Liam McCarthy Cup after Clare won the All-Ireland for the first time in 81 years. Clare v Offaly. Croke Park.

28 June 2008: Galway manager Ger Loughnane on the sideline watching the All-Ireland hurling qualifier, Round 1. Antrim v Galway, Casement Park, Belfast.

21 June 1987: Clare half-back Ger Loughnane clears under pressure from Tipperary's Donie O'Connell. Clare v Tipperary replay in the Munster Hurling Championship, Fitzgerald Stadium, Killarney.

1983: Ger Loughnane in action for Clare during his playing days.

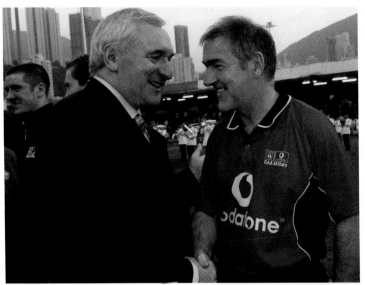

22 January 2005: Former Taoiseach Bertie Ahern TD with Mickey Harte before the game. Exhibition Game, 2003 Vodafone All-Stars v 2004 Vodafone All-Stars, Hong Kong Football Club, Hong Kong, China.

22 May 2005: A delighted Tyrone manager Mickey Harte at the end of the game. Ulster Football Championship, Tyrone v Down, Healy Park, Omagh, Co Tyrone.

31 May 2006: Mickey Harte speaking at the official launch of the Cormac Trust website. The website is an information point for people from all over Ireland and far beyond about the Cormac Trust Fund which was set up after the sudden death of GAA star Cormac McAnallen on 2 March 2004. It covers Cormac's life, career and death and the heart condition which so cruelly cut him and other very healthy and talented young people down. It was largely due to the death of Cormac, Irish youth rugby international John McCall and other subsequent cases that the Irish public became aware of the issue of sudden cardiac death among young people. Wellington Park Hotel, Belfast.

25 September 2005: Tyrone manager Mickey Harte celebrates with his daughter Michaela after the final whistle as Tadhg de Brún, RTÉ Sports floor manager, looks on. All-Ireland Senior Football Final, Kerry v Tyrone, Croke Park, Dublin.

21 September 2008: Tyrone manager Mickey Harte is lifted shoulder high by supporters at the end of the game. All-Ireland Senior Football Final, Kerry v Tyrone, Croke Park, Dublin.

September 1982: Páidí Ó Sé, the Kerry half-back.

22 September 1985: Páidí Ó Sé, Kerry, being marked by Barney Rock, Dublin, in the All-Ireland Senior Football Final. Kerry v Dublin, Croke Park.

2 September 2000: Kerry manager Páidí Ó Sé celebrates with Seán Walsh, Chairman of the Kerry County Board and Selector Eddie O'Sullivan (facing away from camera) at the end of the game. Kerry v Armagh. All-Ireland Senior Football Semi-Final Replay. Croke Park, Dublin.

27 June 2004: Páidí Ó Sé, Westmeath manager, celebrates at the end of the game with players John Keane and goalkeeper Gary Connaughton after victory over Wexford. Leinster Football Semi-Final. Westmeath v Wexford. Croke Park.

9 December 2004: John O'Donoghue TD (left) Minister for Arts, Sports & Tourism, Páidí Ó Sé (centre) Westmeath manager and winner of the Philips Sports Manager of the month award for July and Cel O'Reilly (right) managing director of Philips Ireland. Berkley Court Hotel, Dublin.

8 February 2009: Comórtas Peile Páidí Ó Sé Weekend: from left – Páidí Ó Sé, An Taoiseach Brian Cowen and Shaun Guest of Cadbury Ireland, celebrating the 20th year of the weekend which took place from 27 February – 1 March 2009. Burlington Hotel, Dublin.

28 July 1982: Billy Morgan playing in goal for Cork.

September 1990: Cork manager Billy Morgan (right) watches the final moments of the game from the sideline. Cork v Meath All-Ireland Senior Football Final. Croke Park.

19 August 2007: Cork manager Billy Morgan (right) celebrates with Pearse O'Neill at the end of the game. Meath v Cork. All-Ireland Senior Football Semi-Final. Croke Park.

1977: Joe Kernan celebrates a goal he has just scored playing football for Armagh.

17 March 1999: Crossmaglen Rangers manager Joe Kernan celebrates after the final whistle. All-Ireland Club Football Final. Crossmaglen Rangers v Ballina Stephenites. Croke Park.

22 September 2002: Armagh manager Joe Kernan celebrates with Paul McGrane after the game. Kerry v Armagh. All-Ireland Senior Football Final. Croke Park.

12 December 2002: Armagh manager Joe Kernan is named Philips Sports Manager of the Year 2002. Burlington Hotel, Dublin.

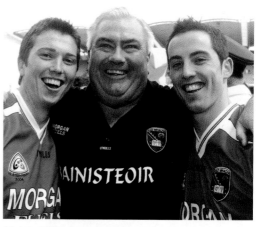

11 July 2004: Armagh manager Joe Kernan pictured with his sons Aaron (left) and Stephen. Armagh v Donegal. Ulster Senior Football Final. Croke Park.

7 May 2003: Armagh manager Joe Kernan (left) holds the Sam Maguire Cup with Des Crowley, Bank of Ireland (sponsors), celebrating ten years' sponsorship of the Football Championship.

1981: Jimmy Barry Murphy playing hurling for Cork.

13 June 1999: Cork manager Jimmy Barry Murphy is congratulated by Cork fans after Cork's victory. Cork v Waterford. Munster Senior Hurling Championship. Semple Stadium, Thurles.

7 September 1986: Jimmy Barry Murphy, Cork (centre) is blocked by Sylvie Linnane (No 2) and Gerry McInerney, Galway. Cork v Galway. All-Ireland Senior Hurling Final. Croke Park.

6 September 2009: Jimmy Barry Murphy waves to the crowd after being honoured as a member of the 1984 Cork Jubilee team during the Senior Hurling Final. Kilkenny v Tipperary. Croke Park.

1 July 2007: Former Cork star and manager Jimmy Barry Murphy watches the Munster Football Final. Cork v Kerry. Fitzgerald Stadium, Killarney.

a free. In it came and before we knew it Tadhgie Murphy had scored a goal. He's dining out on it ever since, I believe. Seconds later it was all over. I could hardly believe it, but then considering what happened Cork in 1976, they were due one.'

That was Kerry's first defeat in a Munster Final since O'Dwyer's first match in charge back in 1975. Was there pressure on O'Dwyer to quit after those defeats?

'Not really, a few murmurings that's all. We quickly regrouped and went on to win another three All-Irelands in a row.' Two of these were special – in 1984 the Centenary Year of the GAA, and one year later in 1985 the ultimate accolade for Ó Sé.

Captain Ó Sé

'Yes, that (the 1985 All-Ireland win) was extra special. West Kerry were county champions in 1984 and I had the honour of captaining Kerry in the following year, 1985. It is one thing to play with Kerry but to captain the team is really special. It was made all the sweeter by lifting the big "canister" over my head – my proudest moment.'

With the exception of one year, Páidí's career ran in tandem with O'Dwyer's reign as manager and there is no hiding his admiration for the genial man from Waterville.

'A brilliant man and Kerry football is indebted to him for his contribution. I have huge respect for the man. A genius really.'

What made him special? 'Two things: one – his ability to motivate a player. No matter who we were playing he had the capacity to drive you on. Then his discipline. He was big on that and no-one dared step out of line with him.'

There was criticism of O'Dwyer late in his managerial career as some observers felt he stayed too long in the position without developing any replacements for his ageing team.

It's a criticism Páidí rejects.

'Not at all – he firmly believed in the team but I suppose, like all good things, it had to end sometime and it did. But boy, we got some run out of it.'

1986 saw the beginning of the end of the great Kerry team, as Cork finally emerged from their shadow in Munster and also at All-Ireland level. Páidí would play in one more Munster Final – the loss to Cork in 1987, after which he called it a day.

He left the playing arena with a remarkable record: eight All-Ireland medals, one as captain, and in ten finals he conceded only one point to his direct opponent. The one blot on the record is his sending-off in the 1979 Final.

Páidí also won 11 Munster Senior Championship medals, 4 All-Ireland under-21 medals, 4 National League medals, 4 Railway Cup medals with Munster and 5 All-Star awards (1981 to 1985).

A Manager in Waiting?

To this day players from the Kerry v Dublin era remain great friends and regularly meet up for reunions. As Páidí explains, 'In all the games we played there was little rancour. Okay there was the odd scuffle but nothing serious. Nowadays we get together for golf and a few drinks and enjoy each other's company. One of the great strengths of the GAA is the friends you make for life.'

With football having dominated his life for so long and now in retirement, the next challenge was an obvious one – management – and he did not have too long to wait for his chance. Ironically enough it came from an unlikely source and in Cork at that.

'UCC was my first shot at managing a team. I really enjoyed it and put a lot into it, unfortunately with little reward. The students were great to work with. Full of enthusiasm and energy and the Sigerson Cup is their big competition. But it did give me invaluable experience in dealing with players and it stood to me later on.'

There was one job he craved and he made no secret of his desire to land it one day.

Managing Kerry.

'No question I wanted it badly. In fact when O'Dwyer retired I applied for it, but Mickey Ned O'Sullivan got it.'

That rankled!

'It did really – I was disappointed. But Mickey was coming from a stronger position. He was a physical education teacher and there was a moving away from the type of training that was done under Micko. It was the start I suppose of the more scientific training methods.'

There was one other factor in O'Sullivan's appointment. 'Mickey had been out of football for a period and had no link with the players who were there then and that might have swung the county board in his direction.'

Three years under Mickey Ned brought little reward – the All-Ireland was not won, and Kerry suffered a humiliating defeat to Clare in the 1992 Munster Final. O'Sullivan was soon on his way.

Once again Páidí's name was in the hat as his replacement. However for the second time in four years he was overlooked for the job. This time it was given to Denis 'Ogie' Moran. Like O'Sullivan before him he met with little success.

Was Páidí annoyed?

'Annoyed? That drove me bonkers altogether.'

He is in little doubt why he did not get the job. 'There was a fear among the County Board that I was a bit of a loose cannon. But the reality of the situation is that in 11 years, there was no All-Ireland won.'

O'Dwyer was at the helm in 1986 when Kerry won the All-Ireland. The next time the Sam Maguire would be claimed by Kerry was in 1997. By then, the Board had relented and Páidí had finally got the job.

While waiting in the wings for the call, Páidí guided West Kerry, his Divisional side, to two County Senior titles. He then took control of the Kerry under-21 team and duly delivered an All-Ireland title.

Finally the Call Comes

The pressure was mounting on the County Board to appoint him to the one job he craved. His case was strengthened by Kerry's inability to break Cork's grip on Munster, with Moran failing dismally in that regard. Now it must be said Cork had a very good team, but the Kingdom supporters were getting restless.

Eventually the call came, and one wonders was it a case of, 'We've tried everyone else, we'd better offer it to Ó Sé'?

'I am not so sure about that,' says Páidí, 'but I do know I wanted it and wanted it badly, because I felt I could make a go of it.'

He immediately set about building his backroom team, and his choice of selectors was crucial.

'I brought Seamus Mac Gearailt, a great coach, Jack O'Connor and Bernie O'Callaghan on board. We had all worked together at under-21 level and we were comfortable with one another. My philosophy as a manager is to bring good men around me, not "yes men". I think my selectors eased the mind of the Board because they knew I had sound men working with me.'

So his journey as Kerry manager was at last underway. It was to have many twists and turns along the way.

Páidí's appointment as manager was an almost instant success.

'In our first year, 1996, we beat Cork to win the Munster Championship, but we were outplayed by Mayo in the All-Ireland semi-final.'

Mayo rarely beat Kerry in Croke Park, but it was a lesson learned and Kerry came back stronger as a result.

'I learned quickly to always be on your guard and to keep your distance from players and I can tell you we were better equipped the following year.'

1997 was the year in which Páidí was to end Kerry's 11-year wait for Sam, and along the way the cards fell neatly into place. First Cork failed to reach the Munster Final, and then Cavan emerged from Ulster. Kerry disposed of Cavan and then Mayo awaited the Kingdom in the All-Ireland Final.

'It was a relief to finally win the All-Ireland, but in the immediate aftermath of that win, my selectors, apart from Bernie O'Callaghan, abandoned me. Whether it was deliberate or not I don't know.'

Páidí set about replacing his selectors and moved on.

Winning the Second All-Ireland

'We retained the Munster Championship before meeting Kildare in the 1998 All-Ireland semi-final.'

It was a hugely emotional day as the manager in the other corner was his long-time friend and mentor – Mick O'Dwyer. It was the classic Teacher v Pupil clash. Little did either man realise that they would meet again as managers with two different counties, a few years later.

'Very emotional indeed. I learned a lot from O'Dwyer but we lost by one point in a game we could have won. I was a bit rattled that year after the selectors had stepped down and under the circumstances we did well to get so far.'

Even to this day Ó Sé is unsure why they resigned. 'We had worked well together and I felt as a group we had a lot more to offer. In this regard it is only right to pay tribute to Bernie O'Callaghan. A great man, sadly no longer with us. His illness had just kicked in in 1997, but he did not desert the cause and for that I was grateful.'

1999 was another year when honours eluded Kerry. On a dreadful day in Páirc Uí Chaoimh, Cork ended their reign as Munster champions.

But one year later the Kingdom and Páidí bounced back.

'I had a good feeling about 2000. We regrouped after 1999 and we were going well. We won the Munster Championship, but had a couple of draws in the All-Ireland series that tested us.'

Armagh should have won the semi-final. 'Well they could have, but they didn't. In fact in the last minute one of their lads had a chance. Not only did he miss but the ball did not even go dead. It meant we had possession, won a free which Maurice Fitz scored, and we won the replay.'

The 2000 final was against Galway and in an unusual way created its own piece of history. As with the semi-final, it ended in a draw. The replay was fixed for a Saturday to facilitate the playing of the first game in the Compromise Rules series, Ireland v Australia. It was a decision that did not sit well with the teams as it presented its own problems. As Páidí explains, 'It was my job to prepare the team but I was dead against a Saturday afternoon match. Look! In my opinion it devalued the Final, for a game that has no relevance to our own. It also made it difficult for supporters as Saturday is a working day in Kerry.'

That aside Kerry won and now Páidí had his second All-Ireland as a manager and the cup famine in the Kingdom appeared to be over. It seemed as if the pressure was now off Ó Sé, but Páidí has a different take on matters.

'There is a high expectation level down here, which brings its own pressure.'

These words would certainly ring true a couple of years later.

Throughout his playing career Páidí came up against Dublin on an almost annual basis. Yet when he was Kerry manager the two teams met only once and at a strange venue for a Dublin v Kerry Championship encounter.

It was also the first year of the quarter-finals in the Football Championship and the game's biggest rivals went head to head in Semple Stadium, Thurles. A venue more accustomed to hosting hurling games.

The occasion was one he enjoyed. 'A great atmosphere in a wonderful stadium and a cracking game to match the occasion, which we were lucky to survive.' Indeed it took a moment of magic from a genial footballer to force a replay.

Páidí takes up the story, 'Dublin led by one point and time was almost up when we won a sideline kick. It was right under the old stand and about 50 yards from goal. Huge pressure. But what a man, if ever you needed a guy to nail it, Fitzy was it. He did and we won the replay, which was also in Thurles.'

With the Dubs out of the way, it looked odds on that another All-Ireland title was bound for An Ríocht. However it all fell apart like a house of cards in the semi-final when Meath filleted Kerry. The Kerry manager has no doubt it was his worst day ever, as a player or a coach, and he was powerless to do anything about it.

'Meath just blew us away. We were flat and clueless on the field and off the field we weren't much better. It was the only time in my career that I wished for a game to be over. The full-time whistle came as a relief to a lot of us that horrid afternoon.'

Personal Tragedy Strikes

2002 arrived with renewed optimism, but it ended in huge disappointment and a personal tragedy.

Cork and Kerry were all set for the Munster Final, when a few days before the game Páidí's brother Míceál died suddenly. There was talk that the final would be postponed. As well as Páidí, Míceál's sons – Darragh, Tomás and Marc – were on the Kerry team.

A frantic few days followed. Eventually it was decided the game would go ahead, at the unusual time of 7 o'clock on the Sunday evening in Páirc Uí Chaoimh (it was originally scheduled for a 3.30 p.m. start).

There was anger in Kerry, whose supporters maintained that out of respect for the Ó Sé family, the game should be postponed. Much of that anger was directed at Cork. Kerry supporters showed their disapproval by staying away in large numbers.

Throughout it all, the Ó Sé family maintained a dignified silence as they grieved for their father and brother.

Cork did not come out of it well, as many felt they were insisting that the game go ahead. The view from the Rebel County was simple, according to a source involved at the time – 'Whatever the Munster Council decides, we will abide by'.

There was a feeling that relations between the counties suffered as a result.

Páidí acknowledges that it was a very tough time. 'Naturally it was a sad time but we as a family dealt with it in our own way. We would be a close and private family anyway but it was a very emotional day. Especially for the three lads who under the circumstances were brave in playing in the final.'

There was a strange, subdued atmosphere that night on the banks of the Lee and it came as no real surprise that Cork won a low-key decider. As for the suggested strained relations with their neighbours from across the county bounds? 'Not at all – the game was played and we all know what happened a few weeks later in Croke Park.'

Was motivation a factor that day?

'Kerry never lack a motive when playing Cork – especially in an All-Ireland semi-final.'

Kerry won with a bit to spare to reach another final, this time against Armagh.

Kerry were expected to win, and for long periods they looked likely winners.

But somehow the game slipped from their grasp and the title was bound for the Orchard County for the very first time.

That weekend Páidí had an uncomfortable time and the signs were not good.

'Funny enough that was a game I never felt confident about. The morning of the game was the toughest morning I ever endured before a match. Even the night before, I got very little sleep. I worried right through that game.'

Could it be that the emotion of his brother's death finally caught up with him?

'I don't know that it did, but I had a bad feeling the entire weekend. In the end my feeling was right, we were not going to win.'

There was criticism after that defeat, some directed at the decision not to replace Marc earlier than he was substituted. But Páidí is adamant that his nephews were treated just like any other members of the panel.

'No, that never entered my thoughts or influenced selection. I always felt they were good enough to be on the team. Okay they, no more than any player, have had the odd off-day but they still are an important part of the Kerry set-up.'

His admiration for all three is obvious, but he has special words for midfielder supreme, Darragh.

'A superb player and without doubt the most influential player that Kerry have had for a long time. When he retires they will be hard pressed to replace him, that's how important he is to the team right now.'

If 2002 was tough then, it got no better in 2003. It could well be described as his *annus horribilus* – even if Kerry did retain their Munster title. It all began to unravel after the All-Ireland semi-final defeat to Tyrone. Kerry were outfought, outthought and outmuscled on that afternoon. It was the day of the zone defence.

Near the end of that game an irate Kerry supporter made a lunge at Páidí on the sideline in Croke Park, which was a shock. 'It was alright, but I suppose he was as frustrated as I was, but I made little of it after.'

The Worst Kind of Fucking Animals

But it was his comments in January of that year, 2003, which sowed the seeds of his dismissal as Kerry manager. Of that he is in no doubt. 'Well, they didn't help, you can be sure. I might have made it easier for me to be replaced.'

The comments cropped up in an interview with journalist Kevin Kimmage at Christmas. In it he called the Kerry supporters, 'the worst kind of fucking animals you could ever deal with' before adding, 'you can quote that'.

There was outrage in the county. Ironically the interview took place in Ventry, but only appeared in print while the team were on holiday in South Africa. While there Páidí was tracked down by RTÉ's Marty Morrissey. This is where he admits he made his second mistake.

'Well I regret the amount of embarrassment and hurt it caused. The amount of coverage and press time it got was in my opinion over the top.'

As for the interview with Marty Morrissey: 'I shouldn't have given the second interview, it only gave the thing more publicity.'

But it was the comment that upset Kerry people.

'I know it did, but it was taken out of context. I meant it as a compliment; because they demand, indeed expect, success. Look Kerry folk only want to be in one place in September and that's in Croke Park. If you don't deliver they consider it a failure.'

As for the remark itself – to this day he is non-repentant.

'I stand over what I said, as I was being complimentary.'

While the team were still in South Africa pressure was mounting back home in Kerry. The County Board issued a statement disassociating themselves from Ó Sé's comments. The Kerry supporters club also condemned the remarks. Meanwhile two polls on Radio Kerry were in favour of Ó Sé stepping down.

Under increasing pressure, Páidí issued an apology in which he said, 'What I meant to say was Kerry fans were "hard to please" and are "always demanding of the highest standards", as we are a proud race of people.'

While all this was going on there was a falling-out with team trainer John O'Keeffe after Páidí said he himself 'would be taking on a more hands-on approach with the training this year'. O'Keeffe hinted he was not happy and he would not be taking a couple of planned training sessions. It made for an uncomfortable period in Kerry football, which had an unsettling effect.

'It was upsetting for a while as we all wanted the one thing – the best for the team.'

Eventually Ó Sé and O'Keeffe had a face-to-face meeting.

Páidí explains, 'Johnno and myself go back a long way. He was a vital part of my backroom team. We sat down had a chat, put it behind us and moved on.'

After the defeat to Tyrone, the knives were out again, but this time, the silent assassins would have their way.

Ó Sé made an attempt to remain in the job. 'I did, because I felt I had something to offer and wanted to continue.'

The end effectively came at the County Board meeting on 26 August 2003 when Kerry Chairman Sean Walsh announced, 'The term of Páidí Ó Sé is up and we will be appointing a new management team.' This would be done at the October meeting of the Board.

It was the sack.

And he did not even learn the news from a Board officer but from an intermediary.

Another war of words erupted between Ó Sé and Walsh with Ó Sé annoyed that since the Tyrone game no-one from the County Board had been in contact with him.

'Badly handled is how I would describe it. Surely after 33 years' service to the county, as player and manager, I was entitled to more than just a phone call to tell me I was out?'

'I was told resign or be fired,' says Páidí.

In the end he called a press conference for Killarney and fired a broadside at the Board.

'Of course I was annoyed at the way it was handled. At the time I thought it was the end of the world. But as everyone knows, life moves on quickly in the GAA.'

Páidí had support from a group of senior Kerry players who issued a statement criticising 'the treatment of Páidí Ó Sé, considering his service to the county as a player and trainer.'

That pleased Páidí.

'It was a nice gesture by the players and I appreciated it, but I wouldn't have expected anything else from such a loyal group.' The support from his family was also 'rock solid'.

'Tremendous; my wife Máire was one hundred per cent behind me at all times. That, and my loyal friends, helped me through a tough time. But I am made of strong stuff and not easily put down.'

So his eight-year reign, in which he won two All-Irelands and six Munster Championships, was finally over. But the ink had barely dried on the story when another chapter in an incredible career was about to unfold.

The New Westmeath Manager

Within a week, he was back in management, taking the reins in Westmeath.

It was a move that shocked many. 'I suppose it did, coming so soon after Kerry. But I can tell you now it was the best thing I ever did. It was the best 12 months of my life.'

Unlike his appointment in Kerry, which was low-key, this new appointment was the opposite. He was ferried by helicopter to Mullingar with the traffic brought to a standstill as he made his way to a press conference.

How did it come about?

'Well when Kerry lost to Tyrone, a few feelers were sent my way. But as I was still Kerry manager, I shrugged them off. Then when I was no longer in charge, they came looking again.'

Was it a difficult decision to make?

'Not really. Football is my bug and I was bitten once again. I decided to have a go.'

It was one decision that he was glad he took – even though it did not start well!

'A wonderful time working with great men. A very infectious group of players I was very comfortable with. I also had marvellous selectors who were very supportive.'

There had been a good degree of success at minor and under-21 level and they all pulled together to make it work at senior.

'Tomás Ó Flatharta from here (Ventry), Paddy Collins and Jack Cooney and the back-up team were brilliant.' A key man also was – 'a guy by the name of Mick Duffy. Mick was the communications man, a brilliant worker.'

After a shaky start things were slowly coming around – just in time for the Leinster Championship.

How different was it training a team in Leinster as against in Munster?

'Well the football was tougher for a start, but sure it's the same game. The rivalry is intense though.'

Managing Westmeath had one big difference to Kerry – the travelling. Surely it must have impacted on business and family life.

'It was strange, but my family, as they did before, rallied around and gave me great support as well as helping with the business.'

Páidí also puts an end to the rumours that he made money out of Westmeath.

'There is this fantasy that I made a fortune, but nothing could be further from the truth. If any guy, not just me, goes to the trouble to train a team far away from home, the least he is entitled to is reasonable expenses. That is all I got from Westmeath; it was the same in Clare, and that is all I looked for. Travelling expenses and a few bob for grub. No more no less.'

Ironically during our chat, Páidí takes a call from *Newstalk.* It was to discuss the very same subject, coming a day after GAA Director General Páraic Duffy claimed a well-known Ulster-based coach made a 'fortune' from training teams in the province.

Winning Leinster with Westmeath

Optimism within the county of Westmeath was growing as the

Championship opener with Offaly drew nearer.

The rivalry in Leinster is big, 'All the counties are practically bordering one another and for us (Westmeath) to win it was a major achievement.'

Along the way they took some big scalps.

'Offaly – we beat them for the first time in 55 years.'

In the next round, Páidí's old rivals Dublin were waiting.

'That was some day! Can you imagine a small county beating Dublin? A wonderful occasion as it always is with Dublin. A full house as well. But I got greater satisfaction out of the next match.'

The next match happened to be the Leinster Final. Laois were the opponents and they were also the reigning Leinster champions. And their manager was none other than his old friend from Waterville – Mick O'Dwyer. It was an encounter Páidí relished.

'I got great pleasure out of that game. I kind of "did a Dwyer on Dwyer" if you like. I kept telling everyone we had no chance but I knew we were capable of winning. I also was aware that some of the Laois players didn't fancy playing against Westmeath.'

The first game ended in a draw, but in the replay and on an emotional day in Croke Park, Páidí put one over on his former mentor.

'It was a great occasion and a good match, but we were well prepared. I took the team to Inchadoney in West Cork and over to Sunderland. The whole Championship experience was a journey to savour.'

Having won the Leinster title, there was then the trip back to Mullingar. A trip he will never forget.

'Over the years I returned home with many a cup, but this was special. The joy on people's faces, young and old, made it all worthwhile. Wonderful, really wonderful. The only pity is we didn't take it a stage further – but to win a Leinster Championship was something beyond their wildest dreams.'

Páidí stayed one more year in the Lake County. But after early exits from the Championship and the qualifiers he moved on.

'I had taken the team as far as I could and felt a change would help. There was no animosity – it was an amicable parting. I will tell you this though, it was a fabulous two years up there and I have nothing but happy memories.'

But in circumstances similar to when he left the Kerry job, another job offer arrived quickly at his door. This time the Clare County Board came calling, and once again he said 'yes'.

Unlike Westmeath, though, there was to be no fairytale ending. Relegation to Division 4 in the League and a surprise defeat to Waterford in the Championship ensured it was a short stay. Another loss to Antrim in the Tommy Murphy Cup brought his tenure to an end.

Did he regret going to the Banner county?

'No, not at all, but there was a big job to be done there. A two or even three-year plan, and I was not prepared for that type of commitment, so off I went.'

A Back Looks Forward

In a long and chequered career, Ó Sé has been never shy to express his opinion on various matters.

On the GPA?

'They are here, recognise them and all work together for the good of the association.' But he is adamant on 'no pay for play'.

'As an organisation we could not sustain it. More importantly it would kill clubs, who are under enough pressure as it is.'

Was it the right decision to open Croke Park?

'No question – apart from the revenue it generated. Why have such a wonderful stadium empty, when it could be full with people supporting Irish teams?'

The ban on winter training concerns him.

'Especially for the weaker teams. They have more ground to make up than the successful counties – it makes it harder to bridge the gap.'

His friendship with Taoisighs is well documented as are his links with the late Charles Haughey.

'Yes, he was a great man and I lost a true friend with his death. My association with Fianna Fáil is well known. I count Bertie Ahern and Brian Cowen among my friends. It's a bit rough for them now, but look – they'll survive.'

In fact every year Páidí runs a football tournament 'Comórtas Peil Páidí Ó Sé' and over the years the Taoiseach of the day has presided over the official launch. This year it was Brian Cowen and it brings in much welcome visitors and revenue to Ventry at a time of the year (January), when they are about as rare as swallows in wintertime.

Páidí's last managerial job was in July 2007. Since then he has been linked with several jobs. Dublin was one and even a return to Kerry was hinted at. Nothing came of either.

But would he be tempted back?

'They say, never say never. For 40 years football has consumed my life. Right now I am busy with the bar and a bit of media work. But you never know what lies around the corner.'

In the week he lost the Kerry job Páidí said he 'would never again train Kerry', but you sense the lure of the 'green and gold' would be too big an offer to turn down.

Leaving Ceann Trá that May afternoon, I sense Páidí Ó Sé has mellowed and is in comfortable surroundings – dealing once again with the public, but without the pressure which management brings.

For now, his business and family consume his life. Football still courses through his veins. After 40 years he is entitled to relax. It's the least he is entitled to, considering the enjoyment and excitement he brought to the game he loves – both as a player and a manager.

As they say in our native tongue – *Ní bheith a leithéad ann arís.*

8

Billy Morgan

The Early Influences – Hurling, Christy, Celtic

It is fair to say that Cork football has always lived in the shadow of its hurling counterparts. A look at the record books tells its own tale – 30 hurling titles with a mere 6 in football. A closer look at that statistic reveals that of the six Championships, Billy Morgan had a direct involvement in three. In 1973 Billy was the captain while in 1989 and 1990 he was the team coach. Is it any wonder then that Billy is often referred to as 'Mr Cork Football'?

Over a period of 40 years his contribution to the game in the Rebel County is unrivalled. As a goalkeeper he had few equals; indeed he is without question the best Cork has produced.

What he brought to the game as a player – meticulous preparation, dedication and bravery – he maintained and surpassed as a coach. A player's man to the last, he had more than one confrontation with officialdom, in Cork and at times beyond.

Yet Billy's first love was hurling.

'It was really. It's the greatest field game in the world. The love of the game was fostered from my home. My late parents came from Galway. My father and his brothers played hurling for the county and from them I developed a huge interest in hurling.'

The first part of our interview took place in the Christy Ring room in Páirc Uí Rinn, Cork GAA's second ground, called after the greatest hurler of them all.

'I grew up listening to the radio. The Cork three-in-a-row team of 1952 to 1954 was special and Christy was the star among stars.'

Billy himself was a very good hurler, even though his club Nemo Rangers are more renowned for their football exploits.

'Nemo would have been very good at hurling in the formative years. But as the football got stronger, hurling suffered. Then the majority of our players, me included, were attending Coláiste Chríost Rí and that was a football stronghold.'

That said, Nemo enjoyed some good days in hurling and Billy reckons he could have made the Cork minor hurling team.

'I was on the minor football team but missed the hurling match as I was suspended having been sent off in a club game.'

His best year in hurling?

'That's easy. In 1974 Nemo had a great run in the Senior County Championship. We beat a powerful Glen Rovers team in the quarter-final. Then we lost narrowly to an equally strong Blackrock team in the semi-final.'

To put this into perspective, Nemo Rangers beating Glen Rovers in hurling at that time would be akin to Kilkenny defeating Dublin in football today.

'Well maybe they (the Blackrock hurling team) weren't that strong but it was a huge upset and a great result for us at the time. Had we managed to win a senior hurling county final it would have really established hurling in the club.'

'Georgie Allan was in charge of the team and I was in midfield with Jimmy Barrett. The Blackrock midfield pairing was Frank Cummins and a young Tom Cashman. Before the game Georgie asked us who would we like to mark. When Jimmy said he would take Frank I was thrilled. But boy was I given a lesson by Tom that day! He took me to the cleaners. He was so good that I ended up being taken off.'

Even now, despite his football commitments, Billy is involved with hurling at the club.

'I'm a selector with the junior team. Hopefully we can make progress in the Championship. Obviously football is our number one game but we have a lot of good hurlers who are very committed.'

Like so many goalkeepers, Billy began life as a forward, lining out at centre-forward with the Cork minors in the Munster Final of 1963.

'I did, but after a disagreement with a club mentor I went off playing soccer for a year. For some reason, I suppose it was because I played Gaelic football, the soccer coach put me in goal and there I stayed.'

Billy always enjoyed playing soccer and once spent a week on trial at the famous Glasgow Celtic club.

'I did, and like any young fellow I would have jumped at the opportunity to play at that level. I had a good week there and was well looked after. Seán Fallon was very helpful. I came home and was told they eventually had signed another goalkeeper. But it was an interesting and enjoyable experience.'

Even today Glasgow Celtic is still a passion of his.

'Yes, big time! I travel over a few times a year, especially to the big European Cup nights. It's a magical atmosphere at those games and it's something I look forward to every season.'

Interestingly, at one stage in 2008, Billy's name was being mentioned as a possible manager of Cork City FC in the League of Ireland.

Early Days

Billy won his first Munster medal when Cork won the under-21 title in 1965 but surprisingly lost to Kildare in the All-Ireland semi-final. His career with the senior team was about to begin.

'I was the sub goalie for the National League in 1965/66. Then I got picked for the Munster Senior Football Championship in 1966.' It was a good start.

'Yeah, we won the Munster Championship but Galway beat us in the All-Ireland semi-final. That was a very good Galway team who went on to win the final.'

The 1966 Munster Final set in train a record that is unlikely to be surpassed, let alone equalled. Billy played in the next 17 Munster Finals and in the process picked up 5 winners' medals.

'It's unique all right I suppose, but in those days we had the seeded draw and then the other counties were not that strong.'

Morgan has huge admiration for Kerry.

'They hindered many a good Cork team by beating us regularly. But they had some of the best players in the game and they were hard to beat. That said, I have great friends in Kerry and meet up with them on a regular basis for a round of golf and a few beers.'

Despite his admiration for Kerry, he loved beating them – as a player and as a manager.

'I always felt we had players as good as Kerry and beating them was extra special. Believe you me, they feel the same about beating us. It's a tremendous rivalry and one we all enjoyed playing in. As a player and a manager I got great satisfaction out of beating them. In many ways it made our summer.'

Interestingly Billy is not a fan of the current Championship format.

'No, I am not. I feel there is nothing like the cut and thrust of knockout football. The Provincial Championship is diluted and it militates against the lesser counties. Look, take Munster for instance. A weaker county might beat Cork or Kerry but it doesn't knock the losing team out of the Championship. That, in my opinion, devalues the win. Then more often than not, Cork or Kerry will go further in the Championship than the team that beat them.'

He accepts that the new format is here to stay.

'Oh it is! The GAA won't change it now, and the counties have embraced it – so the day of the "one chance" in Championship football is long gone.'

On the field Billy picked up his second Munster senior football medal in 1967 and this time Cork made it to the All-Ireland Final.

Waiting there was Meath. It would be the first of many an encounter between Morgan and the men from the Royal County.

Billy does not have happy memories of the 1967 Final.

'Well we lost for a start. It was a poor game and Meath won by a goal; 1-9 to 0-9. I really should have stopped the goal. But we kicked the game away. We hit wide after wide and some of them (the wides) were awful.'

The goal itself was the subject of much debate as it came in a somewhat bizarre way.

'The Meath player Terry Kearns was taking a breather near our goal. He was just recovering when a high ball came in. I went to collect it, and it looked easy enough. Then from nowhere Terry appeared and the ball glanced off his fingertips and dropped into the net. I knew he was there but felt I had it covered. There was a touch of the fluke about it.'

For a young player appearing in his first All-Ireland Final it was a huge disappointment.

'Very much so! But look – you learn from every game. I was very annoyed at conceding the goal, but there was little could be done about it.

That's the joy of being a goalkeeper – one mistake could be fatal.'

It was 1973 before Cork would appear in an All-Ireland Final again. This time though the landscape had changed. Nemo Rangers had won the Cork County Championship for the very first time in 1972. Billy was appointed Cork captain and he sensed 1973 could be special. The late Doney O'Donovan of St Nick's was enticed back as manager. Billy had huge admiration for Doney.

'Doney did more for Cork football than any man I know. When he agreed to coach us in 1973 I felt we had a chance of winning the All-Ireland. Now we had a good team, but Doney was the key.'

Even when he retired from playing and moved into coaching himself, Billy would always refer to Doney for advice.

'He had the greatest influence on me as a player and a coach. I used to ring him regularly for a chat and he would look at teams and players for me. He had a vast knowledge of players and how they would play. He knew every player in the county, their strengths and weaknesses. I could not say enough about Doney and the help and support he gave me over the years. He was also very calm in the dressing room before a match. He was soft - spoken, but when he spoke you listened. His attention to detail was something I took on board when I was manager. The small things make the difference, he would say. He commanded huge respect. A real players' man – that set him apart in Cork football.'

Back then (1973) if Cork beat Kerry in the Munster Final some would see it as the job done, but this team was different. They were driven by a manager and a captain who had only one ambition: Cork in Croke Park on All-Ireland Football Final day.

'We had a great win over Kerry in the Munster Final down in the old park. That was the day Jimmy Barry Murphy banged in two goals. Doney came up with a great switch just before the throw-in. Jimmy and Ray Cummins swapped positions in the full-forward line. Before Kerry knew what hit them they were well behind.'

They might have been. But in keeping with their tradition, Kerry battled back and it took a great save from Morgan to ensure Cork won.

'I remember it well, but we probably would have won anyway. We had a serious team and now we were on a roll.'

Cork went on to beat Tyrone in the All-Ireland semi-final. It was Cork v Galway in the final. Cork were chasing their first title since 1945.

Unlike 1967 this final would provide Billy with the highlight of his playing career.

'It's up there with the best of them. We had been very well prepared and played brilliantly in the final. Galway too played their part. It was actually a very open and free-flowing game, but we were not going to be stopped.'

Cork won by 3-17 to 2-13 and it was a proud Billy Morgan who climbed the steps to lift the Sam Maguire Cup.

To go with his cherished Celtic Cross, Billy also won an All-Star award at the end of the year. He was also named the Texaco Footballer of the Year. To this day he remains the only goalkeeper to pick up that accolade. Yes – 1973 was a special year.

'It was a hugely emotional day for football in the county – tinged with sadness though as a great football man had passed away earlier in the year.'

Billy did not forget him in his speech.

'Weeshie Murphy, father of present team doctor Con, was a selector in 1967 and I felt we had won this one for him. The selectors too were brilliant. Dinny McDonnell from Nemo was a great ally of Doney's and anything they wanted they got.'

An interesting little footnote.

The 1973 All-Ireland Final was refereed by John Moloney (RIP). Three years later, Moloney, one of his umpires and Billy would meet again. It would be a controversial meeting.

The homecoming in 1973 was special. The team had won the hearts of the people of Cork.

'The biggest crowd ever for a returning Cork team. It set in train huge celebrations, and boy did we celebrate.'

In a strange way the winning of the 1973 All-Ireland, instead of being the beginning of something special, was in many ways the beginning of the end. This was a great Cork team, but one that undoubtedly underachieved.

Billy agrees and knows exactly why.

'It's simple really. We celebrated too much and took our eye off the ball. You must remember football wins were rare in Cork and we were heroes. Doney kept warning us, but we just did not heed the warnings.'

The Phantom Goal

Training for the 1974 Championship was only moderate. Despite this Cork beat Kerry in Killarney to retain the Munster title. Then came the ambush. Dublin in the All-Ireland semi-final.

'Without doing a whole lot we beat Kerry handy in the Munster Final. That probably gave us a false impression of where we actually were. Now Dublin were unrated at the time and we were very complacent going into that match.'

Billy saw the signs but could do little about it.

'We were doing okay. Then about 10 minutes from time I remember saying to myself, "Jaysus, if we don't cop on here, we might lose". Well we did. It was a huge shock at the time. Still hurts, not helped by the fact that Dublin went on to win the final. We had blown a great chance to win back-to-back titles.'

Billy's friendship with a number of Dublin players, particularly Jimmy Keaveney, means he is constantly reminded of that fateful day.

'Jimmy never lets me forget. "Ah", he says, "ye thought ye had nothing to do only turn up to beat the Dubs."'

In 1975 Kerry's young guns shocked Cork in the Munster Final and the team began to break up.

'That loss to Kerry saw the end of the team and it is a huge regret for a lot of guys that we did not win a second All-Ireland.'

An opportunity lost?

'No question about it. Little did we think what would happen next.'

What happened was that Kerry were back with a vengeance. The Kingdom would dominate football for the next 10 years. Cork and others were left in their slipstream as the greatest football team ever emerged under Mick O'Dwyer.

However the 1976 Munster Final could have changed the direction of Gaelic Football. It was laced with controversy. Referee John Moloney was a central figure.

Billy takes up the story.

'We were really stung by the defeat in 1975. Doney got us together early for the 1976 Championship. Training went very well and I had a good feeling coming up to the Munster Final against Kerry.'

The match itself marked the opening of the new Páirc Uí Chaoimh. The replay was a week later. Cork were still confident.

'Even more so after the drawn game. We played brilliantly and led by eight points early in the second-half. I could not see us losing.'

* * *

Let's now return briefly to the 1973 All-Ireland Final and the second goal Galway got.

'Yeah I can't remember who took the shot, but I didn't think it crossed the line. But the umpire waved the flag and the goal was given. I gave an interview to a newspaper and said I didn't think it was a goal. I then saw the tape of the match and it was a goal. So I had no problem with it.

'During the second-half of the 1976 match I got talking to the umpire. It turned out he was the same man who acted as umpire in the 1973 All-Ireland Final. He reminded me of what I had said about the goal by saying,

"You were wrong – it was a goal!"'

Billy thought no more about it as Cork were well on top. Then it happened.

'Kerry got a free. Mikey Sheehy took it. He went for a goal but Brian Murphy caught it. Great I thought, that's it, we'll win now. Then I saw your man, the umpire, waving the green flag – a goal for Kerry. I looked at him, and before I could say anything he shouted, "Be quiet! You were wrong before and you are wrong again. It (the ball) was over the line!"

'I couldn't believe it when the referee gave the goal.'

Thirty-three years on, Billy is adamant the ball had not crossed the line.

'Nowhere near it. Brian's feet were on the line when he caught the ball in his midriff. The ball was well outside – it should not have been given.'

That was bad enough, but it got worse for Cork.

'We actually recovered from that and we were still ahead and looking good. I was still confident we would win.'

Then Referee Moloney intervened at the other end of the field.

'It was crazy really. He disallowed a perfectly good goal scored by Deccie Barron. That meant a six-point turnaround in Kerry's favour. It swung the match in their favour. We were shattered.'

There was to be one other twist and it threw Cork a lifeline.

'It was level with time up. Kerry's Mikey Sheehy hit a great ball. It was going over the bar for the winning point when Moloney blew for full-time. I had never seen that before – a referee blowing when the ball was in flight. I think he was trying to make up for the disallowed Cork goals.'

The match went to extra-time, but Cork were spent.

'We never recovered from the goals and Kerry won comfortably in the end.'

Billy is certain the outcome of that match changed the course of Cork and Kerry football for the next 10 years.

'Without a doubt. We should have won. I am convinced of that. Had we won, then the best team ever (Kerry) might never have been heard of.

Kerry people even accept that. They kicked on, broke all records and we went into a bit of a decline.'

In 1977 Cork football was embroiled in controversy due to the 'Adidas gear' incident. Billy and team captain Jimmy Barry Murphy were central characters.

'Early in the year Adidas offered us some gear in return for posing for a photograph of the team. In those days you just got a jersey from the County Board and nothing else so we said, "Yeah, why not?"'

There did not appear to be any problem initially. However in the run-up to the Munster Final with Kerry, the Board officers got involved.

'They said we could not wear the shorts and socks and produced their own gear for us. We had a team meeting and the general opinion was, "okay, let's wear the gear the Board provided and concentrate on the match".'

In the midst of all this, Doney O'Donovan was a calming influence.

'Doney was solidly behind us in whatever we decided. His suggestion was, "Wear the Board gear, beat Kerry and then to a man head to the County Board meeting on Tuesday night" and let them know how strongly we felt.'

That seemed to be acceptable to the players.

'We had more or less agreed to do that. The meeting was nearly over when one of the selectors walked in. Now the same individual had a dreadful attendance record at training. Then to make matters worse he said something like, "Typical footballers, always looking for free gear". Well that drove us mad. Jimmy shot up and said, "That's it, we're wearing the Adidas gear," end of meeting.'

While all this was going on, the players got another shock in the post on the Friday morning before the game.

'We were all informed if we wore anything other than the gear provided by the Board we would be suspended.'

'This meant that although the Board claimed it was trying to sort out the row, in reality it had already decided on a course of action. This only strengthened the resolve of the players. We were not for turning. I understand they (Board officers) spent all Saturday night trying to contact Jimmy but he was probably at the greyhound track as he was every Saturday night.'

In an unusual move Cork travelled by train to Killarney the following day to play Kerry.

'It was the only time I ever remember going to Killarney by train. The officers spent the entire journey trying to get Jimmy to persuade us to wear their gear. Then when we got to the hotel we were brought upstairs to a room. In there they produced a set of white shorts. But we stood firm and refused to alter our stance.'

This surely was not the ideal preparation for a Munster Final?

'The worst ever. Mentally we were gone. All the good work was down the drain. It came as no real surprise that we were hammered. We had no chance really. Our chance went when the selector criticised us.'

Three days after the match the entire panel were suspended. But in a typical Cork move it was only from football. This was to allow Jimmy Barry Murphy and Brian Murphy to play with the hurlers in the All-Ireland semi-final.

'There followed a few lively days and the two lads were prepared to miss the hurling match. They did not want to leave their football colleagues in the lurch although we wanted them to play in the hurling match. It was eventually resolved and the suspension was lifted. The lads played and Cork went on to win the All-Ireland Hurling Final.'

A few months later, both parties (the Board and the players) signed a document whereby only official gear would be used by all Cork teams.

'We were fed up with all the hassle. We just wanted to play football and for that reason we signed it and moved on.'

Billy's inter-county career was drawing to a close. Ironically enough his last Munster Final was in Killarney in 1981. It had a familiar ending.

'Kerry won but I did not finish the match. I think it was just before half-time I was in a collision with Eoin Liston. Purely accidental now it must be said. But given Eoin's size there was only going to be one winner. I was concussed and carried off – not a nice way to end your Championship career.'

On a lighter note.

'Funny really as Frank Cogan said it was the earliest I ever left Killarney after a Munster Final.'

Billy tells a good tale about three Nemo men who were at the match.

'Paddy Quinn and two others, Mick Dunlea and Bernie Murphy, both sadly now no longer with us, decided to stay in Killarney on the Sunday night and they used my injury as an excuse. They phoned home to say I was in hospital and they were staying with me to make sure I was okay. That was fine until they picked up the newspaper the following morning. There was a picture of me leaving the field on a stretcher and the news that I had returned to Cork by ambulance at 6 o'clock on Sunday evening for treatment. I don't know how they got out of it but we had many a laugh about it afterwards.'

Learning with Nemo

By now Billy had also made another big decision about his career.

'I always had an interest in training and coaching. I wanted to do a Masters in Physical Education and that meant a two-year course in New York.'

Billy, who was a teacher in Coláiste Iognáid Rís (Sully's Quay as it is popularly known in Cork), acquired leave of absence and headed for the Big Apple.

'It was a major move on my part. But I was doing it for my coaching career more than anything. I was also getting itchy feet in teaching and was thinking of moving on.'

A big wrench leaving Nemo Rangers and Cork football?

'A huge wrench. But Mary, my wife, and I discussed it and decided to go for it. The kids, Brían and Alan, were young and we felt it was now or never. I knew what I was leaving behind but I needed to go.'

Billy played two more games in the National Football League with Cork before bringing the curtain down on a remarkable career.

In New York two years turned into four and he very nearly stayed there. It was a very happy period in his life.

'It went brilliantly. I got my Masters but stayed on for two more years as we were enjoying it so much. I made some great friends out there. Played football and hurling and worked in Rosie O'Grady's bar in downtown New York.'

Time then for another big decision.

'Well, my leave of absence from work was up and I either returned to teaching or my job would be gone. It meant a lot of soul searching and we really considered staying. In the end though we came home. The two lads were at an age where it was also probably right for them as well to return. It was a close one though. It would not have taken much for us to stay there. I was glad I went though and after all the years playing with Cork it was a nice break.'

On his return he changed jobs.

'I did. I was offered a position with an insurance company and took it. I felt I needed a break from teaching. I resigned my position and moved into the financial business, which I'm still in today.'

Billy now has his own Financial Services Company with his son Brían and nephew William.

By no means an easy business to be in these days?

'It certainly is not, but look, we're doing the best we can in difficult circumstances.'

With his playing career over, although he occasionally played Junior with Nemo Rangers, Billy turned his attention full-time to management. It was a road he was always going to travel.

'It was, as I was very keen on it from a young age. In my early days with Nemo I would be giving Frank Cogan a hand with under-age teams.'

Of course he had trained Coláiste Iognáid Rís to a Munster Colleges' title in 1974.

'That was very exciting. It was the only time we won the Munster Colleges' title. The young lads were great to work with and keen to learn.'

He also had a brief flirtation with the Cork senior football team.

'Twice actually. In 1979 Frank Cogan was the coach and he asked me to give him a hand. But as ever there was a problem. Paddy Driscoll, a Board officer at the time, "did not approve" of my methods and objected to my appointment. I have no doubt it was over the Adidas affair.'

However a compromise was reached.

'It was. Frank was made manager and I was appointed trainer. We lost the League Final to Roscommon and Kerry beat us in the Championship.'

A year later the Board took a different view.

'Frank (Cogan) gave up and I was asked to train the team. I did and I was actually player/manager. We won a great League Final against Kerry, but they beat us in the Munster Final. I stepped down after that.'

The Cork managerial job though was still the one he wanted. He would bide his time until the opportunity came his way once more. All the while he was building up an impressive CV as a manager with a string of county titles with his beloved club.

When you mention certain GAA clubs in Ireland they are automatically linked to a famous player – Christy Ring with Glen Rovers, Jimmy Barry Murphy with St Finbarr's, Kevin Heffernan with St Vincent's, Joe Kernan with Crossmaglen Rangers. Mention Nemo Rangers and the first name to spring to mind is Billy Morgan.

'This club means so much to me. I have been here since I was about seven years of age and my best friends are here. Apart from my family it is very important to me.'

Only once was his loyalty tested.

'I was studying in UCC. I actually won two Sigerson Cup medals while there, medals I cherish. In 1967, UCC met Nemo in the quarter-final of the County Championship. Now that was very strange for me. But the lads in Nemo had no problem with it as that was the rule at the time. I was glad when the game was over.' (UCC won that game.)

Nemo may be important to Billy but Billy, many would say, made Nemo Rangers. The man himself disagrees.

'I like to think I played my part but there are many others. We have been very fortunate to have had men with vision to lead us off the field. They put in place a structure that has stood the test of time. On the playing side we work hard and thankfully have got our reward.'

A look at the record books will testify to that.

With 16 Cork senior county titles, 12 Munster club titles and 7 All-Ireland club titles (a record), it is hard to argue with that. But it was not always the case.

'No, it was tough at times. It took a long time to win our first senior county football title but once we won it we pushed on from there.'

As a player and coach Billy was associated with so many outstanding victories, but a few stand out for him.

'Obviously the first county title in 1972 was special. Then winning our first Munster and All-Ireland club titles helped establish the club on the national stage.'

That was important?

'Very much so. You look at all the big Cork clubs, the Glen, the Barr's and the Rockies – they're recognised the length and breadth of the country and we've achieved that in football.'

There was a period when the titles had dried up. Billy Morgan changed that.

'In the late 1990s we were struggling. We had not won the county title in six years which for us was the longest gap since winning our first. In

2000 we won the county title but lost the All-Ireland Club Final to Crossmolina by one point. The following year, 2001, we retained the County and Munster titles but were again beaten in the All-Ireland Final – this time by Ballinderry.'

Was the Morgan magic failing?

'I don't know about that but it was frustrating because I felt we had a team good enough to win the All-Ireland.'

Is that what made him stay on when others might have walked away?

'I had no intention of walking away but it was tough getting the lads going again. To be fair though they bought into it and we had another motivation.'

Which was . . . ?

'Believe it or not, for all our success we had never won three-in-a-row in Cork.'

In 2002 that statistic was altered. Three-in-a-row in Munster followed. Back in the All-Ireland Club Final again. Now the unwanted tag of three-in-a-row losses in All-Ireland Club Finals hung over Nemo Rangers. Crossmolina were the opposition. Ideal opponents for the Cork side.

'I thought about the prospect of losing but felt playing Crossmolina would help.'

It did. But it was close. Too close.

'We nearly left it after us. But Colin Corkery hit a fantastic couple of points and the two years of heartbreak were over.'

One of his greatest moments?

'No doubt about it. To lose two club finals and come back and win one – that took some effort. Remember that was three long years on the road. Not many teams have the ability or the heart to do that.'

That victory marked the end of his tenure as Nemo Rangers' manager. Cork came calling and Morgan became the Rebels' boss.

Cork Come Calling

Billy's first term in charge coincided with the most successful era ever in Cork football. It also witnessed the most controversial incident, up to recently that is, in Cork GAA.

The opportunity he always wanted came his way in the autumn of 1986. The County Board appointed five senior football selectors, who then had to pick a manager. Billy Morgan was their choice.

'It was a job I always wanted to do.'

His reason was simple, apart from the ability to do the job.

'I felt for years there was a lack of interest in the football team. Very little organisation, except when Doney O'Donovan was in charge. Individuals becoming selectors just for the sake of it. It led to some very poor years. All because we were not preparing properly. That, and I also felt we had the players good enough to challenge the best in the country.'

Did the fact that he was not a selector hinder him?

'To be fair that was the system, but the selectors were good about it. I insisted that they listen to my opinions on players and they accepted that. I also sat in on selection meetings which helped.'

There was widespread approval in the county at his appointment. Indeed some felt it was long overdue.

Billy set about improving things immediately and the players responded.

'There was a real sense we could achieve something. Cork had enjoyed great success at minor and under-21 level and that talent was now coming through.'

Two other players entered the equation. They were both crucial to the successful era that was about to begin. Kildare natives, Larry Tompkins and Shay Fahy, threw their lot in with Cork. Tompkins was immediately impressed with Morgan's attitude.

'I had met Billy in New York and knew what he would bring to the job. I did not expect to play with Cork as I was only going to play club football with Castlehaven. But I was thrilled to get the opportunity to play inter-county football again.'

Larry felt Morgan was ahead of his time as a coach.

'Billy had huge passion – more than anyone I knew. Tactically he was brilliant and he was a great motivator.'

Nowadays much is made of the use of DVDs and laptops for players.

'Back then it was videos and Billy had an amount of them. Every team we played was discussed and analysed in detail – nothing was left to chance.'

If Tompkins was important to Cork, Larry is in little doubt about Morgan's contribution.

'Billy won those All-Irelands for us. If you couldn't play for Billy Morgan you couldn't play for anyone. It's as simple as that. I consider it an honour and a privilege to have played under him.'

As the 1987 Munster Final approached Billy was in confident mood.

'We had trained well, even if we struggled to beat Limerick in the semi-final.'

There was a feeling that Kerry's reign was about to end. Morgan ensured it did.

'We dominated the Munster Final. Larry kicked some great points. We were two points up and I was pleading with the referee to blow the whistle. Then Kerry got a goal. I was in a state of shock.'

The abiding memory of that Final is Morgan lying prostrate on the ground as his team faced defeat in dramatic circumstances. But there was a twist.

'John Kerins took a quick kick-out while the Kerry players were still celebrating. We won a free and Larry kicked the equaliser to force a replay.'

How did he feel at the final whistle?

'Relieved that we had got a draw which we deserved. I also felt we were good enough to win the replay.'

Tompkins recalls Billy's speech in the dressing room afterwards.

'Brilliant – he said all the right things. Positive and upbeat and he had no doubt we would win the replay, even though it was in Killarney.'

Morgan was spot on. A week later Kerry were blitzed and a new era in Munster football was ushered in. Billy, who had suffered before at Kerry's hands, was thrilled.

'It was a great feeling leaving Killarney that night. We also won convincingly which confirmed what I had thought a week earlier.'

Cork v Meath Epics

Thoughts now turned to the All-Ireland series. After another replay Cork beat Galway in the semi-final. Cork were back in the All-Ireland Final. It was the county's first since Morgan had led them to victory back in 1973. A familiar foe was waiting – Meath. It was to become an almost annual event for the next few years.

Meath won and Cork's wait would go on. Billy had few complaints.

'None really, they were the better team on the day. I still felt there was an All-Ireland in our team though.'

The following year, 1988, brought another Munster title. After beating Monaghan in the semi-final, Cork were back in the All-Ireland Final. For the second year in a row it was Cork v Meath. Cork adopted a different approach to this game.

'I felt we needed to impose ourselves on Meath who play a good physical game. I admired them for that. They played to their strengths and we had to match that.'

Cork more than matched Meath – they outplayed them. Victory was in sight.

'We played great and had the match won. Then the referee Tommy Sugrue gave them a very soft free. I was raging, no way was it a free. Stafford pointed it and that meant a replay.'

Cork's physical approach dominated the post-match reports. The replay was three weeks later and everyone was wondering how it would go. Billy was in no doubt how it would be played.

'It was going to be physical. Meath were a proud team and would not accept being pushed around. Word was that the Meath players told manager Seán Boylan they would play it their way in the replay.'

How Cork would respond would determine the outcome.

'We knew what to expect and were prepared for it. I told the lads if anything happened it was all in, to back one another up. They agreed that was the way to play.'

Cork were well on top, but one incident changed the whole course of the game.

'Meath footballer Gerry McEntee was sent off following an incident with Niall Cahalane. It upset our organisation more than Meath's. But we were still ahead at half-time and I was confident enough.'

However, Morgan admits he made an error in the dressing room at half-time.

'I told the players to keep playing football. What I should have said was, "Get stuck in and hit hard". Meath adopted the 'hit-'em-hard' approach and Sugrue was never going to send off a second Meath player. Some of their tackles were reckless and they went unpunished. In the end we lost by one point and it was very frustrating to come so close.'

Having lost to 14 men the team received some criticism. Was Billy coming under pressure?

'We did receive criticism but that goes with the territory. I didn't really come under pressure. Remember we had back-to-back Munster wins. That had not happened since 1973/74 and it took some pressure off. But I wanted an All-Ireland. Munster did not satisfy me and I still believed in the team.'

Much has been written about the contact, or lack of, between Cork and Meath players during that era. 'Even on holidays when we were in the same hotel there was little or no contact. But I had great admiration for them.

They play above themselves and never believe they're beaten. I wanted Cork to be just like them.'

If friendly chat between the players was non-existent, the same could not be said of the managers. Boylan and Morgan were, and still are, good friends.

'Yes, Seán and I always got on well. We both had jobs to do for our teams and we respected each other for that. And as everyone knows he gave me one of his potions for Mary's sinus problem.'

In 1989 Cork recorded a three-in-a-row of Munster football titles. They then defeated Dublin in a controversial semi-final and were back in the final. An important change had taken place. Morgan was now a selector.

'Nemo had won the county title and nominated me as a selector.

In 1988, forward Dinny Allen was recalled to the panel. Some had doubts about this but not Billy.

'I had no problem with it as I felt we needed something extra in attack. Dinny had a wealth of experience. He actually got the goal that won the Munster Final that year. His experience was also crucial in the 1989 semi-final win over Dublin.'

Mayo were Cork's opponents in the 1989 All-Ireland Final. This time the pressure was on.

'Well we put pressure on ourselves to win. But a third defeat would have been a huge setback. One we might not have recovered from.'

Billy is adamant about one thing.

'Had we lost I was gone. The Board would have ousted me.'

Cork did win, but only just.

'We got a great start – went four points up and we were playing well. Then we lost our way and Mayo battled back. Just after half-time Anthony Finnerty got a goal for Mayo and suddenly we were behind.'

What was he thinking at that moment?

'I was saying, "Oh no, here we go again", but credit to the lads, they regained the lead. And I was happy enough.'

Then a pivotal moment.

'We gave the ball away in the middle of the field. Mayo attacked and Finnerty got the ball again. I had a great view of it and his shot looked goal-bound. But somehow John (Kerins) got a hand to it and deflected it out. I can tell you it was a relief that Finnerty did not score.'

Had Mayo got a second goal would Cork have won?

'I'm not so sure. It would have been a huge blow. But thank God we got out of it with a three-point win. In fact we took over after that goal miss but we just could not put them away.'

It made for an edgy last 10 minutes.

'I aged a lot in that period, but it was a great feeling when it was all over.'

What did it mean to Billy that he had finally delivered Sam?

'I was very proud of the lads and all associated with the team. They deserved it for all their hard work over a three-year period. Remember it was our fourth final, if you count the replay, so we just needed to win.'

The fact that his great friend Dinny Allen was captain only added to the pleasure. However that was secondary. The important thing was that Cork were the All-Ireland football champions. It also completed a double as Cork had won the League title earlier in the year.

But Billy knew there was one more bridge to cross if they were to be remembered as a great team. The year 1990 was going to be a big year for Billy Morgan. There was the nagging doubt that they needed a big scalp to cement their place in history. That scalp would have to be Meath's.

'I felt that our achievements would not be recognised unless we beat Meath.'

So the targets for the 1990 Championship were simple – retain the title and hope Meath would get to the final. But before that there was a fiery National League quarter-final that added fuel to the fire.

'It was a bruising encounter and we came off second-best. Not only did we lose the game, we picked up a few nasty injuries that upset our

Championship preparation.'

With hindsight though, Morgan agrees it was the spur Cork needed. As does Larry Tompkins, who remembers Billy's pleading in the dressing room after the match.

'It was another great moment from Billy. He was practically on his knees saying, "I want to be back here (in Croke Park) in September and never ever will a team do that to us again." It really kickstarted our year. Billy said we might have lost the battle today but we will win the war.'

Ironically enough Tompkins did not play again until the Munster Final against Kerry.

Billy takes up the story.

'I remember the morning of the Munster Final we had so many injuries we literally did not know who was fit until we met in the hotel. I was really worried that we would not perform.'

His worries were unfounded. Colm O'Neill, a player who did not know he was playing until Sunday morning, gave a wonderful display. As did Tompkins.

'Colm O'Neill scored 11 points and Larry gave his best-ever performance in a Munster Final. It was our highest-ever winning margin over Kerry – four-in-a-row in Munster. Tremendous satisfaction. With 15 minutes still to go, I'm sitting down quite relaxed in the dugout. That rarely happens against Kerry. But we still wanted Meath in the All-Ireland.'

Billy got his wish. Yet it was a final that was played in a very sporting manner. Well apart from the hero of the Munster Final, Colm O'Neill getting sent off.

'In a funny way there was nothing really happening. Then Colm got sent off and I thought we could be in trouble here. But no, the lads reacted brilliantly and never lost their focus. In fact they doubled their efforts and at one stage we were four points ahead.'

As ever Meath came back.

'They did, but again we were outstanding – particularly Larry and Shay

(Fahy). Between them they scored 8 points (the match ended 0-11 to 0-9). It was Shay's best game ever for us. While Larry, even with a damaged knee, kicked two massive frees under pressure.'

Cork and Billy were now part of history. The victory completed a historic double for the county while dual star Teddy McCarthy had ensured immortality, winning All-Ireland hurling and football medals in the same year.

For Morgan though beating Meath was crucial.

'Well it wiped the slate clean for all of us. We had defeated Meath, ending years of heartbreak, and did it with 14 men, just as they did to us in 1988. It also meant no one could question the bottle of this Cork team.'

It has been said that were it not for the arrival of Tompkins and Fahy, Cork might not have been so successful.

'It would have taken longer to achieve what we did. Cork had enjoyed good success at minor and under-21. But there is no doubt these were two class players to have in our team. I suppose they were the final piece in the jigsaw.'

Coming home to Cork on the following night was special.

'It was a fantastic feeling. Having the two cups on the platform meant a great bond between hurlers and footballers. I can't see that happening again.'

If he ever had any doubts, Billy was now a hero on Leeside. Football was on a high and he had just presided over the best-ever era for the game in the county.

Kerry beaten in four successive Munster Finals, back-to-back All-Ireland wins – the football folk of Cork never had it so good.

'I enjoyed the celebrations as the players deserved every accolade they got. They were extremely dedicated – a fantastic bunch to work with. The amount of time and effort they put in made it all worthwhile.'

The County Board too played their part.

'They were excellent really, whatever we looked for we got. Very supportive at all times.'

Next on the agenda was the three-in-a-row. And that is what enticed him to remain in charge.

'I was thinking about giving it up. But I met Davey Barry downtown one day and told him how I felt. Davey said, "Billy, you can't leave now – we're going for three-in-a-row". So I stayed on.'

The 1991 Controversy

But as with all sport, things change quickly. Less than 12 months after this memorable triumph Morgan and Cork GAA were embroiled in huge controversy.

'The year 1991 was a funny year. I think the efforts of the previous four years took its toll. We had contested five All-Ireland Finals and I suppose we were drained. Also the open draw had arrived in Munster. That meant we were playing Kerry earlier than usual. Kerry won by two points and in a flash our season was over.'

How did he feel after that defeat?

'Naturally we were all disappointed. Our dreams of three-in-a-row had ended, but it had been a good innings and we could not complain.'

Did he now consider giving it all up?

'I hadn't really thought about it. But I suppose I wanted to stay on. I did not want to go after a loss.'

However that decision was taken out of his hands by an amazing decision by the GPC (Executive) of the Cork County Board. In their wisdom they decided not to recommend Billy for reappointment as a selector. Back then the GPC would nominate four selectors for ratification by the Board. The County champions would then appoint the fifth selector.

And how he found out only compounded matters. In fact he never even saw it coming.

'Ironically enough I was in the gym in Páirc Uí Chaoimh. I met a Board officer, purely by accident, and he told me moves were afoot not to put my name forward as a selector.'

How did he react?

'I was shocked. I could not believe it. I got in touch with Nemo Secretary Dave O'Kelly who in turn rang our Board delegate – a member of the GPC – but he gave O'Kelly no information. The delegate made some reference to it being a Cork thing and not a Nemo thing. In fact he was very unhelpful in the whole process.'

The meeting was actually taking place that same night. Delegates were stunned when Billy's name was not listed. Dave Loughman, Ray Cummins, Bob Honohan and Christy Collins were the four names appointed as selectors. No reasons were given. Without even a vote Billy Morgan was removed as a selector. All this less than 12 months after guiding Cork to back-to-back All-Ireland titles.

There was outrage in the county. It sent shockwaves throughout the Cork GAA fraternity. It also set in train a sequence of events never before seen in the GAA. The Cork County Board made a huge error, totally underestimating the level of support which Morgan now enjoyed. There was inevitable fallout, but not before a lot of dirty linen was washed in public.

It transpired that at the Executive meeting of the Board, Billy received little support.

'I understand that only two members supported me. But as one of them was a full-time official, he did not have a vote.'

All this meant that Billy's own club member refused to back him when his name came up for discussion. This surprised and annoyed Morgan.

'Two years previously the same club member and I had acted as selectors when Nemo won the All-Ireland club title. In fact he wrote an article for the Cork GAA Yearbook in which he praised my contribution to that win. Actually I still have the article.'

Under increasing pressure from clubs and several delegates who were supporting Billy Morgan, the Executive agreed to have another vote.

'At the next meeting, a week later, they added my name to the selectors' list. But at the same time they produced 10 reasons why my name was omitted initially.'

Was Billy surprised by this?

'Of course I was. Some of the reasons were very petty. They said I was drinking with the players late at night. Ah, they were silly things.'

There was also reference to an argument with Christy Cooney, now GAA President, over payment for a specialist in weight training.

'I did have words with Christy. It was over 25 pounds a session for this guy. I told Christy that if the Board would not pay it, I would pay it myself and slammed the phone down on him. The list was designed to undermine me and ensure I would not get elected.'

Billy was right. In the subsequent vote Billy finished last of the five. The four Executive nominees were duly elected. But this saga was far from over. One of those chosen by the Executive to replace Billy, Ray Cummins, is married to a sister of Billy's wife Mary. Ray immediately withdrew his name and wrote a stinging letter to the Board. Dave Loughman, who had always supported Billy, also withdrew as a selector. If the Board had planned to humiliate Morgan it was not working. It was they who were now faced with the humiliation.

Two of their four nominees not only withdrew from the committee, but were highly critical of the Executive. They were quickly followed by Bob Honohan who also withdrew. By now though Billy and Bob had fallen out and Bob was on the opposite side of the argument. That left only Christy Collins of the original Executive nominees standing as a selector. The whole sorry saga had taken on a life of its own. It was to take another twist, as Billy explains.

'All of a sudden, with the whole thing collapsing around them, the Board now wanted me as a selector. I remember I was working in West Cork one day and heard one of the very same Board officials on the Radio pleading with me to come back. I thought to myself, "Is this a joke or what?" At this stage I had no intention of going back.'

But pressure mounted on Billy to return. This intensified with a visit to his house by two County Board officers.

'I was at home on a Sunday night when Frank Murphy (County Secretary) and the Chairman Tony O'Mahoney called to see me. I agreed to speak to Frank but I would not talk to the Chairman. I had a good long chat with Frank that night but I still felt unsure of what I was going to do.'

The players, who at all times supported Billy, then entered the equation.

'I met the players in Bandon, almost a full attendance. They more or less said they would not play unless I went back. I was then in a bind. I didn't particularly want to go back, but I felt I owed the players that much.'

To fill the vacancies left by the withdrawal as selectors of Cummins, Loughman and Honohan, the Board nominated Teddy Holland and Liam Hodnett as replacements. There was another twist.

'A group of delegates who had always backed me had a meeting before the next County Board meeting. They asked me to attend so I could explain my position. I told them I was prepared to return but only if Ray Cummins and Dave Loughman were reappointed.'

That presented another problem. Where did that leave Teddy Holland and Liam Hodnett?

'It was agreed that Liam and Teddy should be informed of my exact position. Two lads at the meeting said they would phone them to explain the stance I was taken. Now I knew the calls were being made but there was a different angle put on the calls. People made out that the calls were of a threatening nature, which was not the case at all.'

As a result of these phone calls Liam Hodnett withdrew his name as a selector. The late Eamonn Young was appointed in his place. There was a Board investigation into the phone calls, but it revealed little and nothing ever came of it. Billy then got a phone call that had a bearing on his next move.

'Dave Loughman phoned me and said, "Billy, you have to go back. This was a war and in a war there are casualties. Ray and I are casualties but the war is won." I understood what he was saying, but I still had not made up my mind.'

Cork had a National League fixture coming up against Armagh. Billy had yet to declare his hand. As it was he decided to return. He received a tumultuous reception that afternoon in Páirc Uí Chaoimh.

'It was embarrassing really, but at the same time very moving. I got a standing ovation from the crowd. It made the whole thing worthwhile knowing I had the support of the public.'

Did he regret going back?

'Yes and no. I was determined to prove the Board wrong in trying to get rid of me. At the same time I was thinking was it worth it?'

It was a difficult and stressful time especially for his family.

'Horrible, it was horrible! The intrusion was the worst. Newspapers, radio stations and even television cameras outside the house – ah, it was awful stuff really.'

The support Billy got from his wife Mary helped him through many a crisis.

'Oh I don't think I would have survived without her support. Good times or bad, Mary has backed every decision I made. She always encouraged me to do what I felt was right at the time. The 1991 saga was the worst of the lot, but we got through it.'

More Munsters but All-Ireland Eludes

Billy remained in charge until 1996 and along the way picked up three more Munster titles. However another All-Ireland eluded him. But they came close.

'The Championship in 1992 was dogged by Larry getting sunburn and an infection a few days before we played Kerry in the Munster Final. We lost a scrappy game.'

In 1993 Larry was again central to Cork's challenge.

'We were flying. We beat Kerry in Killarney, hammered Mayo in the All-Ireland semi-final and we were playing Derry in the Final. I remember thinking while watching the Munster Final that we have a right chance of winning the All-Ireland this year.'

Then disaster struck in a club game.

'Larry done his cruciate and I have no doubt we would have won if we had him. As it was we nearly beat Derry even with 14 men. Tony Davis was sent off, unjustly as it turned out. But Derry used the extra man to good effect and beat us. Very disappointed. But when I heard about Larry's injury I just got a bad feeling about the rest of the Championship.'

Billy decided to retire after that game.

'On the way back down to Cork on the Monday after the game, I said to Frank Murphy that I was standing down. He asked me not to say anything. Then Nemo won the county and with Stephen O'Brien coming in as captain I stayed on. In fact I was given another two years. We won two Munsters but lost to Down in 1994 and Dublin in 1995, both in the semi-finals.'

Prior to the start of 1995, at the behest of Murphy, he had a meeting with Christy Cooney who had just taken over as Cork County Board chairman. It was the first dialogue he had engaged in with the officers who were involved in the 1991 saga.

'Some of them I haven't spoken to since, but I worked well with Jim Forbes when he became chairman. I had a meeting with Christy and Frank. I told them that what they had done to me (in 1991) was horrible. Christy admitted to me that "we got it wrong". Once he said that we became good friends and I thought he was an excellent chairman. In fact he was very supportive of me. I think he will make a very good president and I wish him well for the next three years.'

As for his relationship with Frank Murphy?

'Not bad. In fact we had a good working relationship. We did not always agree but we got on with our business. He defended me often enough. Indeed the last time when I got a six-month suspension he was brilliant. He tied the committee in knots and got my suspension reduced to two months.'

In 1995 he was about to walk away but Christy Cooney encouraged Billy to remain on.

'I was given a two-year term. We lost to Donegal in the league semi-final. Then Kerry beat us with two late points from Maurice Fitzgerald in the Munster Final and I decided to step down. But I wanted Larry (Tompkins) to replace me as I felt his drive would take the team on. I had gone stale myself anyway and the team needed a fresh voice.'

Billy then approached Christy Cooney and Larry with a view to a smooth transition.

Ten years at the helm were about to end.

Larry Tompkins succeeded Billy as Cork football manager.

The Kildare native had a hard act to follow. Little did either of them realise that their roles would change again in a few short years.

In all his years with club and county, Billy is adamant that the game must remain amateur and could not sustain 'pay for play'.

'No, the money is just not there, but the GAA must recognise the GPA and the sooner the better.'

Having been a 'players' man' all his life there is little surprise that he should adopt such a stance.

'We all want what is best for the GAA and the players are no different. Let's get it sorted and move forward together. Players' rights must be recognised. They are, after all, the most important asset the GAA has.'

As for Billy himself making him money out of the game – he laughs at the thought.

'I wish! No, I never took money for training any team and never would. The reality is the only two teams I trained are Nemo and Cork. I was approached by Wicklow some years ago. I was a consultant with them for a brief period, that was all. I went to a few training sessions and a couple of matches but it did not last long.'

Over the years Billy has had a fraught relationship with the media.

'First of all I realise you guys have a job to do. I respect and appreciate that, but I hate inaccurate reporting and that has happened to me a few times. I would be okay with guys who I would trust.'

As for trial by media, especially on TV?

'Sometimes they go over the top. Remember these lads were players themselves and were often involved in a few incidents over the years. They can easily forget that when criticising individual players.'

Billy has long been recognised as one of the most innovative and forward-thinking coaches of his time, always ready to embrace new training methods. Against all expectations the opportunity to do so at inter-county level would come his way one more time.

The Second Coming

In the autumn of 2003 Larry Tompkins left the Cork job. Billy Morgan was immediately touted as his replacement. It took Billy completely by surprise.

'I was amazed really. I had done my stint and did not expect to return. My name was being mentioned in reports but I had not given it much thought. Then Cork footballer Colin Corkery approached me and said a number of the players would be delighted if I came back.'

As he is now, Nicholas Murphy was a Cork player back then. Murphy was excited at the prospect of Morgan's return.

'We were delighted that his name was in the frame. Billy had given so much to Cork football that I, for one, was looking forward to playing for him.'

And when he eventually got the job – for the second time?

Nicholas Murphy explains, 'It created a great buzz among the players. We were down after a poor season and he immediately lifted us. Training was excellent and his approach to players gave us great confidence.

Personally I learned a lot under him. He really made you feel you were the best player in the country. That and the passion he brought to the team, were his main strengths. I don't think I have ever met anyone who had the passion Billy had for Cork football.'

They say you should never come back. Why did he and what convinced him to return?

'The approach from the players was important. Frank Murphy then contacted me. I made it clear to him there was to be no interview – I was available if the Board wanted me.'

One other factor was influential in allowing his name to go forward.

'After the strike in 2002 Cork managers were now allowed to pick their own selectors. That helped me make up my mind. If I didn't have that right I would not have returned.'

So, in the autumn of 2003, seven years after leaving the position, the second coming of Billy Morgan as Cork manager was about to begin. It was a changed Championship now – with the backdoor option there for all teams.

'I made a mistake the first year. I decided to give the players who played in Larry's last Championship campaign a chance. We were beaten by Fermanagh in the qualifiers and I knew then we had to go with the younger players. We scoured the county and picked up players like Ger Spillane and Donnacha O'Connor.'

While Billy enjoyed supremacy over Kerry in his first stint as manager, this time round the Kingdom would hold the upper hand.

'That's a fair comment I suppose but I felt we were making progress. In 2005 after they beat us in Munster we got a good run in the qualifiers. We then had to play them in the All-Ireland semi-final. They completely outplayed us that afternoon. They had obviously got stronger as the Championship progressed.'

If that was a setback, Cork recovered for the 2006 Championship.

'We did and should have won the Munster Final in Killarney, but we got a draw. In the replay we won comfortably. James Masters was brilliant that day scoring 1-7. I thought we were going well.'

However Kerry hit back. The two sides would collide again in the All-Ireland semi-final.

'It was hard enough to beat them once but now we had to do it again. We improved on the year before but still lost by six points.'

Could it be that Cork just did not believe they could beat Kerry in Croke Park?

'I never thought that. Every team I sent out I believed we could win no matter who we were playing against.'

A year later that theory would be tested to the full. September 2007 – the first ever Cork v Kerry All-Ireland Final. By now though Billy was certain this year (2007) would be his last year.

'I remember the morning of the final. I was sharing a room with Frank Cogan and I told him this was my last game. What I said to him was, "This is the very last time I will put on Cork gear". He advised me to hold tough, but I was certain I was off.'

An incident earlier in that 2007 season was also a contributory factor.

'I had decided during the year to have the dressing room cleared 45 minutes before games. As I was addressing the players before the Limerick game, Frank Murphy walked in. He apologised first and then went to close the door – from the inside. Now I was very calm. "No, Frank," I said, "would you please leave us as I want this time on our own." He left. He wasn't happy I can tell you. There and then I am certain I signed my epitaph as Cork manager.'

A Lasting Legacy

Did he regret returning for a second time as manager?

'Not one bit. I can tell you now the four years I spent with the present team were the happiest I had with any Cork team. A great bunch of selectors. Teddy Owens, one of the selectors, was outstanding with the training, while the players were a pleasure to deal with. Not a problem. I really hope they win an All-Ireland.'

As for the 2007 Final itself, Billy was devastated at the outcome.

'It was shattering and yet for a period we were in it. The pressure was all on Kerry, they had more to lose than us. All three goals were bizarre and if we had not conceded the first goal you might have had a different outcome. Even at half-time I felt we still had a chance. But the second goal changed all that. You could feel the tension drifting out of Kerry's game after that and there was no way back. Our players were nervous as well and that was a factor. To be fair the lads kept plugging away but the gap was just too big. The injury to Anthony Lynch did not help – losing such a key player a week before the game was a huge blow.'

It goes down as one of the major regrets of his career.

'Without question. I wanted to win an All-Ireland with that team. I felt they deserved it. That and the 1976 Munster Final are my two biggest regrets.'

Sadness too at the loss of two great players – the untimely deaths of John Kerins and Mick McCarthy.

'Terrible that those two young men should be taken from us. Great players but more importantly – outstanding individuals. I can tell you their deaths put everything into perspective. A very sad time for all who knew them.'

Highlights are easy.

'Three of them actually. 1972 – Nemo's first County title, 1973 – as Cork captain and the All-Ireland club win in 2002 after two successive defeats.'

In the weeks after the 2007 loss to Kerry, speculation was rife as to what Billy's intentions were.

'I actually made up my mind while on holiday with Mary. I discussed it with her and told her I was packing it in. Mary was probably hoping I would give it up, but she did say if you stay on I'll support you. But I had decided to go.'

Then at a County Board meeting a few weeks later a decision was made that convinced him his time was up.

'A motion was passed that the manager would no longer have the right to pick his own selectors. It was passed to make certain I would not continue. Those behind the motion knew I would not accept such a situation. I would not. But one way or another 2007 was always going to be my final year. If it was handled better, a lot of problems could have been avoided.'

The players disagreed with this decision and it led to another Cork strike – the second in five years.

Billy was approached by some players who were prepared to fight his cause in the hope he would stay on. But this time he was not for turning.

'I told the players to concentrate on getting the system changed and I would look after myself.'

A few weeks later as the crisis continued on Leeside, Billy Morgan broke his silence.

'I went to New York and ran the marathon and while there made up my mind to tell the Board of my intentions. On my return I wrote to Frank telling him I could not work under the system and withdrew my name for consideration.'

It brought the curtain down on a remarkable innings with the county. And this time he will not be back. For that matter he will now confine his involvement and activities to Nemo Rangers.

'Definitely not. I will not be back with Cork and I have no intention of training any other team. My sole focus now will be on Nemo.'

Billy, ever the competitor, now does a bit of running, completing several New York marathons. He plays a bit of golf – 'I'm not great now, mind,' he says.

'I enjoy the challenge of marathon running. It's tough but it keeps me in shape. It also allows me return to New York and meet up with the friends

I have there. As for golf I would love to play a lot more, but (he laughs) ask Dinny Allen how good I am.'

Over the course of an extraordinary career as player and manager, Billy Morgan has endured every aspect of emotion. The joy of winning. The pain of losing. Frustration. Agitation. Annoyance. But in the midst of all this he still retains his passion for football. Passion for his beloved Nemo Rangers. Passion for Cork.

His lasting legacy is that he left Cork football in a very healthy state after two stints at the helm. Even now he thinks the good times are on the way.

'I can see us (Cork) being dominant for a few years with a very good and young team. We will be in the shake-up in 2009.'

He may not be the coach but Cork are still his team.

Cork football and Billy Morgan . . . inseparable.

9

Joe Kernan

The 'Boot and Bonnet' Treatment

For over 30 years the small town of Crossmaglen in County Armagh was the centre of attention. Sadly it was for all the wrong reasons. The 'Troubles' in that part of Ireland dominated the news. The local GAA club became a focal point. Their facilities were occupied by the British Army – an occupation that began in 1971 and continued until 2007. It was a very difficult time. The club was struggling on and off the field.

Dressing rooms were damaged. Goalmouths were dug up. Fences were erected by the British Army and pitches were shortened to facilitate watchtowers. Tanks were driven through walls. Helicopters whirled in and out as the teams trained. It was harassment of a different sort. Those were worrying times for a proud club.

The situation was the subject of several Dáil debates. Successive

Taoisigh and Foreign Affairs Ministers raised the club's case with the British Government. Through it all though, Crossmaglen Rangers Gaelic Football Club survived. In the end it thrived. Today they are one of the most vibrant and successful clubs in the GAA.

The 'Cross', as they are popularly known, have many outstanding members. Foremost among them is Joe Kernan. On and off the field he has served his club and county with distinction. Joe was an outstanding footballer, winning five Armagh senior county titles. At inter-county level, he won three Ulster titles and two All-Star awards. Unfortunately the coveted All-Ireland senior medal eluded him. Joe retired from inter-county football in 1987. In 1988 he called time on his playing career with Cross.

Management was the next step and it was not long before 'Big Joe' got the call. Yet but for a decision taken many years ago, the GAA might never have heard of Joe Kernan.

Following the completion of his secondary education in Abbey CBS in Newry, the offer to travel arose.

Joe explains, 'Three members of my family emigrated to Australia and they asked me to go over to them. It was tough back then. Work was a wee bit scarce at the time. I gave it a lot of thought. In the end though, I decided to stay.'

Does he regret now not going?

'No, not at all! I would have missed an awful lot had I gone. Football kept me here and I'm glad I stayed.'

Ah yes, football – where it began and will end.

It all began for Joe over 44 years ago.

'My first ever medal was in the local street leagues. I was 11 at the time. I still have the medal in the house somewhere. Football has been my passion since that day, especially the club.'

The local GAA club is the bedrock of the association throughout the country – even more so in trying circumstances. Yet those circumstances, the occupation of their premises, actually strengthened their resolve.

Joe admits that while it was difficult, it bonded the town.

'It was (difficult) in one way and in another it helped. The club actually turned out to be our sanctuary. Whatever happened in the outside, and there was a lot, the members ensured the club kept going. That was very important. There is little doubt that a number of times the club came close to folding.'

If the club folded, Joe believes it would have been disastrous.

'Without doubt the town would have been devastated. We've a lot of people to thank for its survival. Not least our own members, particularly Gene McKenna who kept our case to the forefront in Croke Park. We're especially grateful to the late and great Con Murphy from Cork. That man was outstanding – even before he became GAA President, he was working on our behalf. What Con did for us will never be forgotten in Cross.'

Through it all, the players continued playing.

'In many ways we became immune to the Troubles and the harassment. We played the football and grew to love it. It was tough but it made us appreciate the importance of the club all the more.'

It must have been intimidating though?

'It was, and there's no point in saying otherwise. In fact you were singled out by the soldiers. Some of them would know you, others would not. Those that didn't were awkward. On the way to training or matches we would regularly be stopped. The minute they saw the football gear, they would delay us.'

The lads had a name for it.

'Yes, we called it the "boot and bonnet treatment". By that I mean it was always "open the boot and bonnet of the car", and then we were held up. It made life difficult for us all. But instead of deterring us, we became stronger individuals as a result.'

Training and matches were also affected, as helicopters regularly entered and left the base while these were in progress. This happened despite an agreement with the British Army that when games were taking place, they wouldn't be interrupted. It was an agreement the army ignored.

'It happened far too often. Training and games had to be stopped to allow the helicopters land in the compound. Then when we would resume they would decide to fly again. There is no doubt it was deliberate. We protested, but to no avail. All we got was the standard reply. The Army reply was, "The incoming and outgoing flight was necessary for operational purposes".'

How did their opponents feel about this?

'Well they themselves had similar problems. Not in an occupational sense, but as regards going to and coming from games. So they knew exactly what was happening and accepted the fact. But of course very few adult games could be played on our pitch – it was too small because of the tower at one end of the ground.'

Sadly it took its toll and members were lost – some in tragic circumstances. Others chose a different route.

'Achh we did! Some lads gave up the football, while a few lads decided to get involved in the "political" side of things. That was disappointing as we lost some great men. Men never got the opportunity to play the game they loved at the highest level. The club was poorer as a result.'

The occupation of their grounds continued for many years. Motions would appear on the *clár* of the GAA's Annual Congress for the withdrawal of the British Army. The motions would receive unanimous support, but such efforts had little effect as they were ignored by the British Government.

What was important, though, was the solid support of all 32 counties to Crossmaglen's plight.

Eventually it happened. It began on a phased basis, helped by the easing of the situation in the North. The occupation of their grounds finally ended in 2007. The watchtower was demolished and at last the pitch was back in its rightful hands. It was the end of a long and protracted campaign.

There was a sense of relief all round.

'We were all glad when it happened. Sadly, some men who fought hard for it had passed on and were not there to witness it. One of these was Con Murphy who had sadly died. That was a great pity. The club was well represented at his funeral.'

Losing My Own All-Ireland

In the midst of all the off-the-field distractions, the football continued. Joe was a key figure on the Cross senior team. Between 1971 and 1988 the club won five Armagh County titles. Joe was on all five teams.

All these wins were special.

'They were indeed, given the difficulties we were encountering. The first win especially, and we enjoyed the celebrations that it brought to the town.'

Nowadays, though, winning county titles is the least of the club's ambitions, as Joe explains.

'Well I won five and I thought that was great. But now my sons have a hell of a lot more than me. They also won Ulster and All-Ireland club medals, which I don't have. They're not shy in telling me as well I can tell you.'

Joe's inter-county career began in a Dr McKenna Cup game in 1971. It was to last for 16 years and he played in 6 Ulster Finals. In those days though, Ulster football was far from the force it is today. Dublin and Kerry were the dominant teams.

Joe did win three Ulster Championship medals. The first was secured in 1977. An All-Ireland Final appearance was to follow in September. It was the first time that Armagh graced All-Ireland Football Final day since 1953. Dublin were their opponents and they were also the reigning All-Ireland champions. It was a fabulous experience, even in defeat.

Joe takes up the story.

'There were good teams in Ulster and we considered ourselves to be a good team. The problem was that Dublin and Kerry were great teams, as the records show. I have no doubt we came at the wrong time. If they (Dublin and Kerry) were not around we would have won a couple of All-Irelands.'

The 1977 Final itself was a special day – while Armagh were well beaten, the day had its special moments.

'I actually scored two goals that day. But the way Dublin played I would have needed about another four to give us a chance. It was, the result apart, a memorable day. We (Armagh) had come from nowhere to win the Ulster title. We were also the first team from Ulster since Down to reach an All-Ireland Final. I remember walking around in the parade and the sea of orange in the crowd was unbelievable.'

On the game – goals win games and Dublin got them. Some of the soft variety.

'I actually watched the highlights the other night and they were soft. In fact I met Jimmy Keaveney recently and he admitted that for one of his goals he went for a point. It took him about 30 years to admit it though. But, look, the better team won. However it was an experience I wouldn't swap for the world.'

Joe is certain that reaching the final altered the mindset of Armagh GAA.

'It changed the lives of Armagh people. It shaped our future and made us more determined than ever to win Sam. It took us a long time to get it right, mind you. But playing in that final in 1977 bore bright in the minds of Armagh people. We wanted to win the All-Ireland and we wanted it badly.'

Joe was to win two more Ulster titles, but alas the big one never came his way – a huge regret.

'Ah sure, it would have been nice to win an All-Ireland medal, but that's sport. At least I got to play in a final, unlike some very good players in other counties.'

One regret though is the system then as against now. In Joe's playing career, it was a case of 'no back door'.

'Maybe we might have made more progress, but at the time I loved the cut and thrust of knockout football. Those were the rules at the time and we never gave it a second thought. I often wonder now though how we would have figured if we did get a second chance.'

What he did not achieve as a player, he was determined to do as a manager – bring the Sam Maguire to the Orchard County.

In 1989, his former playing colleague Paddy Moriarty was appointed Armagh manager. Joe was one of his selectors. However three years later and with no Ulster title won, Moriarty resigned.

'Cross' Breeds Success

Joe did not apply for the job. Instead it was back to his roots. Crossmaglen Rangers would now dominate his life. It was his first shot at management.

The club's fortunes had gone into decline. It was 10 years since the last senior county title had been won. Kernan set about arresting that decline. It all began with the winning of 4 successive under-21 titles. It was the springboard for a golden era for the famed Cross. Joe took over in 1992 and immediately set about changing the way they played.

'For the first two or three years it was a rebuilding process. We changed from a traditional catch and kick. We adopted the possession game and mixed both styles. I looked at the three Ulster teams that won All-Irelands and also the great Kerry team to gain an insight into what was required. You try and pick out phases and get your players to adapt it into their own play.'

It slowly began to pay dividends as the players and Kernan became accustomed to one another. 1996 was the year of the breakthrough, the Armagh county title was won and the 10-year-wait was over. It was the beginning of the phenomenon that is Crossmaglen Rangers today.

In November 1996 the first Ulster Club title was won. The journey though would continue.

'Having won the Ulster title, we just took off. We got to the All-Ireland Club Final on St Patrick's Day, 1997. Knockmore from County Mayo were our opponents and we won. On that team we had 11 under-21 players.'

Kernan traces the success to a field in Mosney, County Meath.

'The team that won in 1997, I remember watching them in a Community Games Final in Mosney. They won the All-Ireland 'B' Final that day. Incredibly, 11 of them were on the team that won the first All-Ireland Club Final.'

It gets better.

'Those 11 players kept playing through all the success. In fact six of them played in the All-Ireland Club Final defeat, back on St Patrick's Day in 2009.'

Let us put this in perspective. Since that first win in 1996, Crossmaglen Rangers have not lost an Armagh Championship game – a record that will surely never be equalled, let alone beaten.

'Fantastic really. At this point in time we are going for our fifteenth successive county title. We have come close a few times to losing, but have survived. Oisín McConville, Cathal Short, Francey Bellew, Paul Hearty and the McEntees, John and Tony, all have 14 county medals in a row.'

In that period Crossmaglen made an art out of winning close games, as Joe explains.

'We did! We could never put away a team. In fact we won several games by just one point. But I got great satisfaction out of winning that way. It showed the character of the lads. It stood to them for many years, as they proved very hard to beat.'

At the same time these lads were on the Armagh county team.

'Indeed they were. But if you look after the players properly and do things right, you will have no problems.'

For the record, Crossmaglen Rangers also hold six Ulster Club titles and four All-Ireland titles. Their loss to Kilmacud Crokes in the final on St

Patrick's Day 2009 was the first time they were beaten in Croke Park.

In 2000, having guided Cross to a third All-Ireland club title in four years, Joe decided to step down. It was an easy decision to make.

'Well you can only take a team so far and I had done that. Also as a club we were lucky to have very talented coaches coming through, so it was in good hands.'

By now of course, his four sons – Stephen, Aaron, Tony and Paul – were making their presence felt in the Cross colours. A fifth son, Ross, will soon join them.

Did that influence his decision?

'Not really! I had them with me for a few years. There was never a problem, so I was comfortable with it. As they were also.'

On the Big Stage

Joe might have stepped down from the manager's job at Crossmaglen Rangers but it would not be long before he would be donning the Bainisteoir's bib once again. Except this time it would be the Armagh one. After an approach from the Armagh County Board officers, Joe Kernan was back on the big stage.

It was November 2001 – the beginning of another incredible journey. It was a job he approached with a degree of trepidation, but buoyed by his success with Crossmaglen.

'Well it's the ultimate honour to be asked to manage your county team. I was privileged to wear the Armagh jersey. Now I wanted to give something back to the county. The driving ambition was to end our long wait to win an All-Ireland. I firmly believed we had the players capable of doing that. The task was to get them (the players) to believe it.'

While he would be considered his own man, he didn't look too far for inspiration.

'Two managers stood out for me. Mick O'Dwyer in Kerry and Seán

Boylan in Meath. I had, still have, huge admiration for the way Kerry play their football, while the spirit in which Meath played was something that I hoped my teams would replicate.'

Although conscious of the need to stamp his own authority on the team, there were aspects of Meath and Kerry's techniques that he used.

'Kerry, for instance, simplified the game. Nelligan (goalkeeper) to Páidí (Ó Sé) to Jacko (O'Shea) who in turn would get it to the 'Bomber' (Liston) near the goal – and that was hard to play against.'

What about Meath?

'I remember one day they were playing Roscommon in an All-Ireland semi-final. With seven minutes to go, they were behind by six points. Now teams in that position often gave up – but not these guys. They went on and won the game. That's spirit.'

So as he set out on the journey, he had the blueprint. It was now time to put it into action.

The Ulster Championship of 2002 was as competitive as ever.

Joe made no secret of his ambition and his priority: To win the Ulster Championship en route to the All-Ireland.

'The hardest part sometimes is winning the Provincial Championship. Okay, you had the cushion of the qualifiers. But I felt the team needed to go on to Croke Park as Ulster champions. That would be setting down a marker.'

Joe's first Championship game as manager was against Mickey Harte's Tyrone. It was the beginning of an intense rivalry that would shape Joe's tenure as Armagh manager. Clones was the venue and at the end of a tense contest it ended level. Joe was happy.

'Well I was, because we didn't lose. And we had another game to sort out a few things, which we did.'

It was back to Clones a week later, and this time Armagh were ready.

'A cracking game! Tyrone scored 16 points, but we got 2 goals and they were crucial and we won by 3 points, 2-13 to 0-16.'

A throwback to his days with Crossmaglen. Win a tight game. It was the tightest test they got in Ulster.

'As the campaign progressed we improved, as I hoped we would. Fermanagh gave us little trouble in the semi-final while we went on to beat Donegal by four points in the Ulster Final.'

So a short few months after his appointment, Joe had delivered the Anglo-Celt Cup to a growing band of Armagh supporters.

A sense of relief then when they were crowned Ulster champions?

'Not so much relief, but delight. It was our first title in three years. The trick now was not to sit on our laurels but to drive on. Ulster titles are great but All-Irelands are the ultimate goal. Many a great player has the Ulster medal in his pocket, but he doesn't have the All-Ireland medal to back it up.'

It was as though he was referring to himself – and those of his own generation.

There was one big barrier to overcome first. It was not Sligo, their quarter-final opponents, but the venue – Croke Park. Amazingly, it was 25 years since an Armagh team had won a Championship game at the venue.

A test for an emerging team?

'It was I suppose. But all the good teams win in Croke Park and we were a good team.'

Was there a fear that they might not be able to handle the pressure of trying to win there?

'No! Once we won Ulster I felt we were capable of winning anywhere and against anyone.'

Sligo were eventually dispatched – but not at Croke Park. It took a replay in Navan to see off the men from Yeats County. The wait to win at HQ would continue. But not for long.

'We were lucky the first day. Sligo could have won. In the replay it was close again – we won by 2 points, 1-16 to 0-17. Now that was a relief. In a way though, it helped, as we were written off as Championship contenders after those games.'

The Jersey & The Medal

And so to the semi-final in Croke Park. This time more formidable opponents were waiting – Dublin and their massive support. Memories of 1977 came flooding back. Revenge for that defeat perhaps?

'Not really! I was the only link with that game, and we wanted to get to a final. Dublin just happened to be in the way of that objective.'

Playing the Dubs on their home patch was just what they wanted. Physically the team had changed – Armagh were now a very strong team. If Joe Kernan was their leader off the field, he had an able general on the field – Kieran McGeeney, who was the heartbeat of the team.

But the team had many people Kernan trusted in, and they trusted him. Tactically they had also developed and were hard to beat. Kernan and his selectors had employed the 'zone defence' (group defence of specified areas of the field). It might not have been pretty but it was effective. Very effective in fact. So much so that other teams soon followed and incorporated it into their own game plan.

'We did not set out to be defensive, but we did our best to be good in defence. There is a difference. Our view was simple. Defending is part of the game and we worked hard on it.

'The forwards in any team generally get the plaudits for winning games. But they won't win anything without good backs. So we said let Number 15 be as good at defending as Number 2 – and we will be hard to beat.'

The stage was set then for a huge day in Croke Park for the semi-final – and the first of Joe's legendary 'stunts'.

Half-time, game in the balance. Armagh retreat to the sanctuary of the dressing room, trailing and in a bit of trouble. Joe had an ace up his sleeve.

In advance of the game the selectors had discussed the possibility of them being behind at half-time.

'We did – and we were wondering how to deal with it. That is when I hit on the idea of producing the jersey.'

Ah yes! The jersey! Not just any jersey though. This was different. It was the jersey Joe had worn in the 1977 All-Ireland Final defeat to Dublin. This was special.

'It meant a lot to me, still does. Anyway I got it out of my bag at the break. I said to the lads, "this is special. I want you lads to have one. A jersey that ye wore in an All-Ireland Final. I think ye deserve it for what ye have done for Armagh football.'

It worked?

'It did. We made a few changes as well, but the boys went out in the second-half and played very well to win the game.'

What did they win by? Yes – one point!

'We were making a habit of it, but it's like any habit, winning is a nice one.'

He enjoyed winning by the one point.

'Winning by one point is the greatest score of all time. Winning by 12 or 13 points never did anything for me – well, apart from allowing me to relax every now and again at a match.' Which, judging by the closeness of some of their games, was not too often.

They also enjoyed a bit of good fortune at the end of the game.

'Ray Cosgrove had a free kick to draw the match, but luckily for us it hit the post and we survived.'

So Armagh were back in the final. Only their second in 57 years. And they had finally won a Championship game in Croke Park. If they could win one more they would be All-Ireland champions.

What did it mean to Joe?

'Fantastic really! Just a few months in the job and now 70 minutes away from winning. It lifted the whole county. We had watched as other Ulster teams won the Sam Maguire. Now we wanted to do it ourselves and for our county. Indeed for all the great Armagh players who had gone before us.'

However there was a major obstacle in their path. Kerry. The aristocrats of football. Yet it was a challenge that Armagh relished.

'For Armagh to be playing Kerry in an All-Ireland Final was great. There was a huge sense of occasion around the county. Everybody was looking forward to it.'

How do you deal with the hype?

'It's not easy in a county like ours as the players would be meeting supporters on a regular basis. They were level-headed enough about it though. We just got on with our own business of preparing the team. It was an exciting time for us all.'

The big day finally arrived and, not surprisingly, Kerry were favourites and that suited Armagh.

'Of course it did as the pressure was off, but we put pressure on ourselves to win. We had come this far and the opportunity might not present itself again.'

Armagh did not start well. Final day nerves perhaps?

'Perhaps,' says Joe. 'It was, after all, the biggest day of their lives.'

Kerry looked comfortable. Then Armagh were awarded a penalty. An opportunity to settle the nerves?

To the consternation of their supporters, Oisín McConville missed. Kerry were still five points ahead.

Joe takes up the story.

'We missed the penalty but almost immediately Diarmuid Marsden tackled a Kerry player right under the Cusack Stand. We gained possession and from it we got a point.'

Was it the pivotal moment in the match?

'Without a doubt – if we went in at half-time not having scored after missing the penalty, we wouldn't have won. But we were hanging in there. The boys had character and I felt good at the break.'

It was a day for hanging in?

'It was, and the longer you hang in there the better chance you have of winning.'

Kerry had a four-point lead. A handy lead in football, and Kerry know how to protect leads.

'They do, and it was still a decent lead, but we were far from beaten.'

They were not – and once again Joe would spring a surprise.

For the second game in a row in Croke Park, Joe had an ace up his sleeve. Or in this case a medal. Like the jersey it was his own. But he did not want his players to have a similar one. Joe laughs as he recalls the story.

'The medal was the runners-up one I got for the All-Ireland Final of 1977. It was a poor imitation really. A bit of silver in the middle on a piece of timber. I had one, but this group deserved better.'

The team talk continued, a few changes were made, and then the medal got a bit of a bashing.

'I said to the boys, "look ye have the All-Ireland jersey. This is what I got for the only final I played in. It's no good to me – it never has been". And I fired it across the dressing room. It smashed into tiny pieces – "now go out there and win yourselves the real thing".'

He then produced a second medal with the help of a member of his backroom team.

'My good friend, Eamonn Macken. Mr Fix-It we call him. He had an All-Ireland medal he bought at an auction. "Now boys", I said, "I want you to have one of these – it's in your own hands from here on."'

It was a different Armagh team that took to the field for the second-half.

The first thing they needed to do was raise the intensity of their game.

'We felt we needed to put more pressure on Kerry to have a chance and that is where our leaders stood out.'

Diarmuid Marsden got a goal and Armagh were ahead by the now customary one point. Could they hold on?

'It was the longest 12 minutes of my life, but we battled and battled, and a few subtle touches along the way helped.'

Apart from the goal there was one particular moment when Joe felt they would win.

'Near the end the ball broke in midfield. There was a bit of "ping pong" as I call it. Eventually one of our lads got it. I turned to the boys on the line and said, "this is our day".'

For the second-half Joe was very animated on the line – his body actions reflecting developments on the field.

'I kicked every ball. I just wanted them to do well. They were, and still are, a special group. I willed them to win.'

An abiding memory. Game in injury-time. Joe with outstretched arms. What were his thoughts?

'I looked at the referee and was saying, "would ye blow the fucking whistle?" '

Fittingly, when the referee finally called full-time, Tony McEntee was in possession for Armagh.

'Yeah, Tony had given great service and broke an ankle early in the season. He made a huge effort and got back for the final. It was appropriate that he should clear the last ball.'

The ultimate had been achieved. Along the way the 'big two' – Dublin and Kerry – were beaten, making it extra special.

'Without a shadow of doubt it's hard to win the All-Ireland – but to beat them both on the way showed the resolve within the group.'

After the Party

The celebrations and the victorious homecoming are something that will stay with Joe for the rest of his life.

'It was an amazing scene both immediately after the match and at the banquet that night in the City West Hotel. The homecoming, travelling over the border. Going through the towns on the way to Armagh City – Keady, Silverbridge, Crossmaglen – magical moments.'

'As we passed through other counties, normally our rivals, we got a welcome. There was huge goodwill towards our team. We really appreciated that.'

It was, and remains, the highlight of his career. The transition from player to manager was complete. Even if he found it difficult at the start.

'Look, there is no substitute for playing really and it wasn't easy at first. But the experience with my club stood to me. That was a big help.'

So too was the outstanding support from the Armagh Board and people.

'My job was made easy by the wonderful support I got from the Armagh County Board. No problems whatsoever, they wanted to win the All-Ireland badly. It was very important for the game in the county.'

Of course his managerial stint at his club, Crossmaglen, left him well grounded for the task.

'The players were fantastic and as I was coming from a winning vein with my club, they realised if we all pulled together we too could be winners.'

There were no issues within the squad and in this regard Joe feels the GPA was good for the GAA.

'They probably came along at the right time. Everybody needs a kick in the backside now and again. We were overlooking certain things that should have been done and were not. Maybe in some counties – but not all. Players, all players, must be looked after.'

But should they get official recognition from Croke Park?

'I think we are at a crossroads. It needs Dessie Farrell and someone from Croke Park to sit down and deal with the issues. Some of the things the GPA were looking for, could not be given – as an association we could not sustain it. The GAA and GPA are there for the benefit of players, but there should be a better working relationship between both parties.'

One thing he is adamant on though – 'pay for play' is a non-runner.

'No question, we as an association could not afford it. Clubs in particular would suffer, we were built on the amateur ethos and we should remember that.'

Having landed the All-Ireland in his very first year as manager it was always going to be hard to replicate that success in his second year. But they made some effort. The celebrations were long and hard, but Joe called a halt in January 2003.

'I decided to stop it all and told the lads, and to be fair they were keen to get back to training. I myself attended over 50 functions and turned down about another 50 invitations. That shows how much it meant to the people of Armagh.'

'We actually lost our opening game in Ulster to Monaghan. That sent us on the scenic route, the qualifiers. But to the lads' credit, they got on with it, determined to prove they were not one-hit wonders.'

After a long campaign, Armagh made it back to the All-Ireland Final. In the opposite corner, an old adversary – Tyrone.

A first-ever all-Ulster Final. Vindication that the province was now the strongest of the four, contrary to the opinion of some. Does it annoy Joe and others from Ulster that they did not receive due recognition for their efforts?

'What upset me more was the view that every time an Ulster team won the All-Ireland, it was considered to be a poor All-Ireland. Yet over the years I have seen some dreadful Championships and not an Ulster team in sight. Ulster sides, my own included, brought their own particular style to the Championship. That's what makes our competitions special. Teams adapt and modify their styles over the years. Ulster was no different.'

It was also hard to imagine that he ever thought he would witness an all-Ulster All-Ireland Final. And the hosting of the Ulster Final in Croke Park.

'Great times to be involved and it showed the appeal of the Ulster Championship. Getting capacity crowds in Croke Park was a testimony to the loyalty of the Ulster supporters. It made for a fabulous sense of occasion. Especially for the families who might not get to All-Ireland Finals. For that the Ulster Council are to be applauded for their foresight.'

Now the stage was set for an epic All-Ireland final. Could Armagh win back-to-back titles? It had not been done since Cork in 1989 and 1990.

It was not to be though, as Tyrone edged a tense contest by 3 points: 0-12 to 0-9. A major disappointment. It would not be the first time that Mickey Harte would get the better of Joe in Croke Park.

Armagh did win the Ulster Championship in 2004 beating Donegal in the Final, the first Ulster decider to be played in Croke Park. However there was another setback in the All-Ireland quarter-final. Fermanagh won by 1 point, 0-12 to 0-11.

'Yes that was a blow but credit to Fermanagh, they played well. Remember they had already beaten Cork. We had no complaints with the result.'

Did that put pressure on his position?

'No, not a bit! As I said, the Armagh County Board never gave me anything but one hundred per cent support.'

The players too were fully behind Joe, and he himself was ultra loyal to them. That loyalty surfaced many times, but once in exceptional circumstances. When his star player, Oisín McConville, went public with his gambling addiction, Kernan had nothing but praise for his fellow Cross man.

'You never know what is going on in a person's life. But through it all Oisín displayed immense courage. It took huge guts to admit that he lost nearly €100,000. The guy has character, but then I always knew that.'

It made Joe and his team all the more determined in 2005 and they targeted the League. In fact Armagh had never won the League. Motivation in itself.

'Well, we felt we needed to make a statement and we adopted a different approach to the League. It went very well for us. The final was a huge occasion with over 40,000 in Croke Park.'

It was an unusual pairing – Armagh v Wexford. Wexford had won the group game, but this time there would be no mistake by Armagh. However it was only a means to an end.

'We won by 7 points, 1-21 to 1-14 in a good competitive match. It was our first League title, which was nice. But there was no celebrating. The cup was parked, and the focus now switched to the Championship.'

The drive and hunger to win a second All-Ireland was still there.

'Good teams win one. Great teams win two and three. We wanted to be remembered for winning more than one.'

Armagh safely negotiated their path to the Ulster Final. Waiting for them was Tyrone.

Another cracking game that Armagh won by 2 points: 0-13 to 0-11.

But Tyrone had not gone away. In fact they would exact revenge in the All-Ireland semi-final. It's the system you see. It goes back to a point Joe made earlier.

'Well in the old days, Tyrone would be gone. Now we had to beat them again to reach the All-Ireland Final. In my time if we had a second chance we would have won an All-Ireland. Now we had to work twice as hard to win a second.

The semi-final will go down as one of the more memorable clashes between these two great rivals. It had everything. Passages of fabulous football, quality scores, a dramatic finish and a controversial substitution.

The McGeeney Substitution

'It was one of the best games I was involved in and unfortunately we lost and by just one point – a scoreline that I had been on the right side of in the past. But that's sport. Fair play to Peter (Canavan) – it was a great score to win the game.'

With the game in the balance, Joe made a big call. Some would say the unthinkable. He replaced his general. Kieran McGeeney was withdrawn. Apart from the game, it was the story that made the headlines the following day. It is said even now, four years on, that McGeeney is still miffed at the decision. Joe though is clear on why he made the call.

'It was a huge call, that I accept, but that's my job. I don't know if Kieran is still annoyed with being taken off. Maybe he is but he has never said it to me. But the facts are simple. Our stats man told us Kieran had not touched the ball in 17 minutes. Now for your main man not to be on the ball for that length of time is not good. In fact when he went off we got a point to go two ahead and then fell asleep for five minutes and lost a match we should have won.'

What about the fact that some say the opposition kept the play well away from Kieran's area of the pitch, aware of his value to your team?

'That could be the case alright, but we still felt, and still feel, it was the right call at the time. We made the change hoping to freshen things up and to get on the ball. That was our call then, and we stand over the decision. But you must remember we only lost by one point and that [substitution] was not the winning and losing of the game.'

It must have given Tyrone a boost to see McGeeney being replaced?

'Maybe, maybe not, but it's done now and we cannot change the result.'

What is clear though is Joe's respect and admiration for McGeeney.

'He was the most driven player I ever worked with. Intense, sometimes I felt too intense. But that is the way he was built and he was a real leader.'

McGeeney stands alongside Mick O'Connell, Mick O'Dwyer and Down's Colm McAlarney as players Joe Kernan admired.

So another bad day in HQ?

'Anytime you lose an All-Ireland semi-final is not a good day. But I was still convinced we could win that second All-Ireland.'

A good enough reason then to stay in charge for another year?

The Ulster Championship was won for the third year in a row in 2006. That was another unique achievement as Armagh became the first team since Down in 1959-1961 to win the three-in-a-row in the Province.

But the All-Ireland title eluded Armagh. Kerry ended their 2006 season in the quarter-final with an emphatic 3-15 to 1-13 win. There was widespread speculation that Joe would call it a day, but he decided to carry on.

'My situation had not changed. I still believed in the team and I had the support of the players and County Board. I saw no need to step aside.'

However the end of Joe's stint as Armagh boss came in July 2007.

Stepping Down

Defeat to Donegal after a replay in the Ulster Championship was followed by a qualifier loss to Derry.

'After that game I gave the matter a lot of thought and spoke to a few people whose opinion I would respect. I could have stayed on but I felt it was right to go.'

A hard decision to make?

'No question. But look, I knew when to retire as a player and you just know these things. The team needed a new voice and a new direction.'

No regrets?

'Just one – that the team did not get the second All-Ireland I felt we deserved, but other than that, no, not really.'

'It was a tough few weeks when I made the decision and then when it became public. But I like to think I left Armagh football in a healthy state.'

Of that there is little doubt. In his tenure in charge, Armagh won five Ulster titles, one National League title and of course the All-Ireland title as well.

In all they played 36 Championship games under Joe, winning 23, drawing 6 and losing just 7.

That in any manager's language is an impressive record.

'It is I suppose, but it's not all about matches. I made great friends the length and breadth of the country and they are still friends today, which is important.'

The highlight was of course winning the All-Ireland.

'Oh yeah, but side by side with that would be the first All-Ireland Club title with Crossmaglen – that too was very special.'

So after a wonderful innings Joe moved on, but he is still very vocal on all aspects of the GAA. The ban on winter training is one he's not so sure about.

'I think it's unfair when the season starts in January. Players with little training behind them could get injured and that could hamper their year.'

How do you get the balance right?

'In my view we need to monitor the younger players. Especially the lads playing under-21 and third level. Our young players serve too many managers and that's not good. Any serious athlete will tell you – give me two or three weeks off at the end of every year and that will do. But a two-month break serves no real purpose.'

Having been involved for so long, Joe built up a good relationship with the media.

'I always took the view that the lads had a job to do. I was never one for banning media nights or such like. But I'd protect players and always got the co-operation from the press for that.'

Now he finds himself a member of the media as an analyst for TV3. Just as he did as a player he pulls no punches. However he is conscious of players and what they endure.

'You must call it as you see it, but at the same time show the players some respect.'

In fact the day we met was just 48 hours after an ill-tempered 2009 Ulster Championship match between Derry and Monaghan. But Joe had little time for what went on in that match.

'I understand the physicality in the game but that was over the top. It did little for the image of Ulster football and must be stamped out. I have no difficulty in being critical of players and teams if they break the rules, but at all times it must be balanced. Fair and balanced, that's the way I deal with incidents.'

One major gripe with Joe is players feigning injury to get others sent off.

'I hate that. Many a time I got a belt but I wouldn't go down. Now I see players getting a belt, a fair one, but trying to get opponents sent off. This is the worse aspect in our game. It needs to be stamped out. I'd like to see referees deal with these guys swiftly. They'd soon cop on. That, and the 'verbals' some guys go on with, annoy me.'

Of course since giving up the Armagh job, he has been linked with every managerial vacancy that has arisen in the GAA. Will he return to the inter-county scene?

'Unlikely! I've my time done and I couldn't see myself training another team that could end up facing Armagh.'

He's back in management in a small capacity as manager to the Ulster team.

'Well I always loved playing in the Railway Cup as it was then known, so I was delighted to accept the invitation from the Ulster Council to do the job. We will see how it goes. It's only for a couple of weeks at the end of the year so it's not too time consuming.'

As for the reputed big money on offer to some managers?

'There might be, but I never got it. Nor would I want it. Football has been good to me at club and county level and I was just glad to give something back. Even now when I visit clubs to give the wee lads a training session, I get insulted if I'm offered any sort of payment. I was glad when I was a young boy to get coaching so I appreciate what clubs are trying to do.'

His main involvement now is with his beloved Crossmaglen Rangers.

'I'm doing a bit of coaching with the young lads, but mainly I'm on the Development Committee. We have a lot going on, putting in a new pitch and dressing rooms and terracing the entire ground, along with floodlights. It makes you proud to see what we now have compared to when the place was occupied by the army.'

Joe now runs a successful auctioneering business in his native Crossmaglen, but admits it's tough going. 'It is a bit quiet right now, but hopefully things will improve soon.'

As a pastime Joe plays a bit of golf and in 2008 he was instrumental in setting up the GAA Legends Golf.

'You have to have played with your county to be a member and in our first year we raised €92,000 for charity. In 2009 it was down a bit, understandable given the current climate. Hopefully we will get it back up next year. We have official recognition from Croke Park and we go to Spain every year to play. It's fabulous.'

'Players I had many a tough tussle with on the field are involved. We have great craic and at the same time raise some money for worthy causes.'

Throughout his career, Joe has enjoyed the support of his family.

'I could not have stayed involved for so long without it. They may not have liked my moods on the morning of a match. My wife, Patricia, has been a rock of support. Now it's starting all over again with the five lads. But in good times and bad, they were there and that is important.'

Mentioning family reminds me that Joe's cousin is the renowned International Show Jumper, James Kernan.

'I see him on a regular basis. We're neighbours in fact. We're all very proud of what James achieved jumping for Ireland. Being a close-knit family, we were delighted for him.'

The international dimension to the GAA is also important, even if at times it resembled boxing rather than football.

'The series last year was very good. I think it's important that our players get an opportunity to represent their country. It's the ultimate honour. But unless Australia improves in the next couple of years, the series could be in trouble.'

It is somewhat ironic that we finish with Australia. His sisters are still out there and as he says himself, 'The Australian dog still hasn't barked.'

The GAA in Crossmaglen, in County Armagh and in the country as a whole are better for having Joe Kernan in their midst.

As a player, and then as a manager, he has left an indelible mark on Gaelic Football.

Note: In September 2009 Joe Kernan was appointed manager of the Galway football team.

10

Jimmy Barry Murphy

In Family Tradition

Jimmy Barry Murphy – even the name has a ring to it – has been an iconic figure in Cork GAA since first bursting onto the scene as a 19-year-old in 1973.

In a never-to-be-forgotten season, he was an integral part of a Cork football team that swept all before them as they bridged a 28-year-gap to win the All-Ireland title in 1973. Yet he is best known for his hurling exploits, not surprising when you consider the family background.

Jimmy's GAA lineage makes interesting reading. His uncles and his father, John, played with Cork. In fact John won an All-Ireland hurling medal in 1940. His grand-uncle Dinny captained the Rebels to an All-Ireland hurling win in 1929. Little wonder then that the GAA was Jimmy's calling, even though as a young lad he dabbled briefly in League of Ireland soccer with the now departed Cork Celtic.

'It was really hurling which was special as I grew up around the game. There are family connections with Cloughduv and, of course, St Finbarr's. In our house the talk all the time was of hurling and football. It was very easy for me to start playing the games. Of course I got great encouragement from everyone around me.'

There are numerous sporting events that are etched in Cork people's minds. Jimmy is in no doubt that 1973 ranks among them. 'It certainly is (etched), along with 1966, the three-in-a-row from 1976 to 1978, the double in 1990 and the 1999 win, but that football win in 1973 was special and I consider myself fortunate to have been part of a fabulous team. I was actually picked for the footballers before the hurlers, a team that had been knocking on the door for a few years, but it all came together under Doney O'Donovan. I suppose I was lucky to be there as some of the players were coming to the end of their careers and really deserved a senior medal.'

'It was an exciting campaign, beating Kerry in the Munster Final down at the old park (Cork Athletic Grounds). We got five goals that day, then we got another five in the win over Galway in the All-Ireland Final. The pity is of course that the team did not go on to win more. But if the truth be known, as a group the celebrations went on too long. And while we beat Kerry in the Munster Final in Killarney the following year (1974), which is never easy, Dublin beat us in the All-Ireland semi-final. In a few short years the team broke up and then along came the great Kerry team and Cork had to wait all of nine years for another Munster title. By then I had retired from inter-county football.'

A Dual Player Chooses

One of the first of the game's dual players Jimmy combined both for a few years, but when the choice had to be made, hurling was always going to win out.

'Yeah it was! I must say now I enjoyed playing football but the calls grew and when I finally gave up in 1980, the Munster Final that year was my last football game with Cork. It was an easy decision as the demands on a dual player were too much.'

Jimmy's career is littered with honours.

'I had a great career really in terms of winning medals, but also the friendships I made. I suppose in hurling it came in two phases. I broke into the team in 1975 when we won the Munster Championship but we lost a sensational match to a John Connolly-inspired Galway in the All-Ireland semi-final which was a huge shock. But we went on then to win the three-in-a-row. We missed out in 1982 and 1983 when I was captain – a regret perhaps. It was at the time. In retrospect, I probably made too much of the fact that I was captain and regretted the loss even more as a result – but you get over that and move on. Then 1984 was extra special as we won the Centenary Final in Thurles with John Fenton as captain – a fabulous honour for John. Then in 1986, my last year, we beat Galway in the Final with Johnny Clifford, a great friend of mine as coach – so I have no complaints really.'

In all, Jimmy won ten Munster hurling medals, two football medals and eight hurling medals and of course was selected as an All-Star in both codes. 'It's funny I suppose, but I never lost a Championship match to Tipperary in senior, minor or under-21.'

At club level he was just as successful: five county hurling medals and six football medals in the blue of St Finbarr's and All-Ireland Club medals in both codes. On one famous weekend he played with the 'Barrs in a club final and 24 hours later lined out with both Munster teams in the Railway

Cup Finals, scoring four goals against Ulster in the football decider. Jimmy pulled the blinds down on his career after the 1986 All-Ireland win over Galway.

The 1977 Controversy

Throughout his playing career Jimmy never courted controversy. However it visited him just once. It first surfaced in the Munster Football Final of 1976. On that day the Cork team wore gear supplied by Adidas. The Cork County Board were against such an arrangement. The fact that Cork lost meant it was not pursued by the Board.

Twelve months later the controversy re-surfaced. On this occasion the footballers again defied the Board and wore Adidas gear when playing Kerry in the Munster Final.

Cork lost, but this time the Board took action. After the Final the Board suspended the entire team from football activities only. 'Unusual' is the best way to describe that decision. As a dual player Jimmy was caught in the middle. The Cork hurlers were preparing for the All-Ireland semi-final against Galway. Was there a danger that Jimmy would not play in the hurling game?

'It was a Cork solution to a Cork problem I suppose. There was a lot of tension around at the time. In fact it was nasty for a while. The footballers had a few meetings and these meetings can be draining. It certainly was not a nice business to be involved in. There was a possibility we (Brian Murphy was another dual player involved at the time) would not play. We felt we did not want to let down our football colleagues by going off playing hurling. We were anxious it be resolved before the Galway game. To be fair the football lads did not want us to miss the hurling game. Thankfully it was resolved, the suspension was lifted and it all ended well. We beat Galway and went on to win the All-Ireland Hurling Championship a few weeks later. It was the only time in my career that there was conflict with the Board, and I was glad it did not drag on.'

Time to Leave the Field

Was it the right time to leave after the 1986 All-Ireland win over Galway – and has Jimmy any regrets?

'It was really that I felt I had done enough. The appetite was waning a bit and when that goes you know it's time to move on. I stopped playing with the club as well because if I had played with the 'Barrs, the pressure would have come on to return with Cork and I just did not want that. I knew I'd made the right decision but when I went to the Munster Hurling Final against Tipperary in Killarney in 1987, I was thinking how I would've loved to be playing. I remember a few days after that game, Tom Cashman said to me, "Jimmy, if you were playing we would have won". But, look, that's sport and the urge to play quickly passed. I had done my bit on the field and there were good players coming on stream – as there always is in Cork.'

Having retired from playing the obvious next step for Jimmy was management. When the call came he did not hesitate.

'It was Denis McCarthy, then Chairman of the 'Barrs minor committee, who asked me to give a hand with the minor hurling team and I did. It went well. We won a few county titles and I must say I really enjoyed the experience. After that I took charge of the Cork minor hurlers. Again we had success. Charlie McCarthy was also involved and after a few near misses we eventually won the All-Ireland in 1995. Young lads were easy to deal with. They are keen and enthusiastic, and that makes it a very enjoyable experience.'

Getting the Top Job

In October 1995 Jimmy Barry Murphy was appointed Cork Senior Hurling manager and immediately expectation levels in the county began to grow. It was six years since the last All-Ireland win and supporters were growing impatient. But it was by no means easy in the beginning and Jimmy, for the first time in his career, was the subject of some unkind press coverage due to the fact that he had not managed at senior level before.

In terms of management Jimmy had learned a lot from those he played under.

'I know it's a bit of a cliché but having played under great coaches in Fr Bertie Troy, Canon Michael O'Brien, Gerald McCarthy, Justin McCarthy and Johnny Clifford, I like to think I picked up something from all of them. While individually they brought something different to the job, they all had the same philosophy about hurling – it's a simple game and keep it simple. So my idea was to play the way Cork teams had always played. While no one coach influenced me, I was impressed by all of them – excellent coaches in their own right.'

One other man left a huge impression on Jimmy. He was the incomparable Christy Ring who was a selector during the three-in-a-row years.

'Christy was remarkable and it was fascinating to be in the same dressing room as the greatest hurler ever. His fanaticism for Cork hurling had to be seen. He was quiet during the first year (1976), but for the following two years he developed a unique bond with the players. He became much more involved in the team talks and his eye for the smallest little detail helped swing a few games our way. I thought he was brilliant and it was a huge honour to have known and worked under him.'

Training methods of course had changed dramatically by the time Jimmy was appointed Cork manager. Kevin Kehilly had introduced some revolutionary methods in the late 1970s, but by the 1990s the training regime had moved on again and the transition went smoothly enough.

'Well by now the backroom team had increased to include dieticians, physios and weights training. You adapt for the good of the team. My own ethos in training any team was trust. You must have trust between players and management and that in itself will help team spirit – put the two together and you have a winning combination.'

He has an interesting observation to make of the present-day hurlers and in particular the Cork squad. 'This is only a personal opinion – but I think the fun has gone out of their game. They might not like me saying this, but you must have characters in your dressing room. We had some great guys who had the capacity to relieve the tension on a big day. For me a highlight of my coaching career with Cork was the fun and craic we had in training and on away days. But at the same time we worked hard and the players were very dedicated and in the end got their rewards.'

Fair Play

The next question is the obvious one: is the influence and impact the GPA has had on the GAA good or bad?

'The GPA are going to be part of the Association from here on in. That should be accepted and both parties should work together for the betterment of players as all these things are very important – especially player welfare. I have no problem with that. As a traditionalist I initially had doubts about their motives, but now with goodwill on both sides it can be embraced and there is definitely a place for the GPA within the organisation.'

One thing Jimmy is adamant about though is the 'pay for play' issue.

'Without question, there is no place for that in the GAA and certainly as an organisation we could not sustain it now. Once there is uniformity in the way players are looked after, whatever county they come from, that should be the important thing – and payment for players must never be an issue.'

As Jimmy embarked on his senior management tenure with Cork there was a marked increase in the level of media coverage from his own playing days. He has mixed views on the impact it has on the games, remembering that he was once part of *The Sunday Game* panel when the show was in its infancy.

'The most important thing is that the exposure our games are getting is excellent. It has increased the awareness of the skill level of our high-profile players among so many more people without, it must be said, impacting on the crowds that want to attend live games. That is crucial as spectator involvement adds so much to Championship matches. But 'trial by television' concerns me. It was something that I was conscious of when I was on *The Sunday Game*. After all, players are amateurs, they have families and they have to go to work on Monday.'

Respect is the one word that Jimmy would advocate when analysing games and players.

'Criticism is part of our game and we have all had it during our careers, but it must not become personal. Guys in the studio should, and indeed must, keep a sense of perspective when dealing with players while at the same time not shirking their responsibility if players go beyond what the rules permit and commit fouls that have no place in our games.'

Dealing with the media as a manager surfaced for the first time in 1996 after a heavy opening round defeat to Limerick in his first Munster Championship at the helm. Initially Jimmy found it very difficult.

'There were a couple of issues that I was unhappy with. I felt I was treated unfairly especially by one individual, a journalist with the *Irish Examiner,* who took a particular angle on the defeat. He caricatured me in a certain way – even mocked me at a coaching conference I attended. Also he hammered me on a personal level which I was very bitter about for awhile. I spoke to him about it but we agreed to differ. There is a line that should not be crossed and I felt he did. But we must all live with ourselves, and eventually I got over it and moved on.'

Right Job – Wrong Time?

If he had his time over again, Jimmy would not have taken the senior manager job when it was offered to him in 1995.

'Looking back on it now, it was very naive of me to take the job. Going from minor to senior was something I should not have done because I was not really ready for the senior job. In hindsight I should have gone to the under-21 team for a year or two to gain a bit more experience at inter-county management and then moved up to senior – but hindsight is a great thing.

'What I found was that at senior level you're dealing with elite players in your county and I had no experience of dealing with adult players. It took some time to adjust. I made plenty of mistakes in the first year but the Board had placed their trust in me and thankfully they gave me the time to settle into the job. I must say that in the years in which I was in charge, I got great support from the County Board. I never wanted for anything in terms of preparation. They were very patient and understanding and so were the supporters – a bit different from now.'

In a strange way that defeat to Limerick, and in particular the scale of it (it was Cork's heaviest loss in the Championship for over 40 years and their first loss at home since the 1930s) marked a turning point for Jimmy and his vision of what he wanted for the team.

It was time for change.

'Cork had gone through a period without success and in that first year I made very little change to the panel. But that Limerick result convinced me of what was needed. I had to put my own stamp on the team. Along with the selectors, who I must say were excellent, we identified team positions and areas that needed strengthening and the players who were required to achieve that. We decided to go with a youth policy for the next three years in an effort to win the All-Ireland. Crucially, though, we still had a core of experienced players who were fantastic for us – the likes of Brian Corcoran, Fergal Ryan, Alan Browne and Fergal McCormack. Our team was going to be built around these guys and they would give the younger lads the time and space they required to develop.'

Once again the support of the Board was vital.

'Yes, absolutely! They backed us to the hilt and that was important.

I was given four years in which to do the job and I'm not so sure you would be given that sort of leeway now. Would they be patient? And indeed we have seen here in Cork that it is something the players might not tolerate but back then they were much younger. However the press and the public might not be so patient and expectations in Cork are always so high. But we got the leeway and it worked – although there were a few little blips along the way.'

Clare – the Team to Beat

Clare at that time (the late 1990s) were the hurling team to beat and they stood in Cork's way. They beat Cork in the 1997 Munster Championship on their way to their second title, as they sought to reach the promised land of combined Munster and All-Ireland glory. As Jimmy acknowledges, 'they were a superb side. They won two All-Irelands and probably should have won three but for the controversial ending against Offaly in 2000. They were the benchmark really and for a few years they had our measure in terms of experience, and to be fair in hurling ability also as Ger Loughnane had moulded a fine team.'

The format in those years was also a factor – a case of one defeat and it was season over. While a GAA traditionalist at heart, Jimmy is a huge fan of the present format and has no doubt it would have helped his young team back then.

'First of all let me say there is nothing to match the magic of the Munster Championship – especially a final in Thurles, a unique and special atmosphere unmatched anywhere in sport. But I'm in favour of the present format and without a doubt if it was there in my time as coach we would have benefited greatly – but it wasn't and you play with the hand you're dealt with.'

Hurling, he also advocates, needs its high-profile games especially with all other major sporting events now enjoying huge publicity.

'The reality is that because of its small playing base, hurling needs all the exposure it can get. There is little to be gained from seeing your best players in just one high-profile game every year, where a dodgy call or two or even bad weather could shape your season. Look at Joe Canning, for example. What a great player and under the old system we might only see him play once. So while I am all in favour of retaining the Provincial Championships, the present system, while not perfect, is the best there is and it would be cruel to work hard for three or four months to see it all wiped out in just 70 minutes.'

The year 1998 saw Jimmy pick up his first piece of silverware as Cork senior manager. While it was not the one he wanted, it was a start and it was also important.

'Well for that year we made a huge effort in the League as we felt the young players needed to be exposed to high-profile games against the better teams to find out exactly where we stood in terms of progress. To be fair they worked hard and got their reward. After all there are only two competitions open to senior inter-county players and the best of players cherish a National League medal.'

In Munster, Cork beat Clare in the semi-final and Waterford in the final, but Loughnane and the Banner County were waiting in the long grass come July in the Championship and another year ended in defeat. A disappointment?

'No question it was, but we as selectors felt we were making progress and the next year would be pivotal. It was make or break really – there was a lot riding on 1999.'

And like a good poker player Jimmy played his full hand in the first round of the Munster Championship against Waterford with his former coach Gerald McCarthy in the opposite corner.

There was a sense of disbelief around the county when the team was announced, as it contained six players new to Championship hurling. Jimmy takes up the story.

'It's simple enough really. We gambled because we were running out of time. I knew that day if we lost to Waterford my coaching career with Cork was over. I couldn't go on forever and we and the players just had to deliver – and to be fair they did.'

Cork won and Jimmy in atypical fashion showed huge emotion at the end, racing onto the pitch to embrace his players and with them a legion of fans. Remember this was only a first round.

'I know but it was a huge relief. The players stood up and were counted. Cork were back in the Munster Final and with it into the All-Ireland semi-final (as the format had now changed), where we had not been for a while. It really was the start of something special and it was a fantastic day.'

The Munster Final itself was another huge day and guess who were waiting in the other corner – yes, Clare – but Jimmy was glad.

'I was really, as they were the team to beat. They had knocked us out of the Championship for the previous two years and we were well motivated for the final. With it being in Thurles, I knew we would be ready for the challenge.' They were.

Cork won. Now the wagon was on a roll and it was gaining momentum.

Back to Winning Ways

The winning of the Munster Championship sparked a new generation of hurling heroes on Leeside and they were young and vibrant.

'They were superb and they galvanised the county with huge support, especially the likes of Joe Deane and Seanie McGrath – two players who were brilliant to deal with as they played with a flare I always associated with Cork hurling. You just could not teach those guys some of the things they did on a hurling field – it was great to watch.'

But the train very nearly came off the tracks in the All-Ireland semi-final on a wet and miserable Sunday in August when Offaly tested a young Cork side to the limits. Jimmy appreciated just how close it was.

'We were very lucky and maybe we might have underestimated Offaly a little bit. But at the end of a superb game we just got there and the prospect of being back in the final was fantastic. It was something we were all looking forward to. It was our first final in six years and for Cork that was a long time.'

Expectations on Leeside were high as the big day approached where traditional rivals Kilkenny stood between Cork and the ultimate honour. As it did for the semi-final, it rained and on a dark and dull September afternoon a huge wave of emotion swept over Croke Park as Jimmy's and Cork's final hurdle to glory was surmounted.

As a spectacle it was by no means great but that did not trouble the manager and he summed it up as 'the proudest moment of my career,' even surpassing his own playing days and achievements.

'No question about it – to be part of bringing Cork hurling back to the top was special. The manner in which it was done made it extra special. We won tight games and the players dug deep so many times you just knew they were not going to be beaten.'

At one stage in the second-half of the final, Kilkenny opened up a slight lead. 'Well it was a worry but the way we came back and outfought them in horrendous conditions made it a memorable day. It may not have been a great game, and as a spectacle it was poor, but at the end we won. With Brian Corcoran – a colossus – I just knew we would get there in the end.'

Once again Jimmy's emotions took over and his post-match celebrations surprised even himself as he, not for the first time in his career, was the hero for Cork hurling folk.

Memories of the defeats to Kilkenny in 1982 and 1983 when he was captain came flooding back.

'We had suffered at their hands but it was unrestrained joy and a huge release of emotion, because I knew that my managerial career with Cork was coming to a close. I was just so happy that we had finally won the All-Ireland. The lads I worked with were all good friends and played a huge part in the win – Johnny Crowley, Tom Cashman, Seanie O'Leary, Fred Sheedy and trainer Ted Owens. A great group to be working with.'

The next evening Cork returned home to a welcome unsurpassed on Leeside, the size of which surprised Jimmy.

'Unbelievable really, and when we turned into the famous Paddy Barry's corner the sea of red that greeted us showed what hurling meant to the people of Cork. It was the proudest night of my life when I spoke to the crowd from the stage on behalf of a special bunch of players who made it all possible.'

It was also the start of a new breed of Cork supporter that still exists today. The class of 1999 with JBM at the helm had done hurling a huge favour.

Time to Go

Strangely enough Jimmy contemplated opting out after that win. A case of objective achieved?

'I did as I felt we would find it hard to replicate what we had just done. However I stayed on and to be fair we won another Munster Final beating Tipperary in Thurles which was a great achievement. But when we lost to Offaly in the All-Ireland semi-final I knew it was time to go.'

And as honest as ever, Jimmy knew hard calls were needed.

'I felt burnt out at that stage as the defeats of the early years had also drained me. Also I would not have been ruthless enough to deal with certain players who had delivered the goods for me. So it was time to walk away and enjoy all that I had.'

So after what seemed a lifetime of involvement as a player and coach it was back to some degree of normality and he looked forward to it.

'Well it did impact on my family but coming from such a GAA background they understood what it meant. My wife Jean's father, Mick Kennefick, captained Cork to win the All-Ireland in 1941 so there was no real problem there. With Brian now playing too, they understood.'

It's a source of immense pride to Jimmy that his son, Brian Barry Murphy, now plays soccer with English League Two side Bury FC and of course he has an avid interest in his career.

'We touch base nearly every second day. Then I go over once or twice a year. They (Bury FC) are a very small club and face huge competition from the bigger clubs in the area. They are based very near Manchester. Not a whole lot of money there in the club. They operate off very tight margins. As a club though they are very homely and friendly and make you feel welcome. Brian has had a very successful career for himself. He's enjoying his time there and they are doing well. Hopefully they'll gain promotion.

In 2009 they narrowly missed out on automatic promotion to League One by a goal difference of one. Then in the play-offs they lost out to Shrewsbury Town on penalties – just to rub it in!

'He had success with Cork City and won international caps at under-18 and under-21 level which is a great honour – to represent your country.'

'Brian is in England now over 10 years, well settled and enjoys a good lifestyle there. Hopefully it will continue that way for him. It's a tough game now with the recession but he's done well.'

Having stepped down in 2000, Jimmy to this day remains the longest-serving Cork hurling coach in recent times. After a few years' break he took over his club, St Finbarr's, for three years but the county title so cherished by the senior clubs eluded him.

The Greyhounds

And so it was back to his other favourite pastime – greyhounds, a passion that he has enjoyed for years now, and one that will occupy him for the foreseeable future. As with hurling and football, greyhounds are a big part of Jimmy's life.

'We always had greyhounds, my grandfather and father had them. It was a traditional thing in our house. I inherited that passion from my father. I got involved in owning and training a few greyhounds at home. Then when the new greyhound stadium, Curraheen Park, opened here in Cork in April 2000, it increased my involvement.

'Pascal Taggart appointed me Chairman of the Board of Curraheen Park. It was an exciting time, the building of the new stadium. It meant being in at the start of the development and meeting with local owners and local management.

'Noel Holland had a big input and it was great to be involved. It was a passion for me anyway and I was always going there (Curraheen Park) so to see it completed was exciting.'

Has Jimmy any ambition to win one of the big ones, the Derby or the Oaks?

'Well I still have a couple of dogs in training but it's tough going. It's hard to get a good dog nowadays. Anyway it's more of a hobby than anything else. I still go to the track, especially Saturday nights, and meet up with a few friends and have the craic.'

Jimmy also used the greyhounds as a form of relaxation in his playing days.

'The night before a big game in Dublin can be boring. I found a few hours in Shelbourne Park eased the tension. Some lads went to the pictures or played snooker. I went to the dogs and we had great fun, particularly with Johnny Crowley and Tomás Mulcahy.'

Any big win yet with the dogs?

'No – but the dream lives on.'

Trouble in the Field

In March 2009 Jimmy was thrust back into the limelight when along with former colleagues, Denis Coughlan and John Fenton, he was asked by GAA President Christy Cooney and Ard Stiúrthóir Páraic Duffy to pick a new

Cork senior hurling manager following the resignation of Gerald McCarthy after a protracted and bitter dispute on Leeside. It was a task that gave him little pleasure.

'Certainly not! I had no intention of getting involved in Cork hurling again as I had done my time. It was breaking my heart to see what was going on in Cork hurling and football over the last few years. It was something I thought I would never see happening but for many and varied reasons it has happened. I was involved as a colleague with individuals on both sides in the dispute. I played with and trained under Gerald McCarthy and coached several of the players.'

The decision to help was not taken lightly.

'I thought about it long and hard and was reluctant to get involved, as it is fair to say, there were wrongs on both sides. But in the end I felt if I could make a contribution to bringing Cork forward then I would and hopefully that is the case.'

As for the new manager Denis Walsh, Jimmy is certain that they have got it right.

'Denis will do an excellent job and will be a very unifying figure in time throughout the county. The dispute has left it very divided especially among traditional Cork supporters. He was a great player and hopefully he will be given the support that I got from all sides, players and the Board. Then he will deliver for Cork.'

Jimmy though could not resist one last calling and when it came he just had to say 'yes'.

'I know I thought it was over in a management sense, but Cloughduv is the club of my late father. Many family members asked me at the start of 2009 to give a hand with their junior team and I must say that the lads on and off the field are brilliant to work with. It's a club that I have a strong affinity with – mainly due to the very strong family connections. Hopefully we will have a good year. The main thing is that I'm enjoying it and at the same time helping the lads.'

Jimmy Barry Murphy is one of nature's gentlemen – an outstanding hurler and footballer in his day and a manager that brought glory to a county he served with great distinction over a long and illustrious career. Now he can reflect and say, 'I'd like to think that I made some contribution to the GAA – on and off the field.'

It's a sentiment very few would disagree with.

Seánie McGrath on JBM

As a player Jimmy was idolised by Cork supporters young and old. One such admirer was Seánie McGrath, who considered it a huge honour to play hurling under his idol.

'Jimmy picked me on the Cork minor team in 1993. Unfortunately we were beaten by Tipperary in the Munster Final. That probably broke his heart considering his own record against Tipperary. Then in 1997 he gave me my big break with the senior team.'

It was the beginning of a friendship that is as strong as ever today. Seánie appreciates the support he got from JBM, even when things were not going his way.

'He had a great way of handling players. Always encouraging you to work on your touch. Especially for guys like me. I wasn't that big but if your touch is right everything else will be okay.'

Jimmy also allowed his players great freedom as Seánie explains.

'If he thought you had ability he gave you the freedom to express yourself. He also trusted players and that in turn gained him their trust. And respect. It made you feel honoured to play for him. Okay, we were playing for Cork, but you felt you were playing for Jimmy. When we lost you felt more upset for him than anyone else.'

Jimmy's training sessions were based on skill more than physical contact and his teams played accordingly.

Seánie takes up the story.

'Everything was done at pace. Move. Move. Keep the ball going. Get your touch right. Good ball into the forwards. Great sessions, really enjoyable – that was his theme. Train as you play. He relied a lot on trainer Ted Owens, Ted was excellent. But there was no doubt who was in control.

'The dressing-room banter that year was brilliant. Jimmy, Ted Owens and Dr Con Murphy. Jimmy and the 'Doc' had great craic and were always ball-hopping. It made for a wonderful atmosphere – a factor in our winning the All-Ireland in 1999.'

If the All-Ireland win in 1999 was special for Jimmy, it was equally so for the team. It was also Seánie's only senior All-Ireland medal.

'Yeah but what a year! Remarkable winning it for Jimmy and the few little small touches that made the difference. In the dressing room before the final he personally presented each player with their jersey. Shook our hands and wished us luck. Very emotional. Really motivated us to play for him. Then in the match itself one moment stands out for me. Before the game he told me "just play your natural game and you'll be okay". But I wasn't going well. Missed a few chances in the first-half. Then at half-time he just said, "keep going, you're doing fine". That helped, but it was still not going my way in the second-half. Then it happened. I was out near the sideline on the Cusack Stand side. I caught his eye. He just clapped his hands and said, "well done, keep going". Now he must have been under pressure to replace me. I felt under pressure myself. But after that little cameo I relaxed. A couple of minutes later, my chance came. I knew I had to take it. The ball flew across the pitch, my touch was great and I sent it over the bar for my first point. I got two more points and we won by one point. I felt I had repaid my faith in him by winning the title for him as much as for myself.'

There were other times when Seánie witnessed the respect in which Jimmy was held – not just in Cork.

'In Derry one year after a league game he spoke to the hurling people there. The reaction was incredible – and the respect they had for him. A few years later I met Charlie Carter, who played with Kilkenny in the 1999 Final. Jimmy, he said, came into their dressing room (Kilkenny's) after that game and he never witnessed anything like it. You could hear a pin drop when he spoke. Massive respect for him in Kilkenny.'

When asked what stood out for Seánie in his years playing under Jimmy, apart from his hurling knowledge, the answer was short and to the point – 'his smile, it just lit up the dressing room every time he walked in'.

A fitting tribute to a man who put a smile on Cork hurling as a player and as a Bainisteoir.

ACHIEVEMENTS

Mick O'Dwyer

As Player: 4 All-Ireland football medals, 11 Munster Championship medals and 7 National League medals.

As Manager: 1975, 1978 – 1981, 1984 – 1986: All-Ireland Senior Football titles (Kerry)
11 Munster Championships and 3 National Leagues
Leinster Championships (Kildare, Laois)
Tommy Murphy Cup (Wicklow)

Brian Cody

As Player: 5 All-Ireland hurling medals, 7 Leinster Championship medals, 2 National Leagues and 2 All-Stars awards.
County, Leinster and All-Ireland Club medals

As Manager: 2000, 2002, 2003, 2006 – 2009: All-Ireland Senior Hurling titles (Kilkenny)
10 Leinster Championships and 5 National Leagues.

Kevin Heffernan

As Player: 1 All-Ireland football medal, 4 Leinster Championship medals, 21 Dublin County Championship medals with St Vincent's (15 in football, 6 in hurling).

As Manager: 1974, 1976, 1983: All-Ireland Senior Football titles (Dublin)
5 Leinster Championships, 2 National Leagues

Seán Boylan

As Manager: 1987, 1988. 1996, 1999: All-Ireland Senior Football titles (Meath)
8 Leinster Championships and 3 National Leagues.

Note: Longest-serving inter-county manager - 23 years with Meath.
Also managed the Ireland International Rules team and the Meath Senior Hurlers.

Ger Loughnane

As Player: 2 National League medals and an All-Star award
As Manager: 1995, 1997: All-Ireland Senior Hurling titles (Clare)
                 3 Munster Championships

Mickey Harte

As Manager: 2003, 2005, 2008: All-Ireland Senior Football titles
                 (Tyrone)
                 3 Ulster Championships and 1 National League.
                 He also managed his club, Errigal Ciaran, to Tyrone and
                 Ulster titles.

Páidí Ó Sé

As Player: 8 All-Ireland medals, 11 Munster Championship medals,
4 All-Ireland Under-21 medals, 4 National Football
League medals.

As Manager: 1997, 2000: All-Ireland Senior Football titles (Kerry)
6 Munster Championship titles, 1 National League
1995 All-Ireland Under-21 Football title (Kerry)
Leinster Championship (Westmeath)

Billy Morgan

As Player: 1 All-Ireland football medal, 5 Munster Championship
medals, an All-Star award and 1 Texaco Player of the year
award (1973)
County, Munster and All-Ireland club medals with Nemo
Rangers.

As Manager: 1989, 1990: All-Ireland Senior Football titles (Cork)
7 Munster Championships and 1 National League.

Note: Billy Morgan remains the only goalkeeper to have
received the Texaco award.

Joe Kernan

As Player: 1 Ulster Championship medal and 2 All-Star awards.
5 County Medals and 3 Ulster medals with Crossmaglen
Rangers

As Manager: 2002 All-Ireland Senior Football title (Armagh)
4 Ulster Championships and 1 National League.
3 All-Ireland club titles, 4 Ulster club titles and 5 County
titles.

Jimmy Barry Murphy

As Player: 5 All-Ireland hurling medals, 10 Munster Hurling
Championship medals.
1 All-Ireland Football medal and 2 Munster Football
Championship medals.
Dual All-Star winner with his club, St Finbarrs
County (Munster) and All-Ireland medals in both hurling
and football.

As Manager: 1999 All-Ireland Senior Hurling title (Cork)
2 Munster Championships, 1 National League,
1995 All-Ireland Minor Hurling title (Cork)

Tunnel Vision

Behind the Scenes at Great Irish Sports Events

Tadhg de Brún

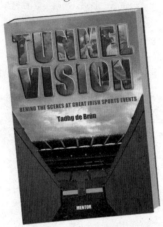

Tunnel Vision takes the reader where no Irish sports book has ever gone before – behind the scenes at great Irish sporting events – from the Irish Open to the Heineken Cup to the All-Ireland Finals. Over 30 years with RTÉ Sports as event/floor manager has given Tadhg de Brún a unique insight into the stories and secrets at all the biggest Irish sporting events.

- Memories of the Irish Open – the golfers, their egos and their problems – and some very rewarding bets placed by the RTÉ crew!
- Snooker Finals at Goffs – the tension and the chaos; how Dennis Taylor was neatly put in his 'seat' after complaining about the facilities.
- All-Ireland Final days – the craziness *not* shown on TV; how the Kilkenny captain emerged from the victorious dressing room dressed in boots and gear and rushed off to church.
- The characters you meet on the road – the managers, players, caterers, cleaners, as well as the rakes of Liberty Square and the security man at the Brandywell. The comedy and tragedy of their lives as witnessed on great sporting occasions.
- Behind the great events of the Charlton Era, including an eventful trip by Tadhg and his crew to the World Cup in America in 1994.

Working On A Dream

A year on the road with Waterford footballers

DAMIAN LAWLOR

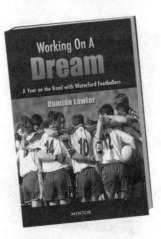

Far from the madding crowds of Croke Park, the inflated egos of star players and boardroom wrangles in the top counties, some GAA teams are fighting for their very existence....

Working On A Dream goes where no Irish sports book has ever gone before - a no holds barred, behind-the-scenes look at an intercounty GAA team struggling to survive at the lower end of the scale: Waterford senior footballers.

With access to all areas, the author, award-winning journalist Damian Lawlor, spent the 2009 season on trains, planes and in the dressing room with the Waterford players as they chase their goals for the year: climbing out of Division 4 of the national league and winning a championship game.

The tale that emerged is an honest, dramatic, sometimes tragic, sometimes comic depiction of what it's really like to be involved at the very grassroots of the GAA.

The Dark Side of Celebrity

Irish Courtroom Scandals of the Rich and Famous

LIAM COLLINS

A journey to the other side of fame – telling the story of Ireland's rich and famous fighting each other across the courtroom floor. The stories of the sexual affairs, the alcohol abuse, the dirty tricks and the greed that ruined relationships and tore friendships apart.

- The beauty queen Michelle Rocca's bitter courtroom battle with Ryanair heir Cathal Ryan over a brawl at a socialite's birthday party.
- Solicitor-to-the-stars Elio Malocco and his dodgy dealings – leading to a falling out with Twink, the de Valera familly and the entire Law Society!
- How Manchester United boss Sir Alex Ferguson fell out with his Irish friend John Magnier over the wonder horse Rock of Gibraltar.
- How the sex of Bono's baby became a central issue in a court case that had absolutely nothing to do with him or U2.
- The Illusionist Paul Goldin disappears from a theatre stage and turns up in Hawaii with 'the other woman'.

Irish Family Feuds

Battles over Money, Sex and Power

LIAM COLLINS

When families fall out, the bitterness that emerges is matched only by the ferocity of their attacks on each other. Family feuds are far more vicious than disputes between strangers, as family members compete to crush each other completely and without mercy.

Cases include many rich and famous Irish families:
- Ben v Margaret – Duel at Dunnes
- The PV Doyle family 'hotel' war
- Comans and the 'Pub brawl'
- Enya, Clannad and the Brennan family feud
- 'Volkswagon vendetta' – the O'Flahertys' family secret

and many more family feuds over money, power and sex.

Larry Cunningham

A Showband Legend

Tom Gilmore

Despite a number of heart attacks, a cancer scare and several attempts at retirement, showband legend Larry Cunningham is still singing in his 70s. His story is a *potpourri* of humour, success, shady deals – as well as sadness, death and murder on the music scene.

Larry Cunningham was the first Irish artist to make the UK Pop Charts – long before U2, the Boomtown Rats, Boyzone or Westlife. His 'Tribute to Jim Reeves' spent over three months in the British hit parade, sold more than a quarter of a million copies and culminated in his appearance on *Top of the Pops* alongside Cliff Richard and others.

When 'Gentleman Jim' Reeves walked off the stage at a dance in Donegal, Larry's singing of Reeves' songs stopped an angry mob from burning the place down. His first No. 1 'Lovely Leitrim' sold over a quarter of a million but the song has sad links to a bloody shooting in a New York bar. The gunfight and deaths, as well as two forgotten song verses, are recalled in this book.

Fascinating reading for those interested in Showbands and Sixties nostalgia, Country 'n' Irish music, the rise and decline of the Ballroom dances and Jimmy Magee GAA All-Stars Football charity.